Transgression and Conformity

Transgression and Conformity

Cuban Writers and Artists after the Revolution

Linda S. Howe

THE UNIVERSITY OF WISCONSIN PRESS

The University of Wisconsin Press
1930 Monroe Street
Madison, Wisconsin 53711

www.wisc.edu/wisconsinpress/

3 Henrietta Street
London WC2E 8LU, England

5   4   3   2   1

Printed in the United States of America

Library of Congress Cataloging-in-Publication Data
Howe, Linda S.
  Transgression and conformity : Cuban writers and artists after the Revolution /
  Linda S. Howe.
  p. cm.
  Includes bibliographical references and index.
  ISBN 0-299-19730-1 (cloth : alk. paper)
    1. Cuban literature—20th century—History and criticism.   2. Cuba—Intellectual
life —20th century.   3. Cuba—Cultural policy.   4. Politics and culture—Cuba—
History —20th century.   5. Arts, Black—Cuba.   I. Title.
PQ7378.H69   2004
860.9'97291'09045 — dc22   2003020571

An earlier version of chapter 2 appeared in *Revista de Estudios Hispánicos* 33 (1999);
I am grateful to Elzbieta Sklodowska for permission to reprint with this acknowledgment.
Sections of chapter 3 appeared in *Afro-Hispanic Review* 15 (spring 1996), *Explicación de
textos literarios* 24 (1995–96), and *Singular Like a Bird,* edited by Miriam DeCosta-Willis.

Contents

Acknowledgments

My sincere appreciation to all the Cuban artists and writers who contributed to this work. I am grateful to Nancy Morejón, Miguel Barnet, Gerardo Fulleda León, Eugenio Hernández Espinosa, Tomás Fernández Robaina, Gisela Arandia, Rogelio Martínez Furé, Inés María Martiatu Terry, Walterio Carbonell, Tomás González, Eloy Machado, Manolo Granados, Marianela Boán, Raul Martín, Alejandro Aguilar, José Mario, and William Luis for much support and patient advice throughout the years.

Thanks to Julie Edelson for her endless editorial and spiritual assistance. Thanks to Emma Claggett for helping with the English translations of the interviews and cited quotes. Thanks to Elizabeth Turnbull for proofreading the text.

Finally, I would like to thank my mother and father for their sacrifice and love. I also owe special recognition to Michael Pratt and Kay Kornovich for their unwavering friendship and faith in me during this project.

Transgression and Conformity

Introduction

Aesthetic Challenges: Officials and Iconoclasts in Postrevolutionary Cuban Culture

No one in Cuba anticipated the disappearance of the Soviet Union, the crumbling walls of communism in the Eastern Bloc, or the sweeping economic and social changes that occurred in the island nation during the 1990s. These events signaled the beginning of a decline in actual Cuban cultural production (since resources were scarce) but not in intellectual activity on the island (e.g., although the country lacked the paper to publish books and magazines, writers continued to write, and Cuban publishers sought out foreign presses to publish their journals and books). Even though the theaters could barely function in the prevailing circumstances, artists managed to produce dance and theater works that required minimal stage production and design. Performance and installation artists, sculptors, and painters also eked out an innovative living with the few materials at their disposal.

Forced by the disappearance of its patron to seek funds elsewhere, the Cuban government weathered the onslaught of capitalist culture with the growing surge of tourism and foreign investment. Prospects for economic betterment of the socialist system waned as the Cuban peso plunged in value, and the glinting island of Castro's revolution steeled itself for the fin de siècle with diminished expectations. As Cuban officials declared the beginning of the so-called Special Economic Period (1990–) and labored desperately to stave off economic collapse, something peculiar began to happen on the cultural scene. In some quarters, the formulaic "revolutionary" rhetoric that had long characterized works produced on the island and that had begun to abate in the late 1980s gave way to works that emphasized citizens' utter disillusionment and the physical and spiritual decay of the country. With the advent of the Special Period, intellectuals still residing on the island audaciously began to explore the chasm that separated the seedy reality they inhabited from the ideal socialist island depicted in the government's propaganda. Cuban intellectuals were increasingly unwilling to deny that the economic and social crisis was real and that its impact was transforming cultural expression.

After 1959 cultural officials unremittingly attempted to shape policy regarding Cuban literary and artistic works. But the revolution Cubans had longed for did not have the outcome anticipated. In the euphoric and chaotic years that immediately followed the Cuban revolution, officials at once began to link culture to political change. Some officials wanted to emulate the Soviet cultural commissar Anatoly Lunacharsky in creating didactic cultural and educational institutions. They insisted that artists and writers accept prevailing values of the revolution, ignore personal material gain, and strive to become the consummate organic intellectual à la Gramsci.

Ironically, in 1965, Che Guevara, who epitomized the socialist "new man," warned that a Soviet-style model for Cuban culture would replicate the "frozen forms" of Soviet socialist realism (*Obra* 378) and attacked other communist countries' institutionalized and mechanical representation of socialist idealism. Indeed, officials and intellectuals disagreed among themselves about the implementation of such an intransigent policy based on the Bolshevik model. Whether from conviction or opportunism, some intellectuals clamored to espouse revolutionary ideals. Those who did were rewarded with privileges and with expanded opportunities for publishing or producing their work, though few would argue that the new system of incentives always worked to the advantage of Cuban literature. Even the Colombian writer Gabriel García Márquez, a close friend of Castro, admits that the Latin literary intellectuals' endorsements of the government were sometimes disingenuous: "Many second-tier intellectuals, without opportunities in their own lands, found a way of acquiring power by proclaiming solidarity with the new regime" (Castañeda 184–85).

The arbitrary, inconsistent, and sometimes even anarchic operations of the Cuban cultural bureaucracy make it difficult to generalize about the degree to which official policy has infringed upon intellectuals' freedom of expression. The ground has constantly shifted, keeping nearly everyone off balance. In the early days, officials obsessed with Cuba's revolutionary ideals called for artists and writers to collaborate in what the officials saw as the noble task of ideological transformation. Canvas and poster art were cramped with scenes of energetic agricultural production, guerrilla victories, and enthusiastic youths scaling mountains to implement literacy campaigns. Using both the Bolshevik and the Mexican revolutions as inspiration, Cuban authorities touted sacrifice and valor and mocked "bourgeois" culture as a decadent, superannuated relic. Like their Bolshevik models, the leaders of the Cuban cultural bureaucracy saw art as a vehicle for the transmission of political ideology. They looked at the socialist realism of the Zhdanov period and conceived of Cuban art as a didactic vehicle with a stunning tropical veneer.

While some intellectuals hurriedly "reformed" themselves and began new careers as progovernment sloganeers, some artists refused to be coopted. Unable to circulate their work openly, they gathered privately and held discussions. Some writers had their works smuggled out of Cuba to be published in other countries, and many artists and playwrights had preliminary showings of their oeuvres before officials banned them.

One should call into question not only the uneven quality of production but also the irregular manner in which institutions and powerful cultural bureaucrats, with differing levels of commitment and various agendas, implemented cultural policies. For example, early on, the more liberal cultural institutions, such as Casa de las Américas, maintained flexible policies toward iconoclast artists. When individuals experienced conflicts at the more politically intransigent institutions, such as UNEAC (Union of Cuban Writers and Artists), they sought refuge at Casa de las Américas, whose director, Haydeé Santamaría, a powerful figure, provided a haven for marginalized intellectuals. Inevitably, Castro's support for Russia's invasion of Czechoslovakia (1968) and the disconcerting Padilla affair (1968–1971) marked a period of stricter adherence to official culture (discussed later in this book). Eventually, as the Cuban government became more politically dogmatic and economic problems increased, authorities forged an ever more intimate alliance with the Soviet Union. The hard-line communists overpowered their less zealous colleagues, and Santamaría eventually felt compelled to knuckle under to the prevailing line. (This was probably prudent, given that, at the time, anything less than absolute submission was routinely portrayed as treason).[1] Several cultural bureaucrats who might have been liberal and "tolerant" of rebel artists during one phase of the institutionalization of culture became intransigent during periods of political pressure to the point where they restricted production by imposing censorship and repression. Likewise, once-defiant and flamboyant writers became subdued after they could not get anything published for several years. This uneven and sometimes paradoxical behavior complicates analysis of cultural production and makes it difficult to determine which officials agreed with institutional policies and which writers kowtowed to them at any given moment.

Ironically, by the 1970s, the fetishism of Che Guevara's "new man" (the nonwage earner who selflessly worked for the betterment of society and a messianic future) had become a symbol for movement toward Soviet-style economic and cultural reforms. The cultural purges of the 1970s indicated that authorities were committed to politicizing culture. In the late 1980s and early 1990s Cuba experienced internal political conflicts and the repercussions from international political military and economic setbacks. The Argentine Jacobo Timerman reiterates that the government's policy of greater social responsibility was a result of Cuba's increasingly close ties to the Soviet Union, which had begun in the 1960s. Armando Hart, the Cuban minister of culture and a veteran of the Sierra Maestra, as late as 1987 publicly quoted a text by Lenin's commissar of culture. Hart indicated that artists must "move toward processes of greater participation and democracy" through greater "social responsibility." According to Timerman, this was a hypocritical statement that concealed opportunistic self-promotion and personal material gain: "The degree of one's 'social responsibility'—a pseudoscientific formula invoked to avoid mentioning party discipline or flattery—is what determines who gets published, who has access to newspaper publication, who speaks on the radio or television, who travels to congresses abroad, who can return from aboard with a television set or air conditioner" (53).

Timerman emphasizes the state's disingenuous expectations of revolutionary commitment when he exposes the artist's accumulation of material goods in return for service to the state. Although this might not have been common practice among Cuban intellectuals, Timerman's revelations call into question the rhetoric of self-sacrifice and idealism as the main motivation for officially sanctioned artistic production.

In this study I examine the relationships among "revolutionary" policies, iconoclast aesthetics, "bourgeois traditions," and diverse and "subversive" cultural elements. Revolutionary culture has its own dramatic effect: among the several factors that contributed to turmoil are politicized expression, struggles among intellectuals and officials over aesthetics, and the shutting down of iconoclastic artists and independent presses. For example, the closing, in 1965, of El Puente (the name of both a semi-independent publishing house and the loosely knit group of young intellectuals whose works were published by that publishing house) signaled an end to the existence of independent presses and to relative aesthetic freedom, part of a process that had begun with the demise of the more established literary supplement *Lunes de revolución.* In addition, the controversies over Afro-Cuban politics and artistic expression brought on in part by the Black Power movement of the 1960s, the writings of Malcolm X, the influx of Black Panther Party members into Cuba, and the government's negative reaction to a localized Cuban-style Black Power movement influenced subsequent writings by and about Afro-Cubans.

I dedicate particular attention to the ways in which the debates about aesthetics, cultural politics, and Afro-Cuban expression impact the works of the poet Nancy Morejón, the ethnographer/novelist Miguel Barnet, and other Cuban artists (some of whom have remained in Cuba and others of whom have become exiles). Their aesthetics reveal a compelling relationship that links cultural and political events such as the closing of El Puente, the controversies over Afro-Cuban expression since the revolution, and the advent of the Special Period.

In chapter 1 I analyze the aesthetic and political clashes that occurred between some independent intellectuals and their political or cultural rivals, which ultimately led to the intellectuals' professional demise as officials put an end to both the liberal literary supplement *Lunes de revolución* and Ediciones El Puente. While much has been written about the closing of *Lunes de revolución,* virtually nothing substantial has been published about the inchoate Ediciones El Puente, even though its closure, in 1965, symbolized the end of an era for autonomous groups of young writers and artists. El Puente published works by both Nancy Morejón and Miguel Barnet, who were closely associated with the literary group. I relate their personal development to the publishing house and to the contentious cultural politics that led to its demise. The politicization of aesthetics, rivalry among intellectuals to secure positions or privileges in cultural institutions, and officially sanctioned homophobia utterly convoluted cultural production. For many years after the El Puente scandal officials implemented measures that eliminated iconoclastic intellectuals from the cultural scene. This was the time of the infamous UMAP ("Military Units for the Aid of Production") forced-labor camps and, later, the purges of several writers, artists, and professors from Cuban cultural institutions. According to Hugh Thomas, the camps "were set up to house large numbers of civil servants, homo-sexuals, ex-members of the bourgeoisie or potential, rather than overt, opponents of the regime" (*Cuban Revolution* 685). The so-called gray years of the 1970s adversely affected numerous generations of Cuban artists and writers and substantially constricted their freedom.

Official standardization of cultural norms revealed a forced union between a residual, and predominantly white and middle-class, cultural milieu (inherited by the revolutionary government) and the constricted image of the intellectual as the new man of a socialist society. As the Cuban literary critic Victor Fowler Calzada points out, mentions of the rivalries that existed among intellectual groups are a cliché in explan-ations of shifts in Cuban cultural politics since the 1950s (*La tercera* 70–71). How did communist officials hope to advance the utopian theme of Cuba's political independence and nationalism through the cultural realm, and how were artists to manifest these ideas? Which divisions in prerevolutionary Cuban culture did intellectuals inherit, and which did they invent? To what degree did the politicization of aesthetics affect artistic renditions of national identity and define the role of Cuban cul-ture after the 1960s? To what degree is Cuban cultural production in the 1990s and 2000s self-referential with regard to the revolution? What do artists have to say, if anything, about the contradictions produced by official restraints on culture and society?

In chapter 2 I analyze how the authorities restricted sociological studies on contemporary society and problack writings, asserting that they produced "contradictions" inimical to a socialist state. The com-plexity of official systematization and the aesthetization of Cuban cul-ture overlapped with such factors as racism and the U.S.-influenced Black Power movement of the 1960s. These developments came to-gether to produce heightened awareness of Afro-Cuban culture. At the same time, the government cracked down on African-based religious and cultural elements. These contradictions created a dilemma for in-tellectuals with an interest in Afro-Cuban culture.

If Afro-Cubans altered their views under pressure with respect to new racial politics and aesthetics, perhaps revolutionary racial rhetoric, rather than adequately reflect the reality of Afro-Cubans' societal inte-gration, merely fabricates an ideal racial harmony. In the 1990s some Afro-Cuban intellectuals rejected the term "Afro-Cuban." Has the of-ficial "antirevolutionary" stigma attached to "separatist" black politics and identity produced a denial of racial heritage? For example, if the rev-olution purportedly created institutional racial equality, one has to ask why so few Afro-Cuban writers, especially women, are represented in the literary canon.

My study attempts to move beyond the predictable (and sterile) confrontations that mark so much writing on Cuban intellectual history. My intensive interviews with many who participated in the events of the 1960s provide new insights into the delicate and controversial subject of racism and official repression of black expression in postrevolutionary Cuba. These oral histories only begin to reveal the complex relations between Afro-Cuban intellectuals and revolutionary officials. How blacks successfully integrated their works within revolutionary politics and what authorities did to promote black expression within the limits of official racial policies remain to be examined.

Morejón and Barnet are among the most successful of the writers who began their careers in the early days of the Castro government. Morejón's poetry has been widely translated and is often anthologized. Her poems and essays encompass a variety of literary and political topics. She began her career as a poet with her first two collections, *Mutismos* (1962) and *Amor, ciudad atribuida* (1964). Later, she published *Richard trajo su flauta y otros argumentos* (1967), *Parajes de una época* (1979), *Cuaderno de Granada* (1984), *Piedra pulida* (1986), *Paisaje célebre* (1993), *El río de Martín Pérez y otros poemas* (1996), *Botella al mar* (1996), and *La quinta de los molinos* (2000). Barnet's testimonial narrative, *Biografía de un cimarrón* (1966), has been translated into several languages and has sold well internationally. He has published testimonial "novels," as well as collections of poetry. His more recent (and arguably most complex) works are the short story "Miosvatis" and the poem "Hijo de obrero," both published in the 1990s. As a scholar, he is particularly well known for his work on Afro-Cuban religion. In the late 1990s and early 2000s both Barnet and Morejón continued to produce challenging literature that alluded to Cuba's tumultuous political, social, and cultural realities.

Since the 1960s these writers have generally worked within the officially accepted limits in the field of revolutionary cultural production. I link changes in Morejón's and Barnet's personal aesthetics to the shifting policies of the revolutionary government's cultural institutions, with special emphasis on debates about aesthetics, cultural politics, and gender and racial issues.

The French sociologist Pierre Bourdieu's approach to cultural production provides a framework for analyzing how historical and political conditions may have influenced Morejón and Barnet's choices of content and form. Bourdieu sees society as a set of "profoundly buried structures of various social worlds" that also includes "the 'mechanisms' which tend to ensure their reproduction and/or their transformation." Reproduction is ensured by the hierarchical priority of cultural institutions and the "distribution of material resources" to intellectuals, which determine who and what is published; it is sustained by "systems of classification" that practical agents (intellectuals) use in their conduct, thoughts, and judgments (*An Invitation to Reflexive Sociology* 7).

It follows that the "double life" of the intellectual stratum also depends on the fact that intellectuals more or less comply with officially imposed aesthetics and compete among themselves for publications and prizes. Bourdieu exposes the correspondence between social structures and ideas to reveal how institutions uphold official ideology through prescribed cultural expression. As Bourdieu argues, "symbolic systems are not simply instruments of knowledge, but also instruments of domination" (7–13). This is particularly the case in communist Cuba, where the government has explicitly sought to transform art into a tool for constructing a new social order.

Although I do not limit my analysis to Bourdieu's theories, his explanation of how symbolic systems function helps us to understand that commonsensical versions of Cuban reality are, in part, products of the link between the interests of the dominant power structure and "objective" cultural production (13). As Bourdieu asserts, "symbolic systems are social products that contribute to the making of the world; they do not simply mirror social relations but help *constitute* them" (14). I appropriate Bourdieu's idea of going beyond clichés, stereotypes, and classification to make explicit the power relations inscribed in social reality and the cultural realm. Revolutionary officials and the intellectuals who supported the revolution attempted to transform Cuban social reality by "transforming its representation" (14). For example, they produced an array of symbolic systems to promote the revolutionary consciousness of Che Guevara's "new man," whose sense of history and voluntarism were deemed necessary to the construction of a socialist state. Specific themes and iconography of heroism, altruistic sacrifice, and nationalism reflect the aesthetic norm of "revolutionary" commitment; artists and writers competed among themselves to wield the norm in diverse genres.

Barnet's and Morejón's struggles either to preserve or to shift the boundaries of representation that make up literary production reflect how their roles as writers have been marked by contradictions, setbacks, and qualified successes. Their particular ways of expressing commitment and resistance within politicized Cuban culture have undergone several changes. Two key factors contributed to Morejón's and Barnet's early development: (1) their involvement in rivalries with other intellectual groups, who criticized their aesthetics and their association with the publishing house and literary group El Puente; (2) their unique literary representations of Afro-Cuban culture and politics as part of a national revolutionary consciousness.

In chapter 3 I investigate Morejón's ideas about Afro-Cuban culture, her use of the concepts of transculturation, nationality, and "mulatez" or "mestizaje" (racial and cultural synthesis), and her creative use of double entendres and mixed poetic metaphors throughout her literary trajectory. I consider how Morejón has been influenced by the writings of her mentor, Nicolás Guillén, but attempts to go beyond Guillén's literary configurations of the Afro-Cuban woman in such poems as "Mujer negra" and "Amo a mi amo." I argue that her poetry and other writings also indicate tensions and contradictions, but, in contrast to Barnet's preliminary effort to represent heretofore unvoiced black history, Morejón has, at times, effaced herself and made "invisible" her blackness and her femaleness. At other times, she has taken up racial and gender issues with revolutionary fervor. Morejón has alternately positioned herself in relation to race and/or gender, depending on the shifts in the somewhat unpredictable political climate for blacks following the revolution. On the one hand, as a contemporary black woman, she has been careful not to overemphasize her blackness-as-difference by claiming that the development of a black consciousness is merely a step in Cuban society's overall socialist evolution. On the other hand, she has utilized her position as a black female writer to push beyond the parameters of revolutionary rhetoric about black women in order to revise notions of Afro-Cuban culture and identity. I examine how Morejón, in her desire to merge gender and racial discourses, develops an aesthetic that questions the historical, literary, cultural, and political constructions of the female subject.

Like Morejón, Barnet initiates a political and literary discourse that approaches politics and aesthetics from several angles, calling into question the monolithic view of official rhetoric. In chapter 4 I discuss Barnet's desire to create a discursive site for blacks in his ethnology and poetry. I argue that his research on Afro-Cuban society does, indeed, call into question previous historiography. Moreover, Barnet, as an adherent of the Castro government, conceptualizes Afro-Cuban identity through the lens of Cuba's revolution. In doing so, he may at times exclude black voices that dissent from official policies and erase them (so to speak) from his transcripts.

In his early work, Barnet, while he does not always sufficiently problematize his own ethnological perspective as a white writer who "speaks for" black culture, delves into an area of "black" studies that is controversial within the white intellectual establishment; later, he no longer suggests that Afro-Cuban religious practices would disappear as the socialist programs for blacks progressed. For example, in recent interviews and in the documentary *Nganga Kiyangala* (1991), he states that definitions of black culture and identity cannot be limited by hegemonic Cuban nationalism and revolutionary rhetoric. Barnet's complex positions underscore how he has blended his perspective with official policy toward black expression but, at the same time, rejected society's prejudice against Afro-Cuban societies and religions. As a result, he incorporates aestheticized images of Afro-Cuban elements in his poetry. I study the thematic and formal changes of the poetry in such collections as *La piedra fina y el pavorreal* (1963), *Isla de güijes* (1964), *La sagrada familia* (1967), *Mapa del tiempo* (1989), and *Con pies de gato* (1993). I also analyze some of his most recent work depicting social and political decay of 1990s Cuba. This writing, which is politically as well as aesthetically provocative, reveals Barnet's tensions with restrictive policies on cultural expression.

A study of aesthetic debates after the revolution, coupled with information about political repression of "subcultures" and cultural officials' elimination of "independent" institutions, provide a critical view of Cuban cultural production. Likewise, with regard to subcultures, by evaluating writings about and by Afro-Cubans and evaluating the repression of decadent aesthetics or lifestyles and then considering these conditions against the fate of iconoclasts, homosexuals, and/or blacks in contemporary Cuban society, I hope to cast light not only on Barnet and Morejón's literary projects but also on the reasons those projects encountered difficulties. In the case of Afro-Cubans, Morejón and Barnet accepted the perplexing task of skirting controversial political issues about black expression without devaluing Afro-Cuban culture and society.

Barnet's and Morejón's ability to invent literature that both conforms to and defies the rules of officially sanctioned literature reveals their own participation in the social, political, and cultural changes that took place after 1959. Not only did they differentiate themselves from the previous generation of poets and writers; they also sought ways to express Cuba's radically changing circumstances. Their attempt to represent "subcultures" and their resultant contradictory aesthetics attest to their constant struggles with the realities of Cuba. Morejón and Barnet invented fictionalized versions of the heterogeneous cultures that constitute "Cubanness," under difficult circumstances and in the context of the sweeping historical changes that followed the Cuban revolution.

1

Art in Revolutionary Cuba
What Price Solidarity?

The sharp divisions between supporters and opponents of the Cuban government make it nearly impossible to analyze postrevolutionary culture without offending partisans on one side or another. Opinions about the relationship between politics and culture vary according to one's ideological proximity to, or distance from, political developments in Cuba since the 1959 revolution. Some writers and artists benefited from revolutionary commitment and their adherence to the government; their works were produced or published regularly, and they enjoyed the pleasures and privileges of fame. Others fell from grace or experienced difficult periods of official chastisement before "rectifying" themselves ideologically or leaving the island for good. Still others blossomed as professionals in the late 1970s and early 1980s. They produced fervently before facing multifarious challenges and shortages brought on by the Special Period (1990–), when Cuban officials implemented drastic measures to stave off economic collapse after the disappearance of the Soviet Union. The subsequent social and moral meltdown triggered bold responses from the intelligentsia. Writers and artists moved to reinterpret history, highlight past errors, and portray the consequences of more than forty years of communist control. With privileged hindsight, they illuminated the revolutionary system's crumbling façade and the shortcomings of its messianic projects.

A survey of recent critical work shows that some intellectuals are no longer afraid to examine the ways in which official restrictions have distorted our understanding of postrevolutionary Cuban cultural history.

Most of these limits were justified by appeals to national security: the government asserted that, in a time of crisis, unity had to take precedence over the artist's creative process. Officials had to save Cuba from "imperialism" and from the horrors of capitalism. In recent years the Cuban authorities have worked tirelessly to dispel the idea that they demonstrated excessive intolerance toward refractory artists or their works. The government's current broadmindedness toward many once-forbidden works and promotion of recent appeasing cultural adaptations of past "inaccuracies" create a curious erasure effect. Likewise, the suffering of one-time victims is now downplayed in favor of a rhetoric of recovery and reconciliation. For example, some critics have said that the Cuban film *Fresa y chocolate* (Strawberry and Chocolate) is a double-edged sword. The film depicts the problematic relationship between a sincere but naïve young communist and a homosexual during the 1970s, when officials marginalized many Cuban artists and purged artistic and intellectual centers, particularly the theater and the university. While it criticizes the Cuban Communist Party's intolerance of gays, it also downplays the systematic nature of repression. Does this fictionalized version represent a new, open policy toward gays and other marginalized components of revolutionary society? As the Cuban critic and writer Reynaldo González suggests, this complex issue requires further study simply because a popular film cannot expunge "the transitory nightmare" ("Meditation" 17).[1] González notes the difficulty in presenting palatable versions of insidious political events: "Cuban cultural policy now tries to salvage those writers who, having produced significant works, were not allowed to publish them. Those who died are invoked and homage is paid to them, leaving a bittersweet taste in our mouths when we recall the incomprehension that plagued their years" (17).

In an equally critical review of *Fresa y chocolate*, Emilio Bejel says that the film "illuminates even as it represses the problematic aspects of the relationship between homosexuality and Cuban nationality" ("Strawberry" 69). Likewise, the reconciliatory ending of *Fresa y chocolate*, with its display of love between the protagonists, might snuff out further discussion. In its politically ambiguous (yet *un*ambiguously sentimental) embrace of the ideal of tolerance, the film suggests that dogmatic authoritarianism is now a thing of the past. It is as if the infamous UMAP (Military Units for the Aid of Production) camps of the mid-1960s, where thousands of gays and hippies were sent as punishment for their "deviant behavior," had never existed.

Up with the Revolution / Our Union Makes Us Strong

In the sixties, when the international and Latin American left proclaimed its solidarity with the Cuban revolution, some artists' careers
were launched, some remained tepid, and others were trampled. The
Castro revolution delighted leftists, who enthusiastically embraced
the fledgling Cuban government and its bearded leader's victory over
Uncle Sam and the policies of Manifest Destiny. Supporters of the new
government wanted to eradicate European- and American-dominated
economic markets and cultural trends. The past was a heavy burden for
a society whose economy had been based on sugar and tobacco,
tourism, and international gambling in mafia-run casinos.

Some authorities believed that Cuba's colonial and "neocolonial" histories were also an aesthetic and ideological liability, and the Castro government worked to remake the island's image. In official propaganda it
proposed an innovative culture that would forge an incessant guerrilla-
fighting zone of the utopian left, fortified against imperialism. On the
assumption that to build a communist state it was essential "to build new
men as well as [a] new economic base" (Lumsden, "Ideology of the Revolution" 539), government officials tirelessly celebrated the "altruism"
of Che Guevara and Fidel Castro. With enough repetition and the appropriate dose of prodding they hoped to replace foreign-influenced
culture with a new revolutionary consciousness.

After the relative openness and utopian euphoria of the early 1960s,
Cuba's cultural vitality atrophied as authorities drew skewed parallels
among harvesting sugar cane, fomenting guerrilla warfare, and engen-
dering culture through social volunteerism. Although authorities encouraged a variety of cultural activities, they funded primarily prorevolutionary literature, documentary films, and graphics. Suspicious
of "bourgeois art," some were determined to fabricate a national image
not only with guerrilla iconography but also with the rhetoric of "moral
correctness" based on revolutionary ideals. Official insistence on the
ethical transformation of culture and society brought about purges and
institutional infighting. As artistic freedom faltered and politics took
precedence over experimental aesthetics, some artists and writers competed for government support and cultural prizes, while others resisted
official infringement on their imaginative powers. Writers and artists
who demonstrated an unwholesome partiality for experimental styles
or "cosmopolitan" ideas were punished for their unconventional aesthetics and "scandalous" lifestyles. When disagreements over literary

and critical "taste" came to a head, the government silenced the dissenters whom it judged to be too unruly or vociferous; they either were dismissed from their positions or had to relinquish publishing privileges.

The new government's efforts to bring artists and intellectuals to heel began when Fidel Castro joined forces, however unevenly, with the Communist Party. After the events of the CIA-backed Bay of Pigs invasion (1961), Castro declared that Cuba's revolution was of a "socialist" (i.e., communist) character. The Bay of Pigs fiasco and the Cuban missile crisis (1962) heightened Cuban nationalism and "anti-imperialist" rhetoric as Cuba developed closer ties with the Soviet Union. In the midst of the Cold War, U.S. officials broke diplomatic relations with the Castro government and isolated Cuba from international relations. Such newly established cultural institutions as Casa de las Américas and the Cuban Institute of Cinematic Art and Industry (ICAIC) became weighty substitutes for embassies. Authorities also founded the Union of Cuban Writers and Artists (UNEAC) and the National Council of Culture (CNC) to support more politically committed forms of cultural expression.[2] On a political and bureaucratic level, the official call for orthodoxy brought about the creation of Integrated Revolutionary Organizations (ORI). Hugh Thomas explains that the organization, headed by Aníbal Escalante, gained political control by melding the Communist Party, the 26 of July Movement, and other organizations into a single body.[3] Even though the Castro government was not part of a united party in early 1961, officials simply began to refer to the former movements as a single entity, "revolutionary organizations," and later "ORI" began to appear in the press (*Cuba* 1372). Initiatives such as the government's much-ballyhooed literacy campaign, which constituted a nationwide effort to provide a basic education for the majority of Cubans, reinforced the message that authoritative control of politics and culture was indispensable for the benefit of the society as a whole.

Officials declared that not only was Cuba under siege by a powerful and aggressive opponent (the U.S. government would exploit political divisiveness among the Cuban people) but that it had to contend with such political organizations as the Alliance for Progress (instituted by John F. Kennedy in 1961) and the Organization of American States (OAS, an association of countries aimed at settling disputes that was founded in Bogotá, Colombia, in 1948), which the Cuban government claimed were backed by the U.S. government to implement aggressive policies against communism and Cuba.[4] A public declaration about sinister U.S.

aggression by the contributing editors of Casa de las Américas in the Mexican journal *El Corno Plumado* (1967) reflects some artists' acceptance of the Cuban government's action to curb dissent among artists, allegedly because of their manipulation by external forces: "Militarism with its usual methods and the Alliance for Progress with greater subtlety are continually involved in an attempt to cut short this revolution and to twist it to its own ends. Insofar as concerns culture, the Alliance for Progress as well as the OAS—both instruments of the heightened U.S. policy—have been trying for some time to place our intellectuals in a dilemma, offering them possibilities and opening perspectives" (Pacheco et al. 134). The contributors called for greater ties between intellectuals and the community, particularly in "underdeveloped" countries like Cuba, "oppressed under the fist of North American imperialism, native oligarchies, and the blackmail of highly industrialized nations" (135).

On the other hand, the official demand that writers and artists express "the needs of the community" was a heavy-handed measure. Were not the iconoclasts' creative edge, idiosyncratic style, and sense of honesty integral parts of culture? Were the dismal fates of several artists and writers the appropriate tradeoff to enforce constant revolutionary struggle? Punishment for the slightest ideological dissent or lack of commitment led prudent artists to reach for "revolutionary" metaphors, which lowered standards of artistic judgment. The government's insistence that the proper role of artists was to extend the "revolutionary" political struggle into the realm of culture had lamentable effects on the independence of the art world and on the rich variety of Cuban cultural life.

More than thirty years after the revolution, with the advent of the Special Period, artists and writers reflected on the politicization and proscription of expression. They scrutinized the contradictions of policies and creatively tallied the damage to artistic integrity and human dignity. Artists' dependence on state funds had forged a symbiotic relationship in which official institutions expected them to dutifully perform as cultural engineers of revolutionary souls. They had been brought up in a world in which everything was always a given—an embattled island of clichés, political mottos, national flag waving, and formulas that reigned over personal expression. Disconcerted and in limbo in the 1990s, artists took advantage of the government's overwhelming task—the resolution of economic and political problems, which produced sudden cultural weightlessness.

Down with Everything Else / Which Side Are You On?

Before the revolution, culture was not the exclusive concern of a paternalistic state. Rather, the Cuban intelligentsia was centered in the universities, "in private-sector organizations devoted to research" (Johnson 137). Other intellectuals worked in their professions, while still others toiled in less revered occupations and did their work on their own time. Even though rivalries already existed among intellectuals, after the revolution their differences became more acute, and the political stakes increased with the advent of radical social and political change. The revolution was the impetuous and ardent affair that permeated all realms of society. State authorities and cultural bureaucrats radicalized culture "through speeches, declarations at congresses, appointments to leadership positions, and the allocation of resources" (Johnson 139). While some individuals were either adamantly opposed to or in favor of a nationalist-socialist paradigm, others wavered between aesthetic individualism and political commitment. Mike González explains that at the heart of the polemic was the intellectual's social responsibility, exemplified in the officially sponsored ideal of the guerrilla-poet. Since "uncommitted" art was deemed unacceptable, "critical voices were stilled after 1971 in all areas of Cuban society" (271).

Several factors contributed to the official management of Cuban culture. When Castro delivered his famous words, "within the Revolution, everything; against the Revolution, nothing," he alluded to the intellectual's responsibility to choose his own theme and style (*Palabras* 23). Castro adjoined to the freedom to choose a "favorite theme" the government's prerogative to judge the intellectual's work through "the prism of the revolutionary crystal" (23). Symbolic of the increasing political clout of Communist Party officials, Castro argued for less aesthetic subtlety and more humble service to the masses and to the revolutionary cause.

That same year, Cuba held the First National Congress of Writers and Artists, at which the bureaucrat José Antonio Portuondo announced that although officials recognized artistic freedom, artists and writers were obligated to develop an "integrally formed national conscience" (503). In his report, Portuondo hinted that the militancy of the artist was of the utmost significance: "What is important is that the artist, creator, or critic assimilate, make into his own flesh and blood the experience of this new era in which we are living. That he deeply assimilate the new conception of reality, that he study and work; that he identify with his people, and that he express this new spirit in ways that cannot be given him ahead of time, like a set square, and that cannot be imposed on him by decree, but rather that he has to discover; he has to create art and literature" (76).

Portuondo's words were a harbinger for the future of Cuban letters. Other officials, such as the University of Havana chancellor and veteran communist Juan Marinello, promoted similar ideas that supported Portuondo's call for the intellectual's "self-discovery," which would lead to the creation of a new society. In a speech, Marinello proclaimed that "a committed historical period demands a committed literature" (48). The address came in the midst of bitter polemics over certain intellectuals' worrisome "lack of dedication" to the revolution.

The principal spokesmen for the position that Cuban writers should suppress their personal inclinations in favor of the needs of the new government were Portuondo, Marinello, and the ambitious young writer Lisandro Otero. On the other side were the defiant poet and critic Heberto Padilla and Guillermo Cabrera Infante, already a former editor of the literary supplement *Lunes de revolución* because of his disagreements with leftist intellectuals over aesthetics (Ripoll 500–503; Menton 125–26). In a 1967 article in *El Caimán Barbudo,* Padilla had infuriated the authorities by praising Cabrera Infante's extraordinary novel *Tres tristes tigres,* which had been banned but was nevertheless circulating clandestinely in Cuba. To make matters worse, he contrasted that book's excellence with the plodding mediocrity of Otero's novel *Pasión de Urbino,* which had just won an official literary prize. Padilla would pay a heavy price for his independence.

Caustic disagreements over whether artists should be compelled to subordinate their creative impulses to the demands of intrusive cultural officials created an atmosphere of fear and tension that carried over into the 1970s. On 17 April 1971, in the wake of an independent jury's decision to award a prize to Padilla's collection *Fuera del juego,* the First National Congress on Education and Culture met to discuss cultural policies and to revise criteria for awarding prizes of literary contests (Menton 151). Lourdes Casal lists the tightened controls of cultural affairs that she claims were a direct result of Castro's speeches and of the Declarations made at the First National Congress: "(a) the primacy of political and ideological factors in staffing universities, mass media, and artistic foundations, (b) the barring of homosexuals from these institutions, (c) tighter controls on literary contests to assure that judges, authors, and topics are truly Revolutionary, (d) a violent attack against 'pseudoleftist bourgeois intellectuals' from abroad who had dared criticize the Revolution on the Padilla issue" ("Literature and Society" 462).

Officialdom's insistence on party discipline and "social responsibility" limited the options for writers of fiction (that is, if they wanted their works to be published). For the Party, the Cuban writer's legitimate role was to serve as a foot soldier in the struggle to build communism. Roberto González Echevarría says that officials used the "presentness" ("The Humanities" 112) of the Cuban revolution to eliminate heterogeneous representations of history and literature. The writer, in the image of Che's "new man," was to convert the revolutionary period into an age of beginnings. However, Cuban officials' rhetoric about the need to break with bourgeois traditions was anything but novel. Indeed, the idea of radical creations is a recurrent theme in Western literary tradition:

> Moreover, the peculiar form of conversion that most frequently appears in Cuban literature of the Revolution, the attempt to turn literature into the direct expression of a radical new reality and of a freshly discovered collective consciousness, in these terms, is the most common in the post-Romantic period. The modern tradition is or proclaims itself revolutionary, so how can literary tradition be subverted to mark a new beginning without reasserting the tradition of subverting tradition? How can I become another without really remaining the same? Barnet's *Biografía de un cimarrón* and the documentary novel in general are at the very center of these complex issues. (112)

Rupture always implies continuity and often confirms the very traditions that are being denied. Cuban writers did not and could not make a clean break with Western tradition; Cuban literature is part of the Western tradition, even in its effort to convert literature into revolutionary agitprop. Otherness seeps through the cracks and surfaces despite official attempts to create homogeneous expression.

Official speeches and writings produced a "hortatory criticism" (González Echevarría, "The Humanities" 203) that focused on a new kind of literature linked to the government's political ideology. This current of writing came mostly from older figures, influenced not only by Marxism but also by Sartre and by the kind of populism that produced the regional novel in Latin America. Castro, Portuondo, Juan Marinello, and others "clamored for novels that reflected in the most immediate way the transformation of society" (203).

Roberto Fernández Retamar, director of Casa de las Américas and one of the most enduring of Cuba's cultural bureaucrats, promoted a parallel trend, calling for a "conversational" poetry. In his essay "Calibán," he envisions an intellectual who sheds his petty bourgeois skin to end Cuba's dependency on the metropolis's cultural models. The poet abandons the language as well as the conceptual and technical apparatus of Western culture and replaces it with an intensely personal and revolutionary poetry. According to Fernández Retamar, conversational poetry captured the collective experience, since the poets who produced it renounced their individuality in order to serve the masses.

In deference to the revolution, Mario Benedetti argues that the Cuban government's imperative was to link ideology and culture to domestic policy. Officials nudged citizens toward voluntarism to enable the country to overcome economic underdevelopment. Intellectuals were encouraged to join their comrades in dedicating themselves to "Castroism," with the promise of dramatic change and a brighter future ("Present" 538).

Cuban cultural life in the 1970s reached new levels of rigidity and asphyxiation. The difficult years inaugurated by the Padilla debacle (discussed later in this chapter) were marked by witch hunts for potential dissidents, banishment of homosexuals to marginal posts or reeducation camps, and draconian censorship. Again, in 1975, officials vowed to maintain control of culture at the First Congress of the Communist Party. Johnson summarizes the general trends, beginning with the new constitution of 1976, which "codified much of what had been achieved during the previous decade" (146).

A modest dialogue with exiles began in 1978, however, and after the embarrassment of the Mariel exodus of 1980, the state adopted new tactics to ease up on its rigid position in an attempt to regain control and to diffuse criticism from both off and on the island. From 1979 to 1986, repression "became less systematic and more individualized," and the "rectification process," initiated in 1986, gave intellectuals hope that government restrictions on writing, research, and publication might slowly change for the better (Johnson 146).

At the Fifth Congress of the Union of Communist Youth (1987), Carlos Aldana, a Communist Party ideologue (who was ousted by the Politburo in 1992 for "unethical" business dealings) argued for what he called a "qualitative approach to national culture" and called for "increased importation of foreign works" (Johnson 146–47). Some interpreted this statement as a subtle criticism of the revolution's mediocre culture and a plea to internationalize aesthetics in Cuba. On the other hand, Padula describes several events that reveal problems and tensions as the decade of the 1990s began. In 1989, the same year that the Berlin wall was destroyed, "fourteen officers, including general Arnaldo Ochoa Sánchez, hero of Angola and Nicaragua, were arrested," and, after a swift trial, "Ochoa and three other officers were shot" (32). Carlos Aldana, who also had attempted to reform Cuba in the 1990s by implementing Cuban concepts of *perestroika* (political and economic restructuring) and *glasnost* (openness), was arrested, disgraced, and demoted by the authorities in 1991–1992 (33). The poet María Elena Cruz Varela, who was a young product of the revolution, condemned its corruption. According to Padula, she "subsequently signed—along with ten others—a 'Declaration of Cuban Intellectuals,' which called for an open national debate on Cuba's future" (34–35). In 1992 she was sent to prison. However, there were observable cracks in the political system, and a new generation of Cubans began to show their discontent. The 1990s Special Period made it possible for intellectuals to push the envelope on critical perspectives as a result of the general crisis that faced the Cuban government and its socialist system. After forty years of "revolution," and some daring forays into iconoclast expression in the 1980s, many Cuban artists had become impatient with the perpetual official promise of a better future.

Point Counterpoint: Negotiating Cultural Production

A morass of facts and figures that can be neither substantiated nor denied further confounds an understanding of Cuba's cultural zeitgeist. Cuba had always been a tiny, socially and politically incestuous island of idiosyncratic artists and writers who knew one another intimately and all belonged to any number of cliques. Even individuals whom officials persecuted (e.g., Heberto Padilla, José Mario, and Reinaldo Arenas) often had personal ties with influential cultural bureaucrats.

Rifts, rivalry, and envy among the Cuban intelligentsia brought about the downfalls of several writers and artists. Not everyone was able to conform, and few were able to escape attention. For example, iconoclastic writers such as José Lezama Lima and Virgilio Piñera and defiant Afro-Cuban artists like the playwright and theater director Eugenio Hernández Espinosa, the writer and director of Baile folclórico nacional de Cuba Rogelio Martínez Furé, the playwright Tomás González, and the painter Manuel Mendive also had working relations with cultural officials. Eventually, all of them were restrained for their "aestheticism," their sexual orientation, or their political or social eccentricities. However, after being subjected to different lengths of "silence" in terms of actual publication or production, these ostracized intellectuals were "reintroduced" (albeit posthumously in the case of Piñera and Lezama Lima) into mainstream culture.

Johnson explains how alienated intellectuals were rehabilitated after undergoing official chastisement: "Antonio Benítez Rojo, demoted in 1970 from the directorship of Casa de las Américas Center for Library Research to an entry-level researcher, was 'rehabilitated' in 1976 as director of the Center for Caribbean Studies. Eduardo Heras León, dismissed from the editorial board of *El Caimán Barbudo* for his 1971 book *Los pasos en la hierba*, was 'rehabilitated' in 1977. Antón Arrafat, banned for the 1968 drama *Los siete contra Tebas* (believed to be a veiled criticism of Raúl Castro), succeeded in 1984 in having his partially autobiographical novel *La caja está cerrada* published, even though the manuscript had been completed in 1970" (162).

Another important political figure with cultural clout was Carlos Franqui, who had a falling out with Castro after having made illustrious contributions to the revolution. He was Castro's former close ally, a member of the 26 of July Movement, and editor of the daily *Revolución*. He published in anti-Batista journals, and in March 1959 he founded the weekly *Revolución*, an organ of the 26 of July Movement (Thomas, *Cuba* 868; Szulc 458). An ex-Communist and journalist, he was a member of Juventud Socialista and had participated in an abortive attack on the Dominican Republic in 1947. Franqui explains, in his *Vidas, aventuras*, that he clashed with the Communist Party apparatus and members of the 26 of July Movement in the early 1960s.

Communist Party officials used autocratic measures to eliminate *Lunes de Revolución*, the cultural supplement to Franqui's daily *Revolución*. The supplement espoused liberal views and remained outside Communist Party control. Intellectuals were already divided over aesthetic and political positions when officials banned the film *P.M.* Directed by Sabá Cabrera Infante, Guillermo's brother, this documentary depicts Afro-Cubans cavorting in Havana's lively nocturnal scene. Guillermo Cabrera Infante protested the censorship, but officials permanently removed the film from circulation, labeling it excessively sexy and racy.[5] Menton says that some authorities thought it "featured too many Negroes, and yet others that it was quite the wrong impression of Cuban life and merely provided the enemy with ammunition" (126). The *P.M.*

scandal was a pivotal moment in the communists' struggle to eliminate independent cultural production. The film's suppression confirmed authorities' ever-increasing censorship of expression and unwittingly revealed the state's racist attitudes. Polemics that predated the revolution now came to a head. Since the 1950s, there had been a rivalry between the Communist intellectuals who had found a home at the newly created official film institute, ICAIC, and those from *Lunes*. During Batista's reign, a small group of left-wing intellectuals broke off from Havana's Cine Club of the Cinemateca to form a programmatically Marxist film club. Immediately following the revolution, these intellectuals took control of the newly formed ICAIC, which exacerbated the battle of wills between the Cinemateca (Sabá Cabrera Infante, German Puig, Ricardo Vigo, Néstor Almendros) and the Marxist group (Alfredo Guevara, García Espinosa, and Gutiérrez Alea). Over time, the Marxists won out and ostracized Almendros's group. Néstor Almendros comments that in the rapidly changing political environment, many intellectuals with no previous political affiliation converted to communism practically overnight and set about denouncing former close allies (Luis, "Cinema" 20).

Cultural bureaucrats had found an excuse to close *Lunes* in the controversy over *P.M.* When *Lunes* ceased publication on 6 November 1961, officials at UNEAC replaced it with two new journals, *La Gaceta de Cuba* and *Unión* (Johnson 142).[6] Intellectuals associated with the supplement and implicated in the controversy were assigned to diplomatic posts abroad. Official subterfuge and the displacement of these intellectuals sent a clear message to the intelligentsia that nonconformists would not be tolerated.

The tribulations of the great poet and critic Heberto Padilla constitute another case in point. Padilla's problems began in 1961, with the closing of *Lunes*. He had gained a reputation as an irreverent intellectual, and his troubles escalated when he excoriated Otero's novel. In 1968 he published his daring and ostensibly antirevolutionary poetry volume, *Fuera del juego* (Menton 135–41). The authorities responded by arresting and allegedly torturing him. Apparently, Padilla was forced to give a public confession in which he condemned himself and fellow intellectuals, including his wife, Belkis Cuza Malé, for "bitterness toward" the revolution (Casal, *El caso Padilla* 96). Outraged foreign intellectuals, among them former Castro supporters such as Jean-Paul Sartre, Juan Goytisolo, and Mario Vargas Llosa, quickly concluded that Cuban authorities had staged Padilla's confession and publicly drew the obvious parallel to Stalin's show trials. Even though he was eventually released from custody, Padilla was officially marginalized. He fled Cuba in 1980 (Padilla 234–47). The Padilla affair and the ensuing purges marked poignant moments for writers and artists. They made it clear that the authorities had little tolerance for artistic experimentation, political skepticism, or iconoclasm.

Anecdotes, actions, memoirs, and sketchy and perfidious facts reveal the cultural turbulence of the period and obliquely refer to the tensions that existed between officials and intellectuals. Unpredictable and disconcerting cultural and political activities characterized what Pierre Bourdieu calls "the mood of the age" (*Field of Cultural Production* 32). Bourdieu argues that our understanding of cultural production comes not only from the internal analysis of cultural works (for example, *explications du texte*) but also from analysis of the "connotative aspects" of the cultural milieu at a given moment. When an era is analyzed merely in denotative terms—the intellectualization of the works, biographies of writers and artists, and the history of culture—without the connotative matter—all the commonsensical information, the little ironies, the twists and turns of politics, the silently understood rules— a "de-realization effect" occurs, and writers' and artists' acts and motivations are never really understood. Social histories take into account the "givens." Contemporary stories, chronicles, and memoirs reveal artists' and writers' behavior and the machinations of official institutions. Personal politics, differences, ideas, and enigmatic dynamics are "in the air" and "circulate orally in gossip and rumor" (31–32).

Several writers have attempted to fill in the gaps that Bourdieu alludes to and that are left by the sanitized official history. To cite only the most illustrious examples, Carlos Franqui's *Vida, aventuras y desastres de un hombre llamado Castro*, Néstor Almendros's film *Improper Conduct*, Padilla's *La mala memoria*, and Arenas's *Antes que anochezca* all rebuke government officials for their mistreatment of politicians, writers, and artists through personal anecdote and documentation. In another text, *Las palabras perdidas*, Jesús Díaz describes his own participation in the polemical incidents surrounding *El Caimán Barbudo*, and in *Mea cuba* (1993), Guillermo Cabrera Infante chronicles the challenges faced by Lydia Cabrera, Nicolás Guillén, Vigilio Piñera, and Reinaldo Arenas as writers who fell out of favor with officialdom. In his interview with Emilio Bejel, the distinguished poet Cintio Vitier discusses Lezama Lima's tragicomic difficulties with cultural bureaucrats. These texts portray the precarious nature of individual power in cultural politics and the negative impact political volatility has on individuals' lives and careers. These "unofficial" and personal versions of almost three decades of Cuban cultural histories constitute an alternative point of view to that offered by official versions of history.

Cuba's "Red Desert" Literary Competitions

One example of a potent rumor that encapsulated an intellectual response to the repressive mood of the late 1960s was the caustic label "Red Desert," which came to characterize the results of the 1967 UNEAC and the 1968 Casa de las Américas literary awards. Some Cuban intellectuals bemoaned the official shift toward "dry" Communist aesthetics, the restrictions on literary experimentation, and the increasingly politicized standards for literary prizes. In their opinion, the judges more often than not awarded prizes solely on the basis of a work's "revolutionary" ideology. With very few exceptions, the works that made it past the censors were no more distinguished than the Soviet literature of the Brezhnev years—an astonishing development in the country of Alejo Carpentier, Virgilio Piñera, and José Lezama Lima.

UNEAC and Casa de las Américas controlled literary juries' decisions. The daily paper *Granma,* official organ of the Cuban Communist Party, often refuted "unorthodox" decisions that favored aesthetics over politics (Johnson 144). Johnson elaborates on the state's draconian demand for ideological purity: "Lisandro Otero, in speaking for the government, called for the creation of a new political and literary avantgarde. An official cultural policy was established, one that a cultural commissar interpreted and enforced by selecting and awarding jobs, controlling publishers and bookstores, selecting juries, and granting such prerogatives as foreign travel. Hence, 1968 ushered in a drab, regimented conformity, characterized by heresy hunting and the silencing of unorthodox opinions. In less than a decade, the bureaucracy supported by the state's ideology triumphed over the intellectuals. The cultural offensive marked the end of provocative articles and literary production, as scholarship underwent an intense ideological scrutiny to ensure purity" (144).

The UNEAC and Casa competitions favored ideologically inclined works and marked the beginning of the end of stimulating production. When a literary competition was declared "desierto" (literally desert), this meant that no work had been awarded the prize because the judges deemed none of the works worthy of the award; the competing works received a mere mention. For example, UNEAC judges declared the

1967 competitions "desiertos" and doled out a mention to Reinaldo Arenas's novel *El mundo alucinante* and another to Nancy Morejón's *Richard trajo su flauta y otros argumentos* for poetry. In the 1968 Casa poetry competition, the actual winner was the Spaniard Félix Grande for his politically committed poetry from *Blanco Spirituals*. Among others, Miguel Barnet's *La sagrada familia* and Excilia Saldaña's *Enlloró* received meager mentions.

With a touch of gallows humor, young intellectuals named their cultural malaise after the Italian director Michelangelo Antonioni's famous 1964 film *Red Desert*. The film depicts a neurotic young wife's struggle to overcome spiritual emptiness and to grasp the meaning of life in the vacuous cultural landscape of a modern industrial wasteland in northern Italy.

The Giulianas of Cuba's Red Desert were alienated artists and writers who found themselves in an officially mandated cultural vacuum. Kitschy "revolutionary" iconography saturated the landscape, since the military struggle against imperialism (however elastically defined) played a central role in the government's narrative of legitimation. In the insipid competition, judges awarded literary prizes to texts with socialist-realist themes and rejected works that failed to trumpet the party line. Writers who ranted against the corruption and exploitation of capitalism and who had a penchant for conformity and proselytizing were the revolution's new prototypes. Parables about guerrilla victories and consciousness-raising politics characterized the worst mannerisms of late social realism. In some cases, the level of mediocrity was inversely proportional to the trench-digging commitment evident in the work's content.

Conversely, "pure" aesthetics or foreign-influenced styles offended official sensibility. The dry, tongue-in-cheek image of the Red Desert conveys the paradox of a Cuban culture that became dehydrated during the revolutionary gush. Hence, Red Desert transcends the mere characterization of the literary competition to underscore Cuba's star-crossed embrace with Soviet cultural policies. The desert is a dusty catalyst for a thirsty culture in the aftermath of sweaty political wrath; it also denotes a culture gone dry or awry and conjures an atmosphere where everything rare, subtle, and profound is desiccated. Officials bury culture deep in the desert sand as an ostrich buries its head, and lay to rest cultural sumptuousness.

Beat Poet Ginsberg: "Queen" of the Desert?

Not only did officials curb the glitter from cultural production to create the red desert, but also they attempted to clear out the gay "rabble" that saturated the artistic milieu. By 1965 officials had formed the UMAP camps. The mid-1970s marked the beginning of the so-called *quinquenio gris,* or gray years, which saw increased persecution of gays and other "deviant" groups. According to David William Foster, the official purges against "unruly elements" initiated by the UMAP social program were taboo subjects for leftists. Treatment of alleged homosexuals was viewed as an "infamous transgression of human rights" and an "embarrassment," but leftists did not condemn it. Apparently, their sense of loyalty to the Cuban revolution led many of them to avoid discussion of the government's antigay policies. The government "subscribed to the legendary (nineteenth-century social engineering) antipathy of Marxism-socialism-communism (and parallel revolutionary movements like anarchism) toward homosexuality as socially nonproductive behavior." From the viewpoint of Castro and his hypermacho *barbudos,* homosexuality was the distilled essence of the "bourgeois decadence" that led to the exploitation of the poor and to the growth of prostitution (67).[7]

Not only well-established intellectuals but also young upstarts became casualties of official moral, political, and aesthetic crusades. For example, after José Mario, editor of Ediciones El Puente, was implicated in a series of incidents that spun out of control, authorities sent him to the UMAP camps. His problems escalated when the American Beat poet Allen Ginsberg made an unforgettable visit to Havana in 1965, when Cuban bureaucrats invited him to serve as poetry judge for Casa de las Américas. José Mario and Manuel Ballagas escorted Ginsberg around Havana and spent time in his hotel room. The young men were interested in Ginsberg's poetry. For his part, apparently Ginsberg was flattered by their genuine admiration and tried to seduce the youths. Gerardo Fulleda León says that he even had to "rescue" Manolo (Manuel) Ballagas from Ginsberg. After they met with Ginsberg and with other prominent intellectuals from Spain and Latin America, Fulleda León and Ballagas accompanied him back to his hotel room. In Fulleda Leon's humorous account, Ginsberg is a seductive bell ringer who tries, like the pied piper, to entice Ballagas to cross the threshold into his hotel room that evening:

Lo conocimos a la puerta de UNEAC, José Mario, Manolo Ballagas, Ana María Simo y yo. Nos encontramos adentro con [Julio]
Cortázar, [Mario]Vargas Llosa, Nicanor Parra y Camilo José
Cela. De allí salimos caminando todos al Hotel Riviera, eran
como las cuatro de la tarde. Y nos pasamos hasta la medianoche
tomando tragos en un bar del hotel. Deslumbrados nosotros con
ellos y ellos queriendo saberlo todo de nosotros. Cortázar amable
y sencillo; Vargas Llosa sereno y observador; Nicanor Parra sim-
patiquísimo; Cela insoportable y chusco; Allen apestoso y aluci-
nado y el "típico americano inocente".

Fue una noche memorable, por ahí tengo escrito algo sobre ese
encuentro. A la hora de despedirnos, Allen hizo que Manolito y
yo lo acompañáramos hasta la puerta de su cuarto tocando con
una campanita una salmodia hebra, acompañándola de su canto
peculiar y envolvente, "Come, come" (en inglés) le decía a Manolito (era casi un niño) para que entrara al cuarto. Tuve que ar-
rancárselo para llevármelo de allí a salvo. (interview with the
author, Havana, 28 July 1992)

[José Mario, Manolo Ballagas, Ana María Simo, and I met him
at the door of UNEAC. Inside, we met [Julio] Cortázar, [Mario]
Vargas Llosa, Nicanor Parra, and Camilo José Cela. We all left
from there, walking to the Hotel Riviera; it was about four in the
afternoon. We stayed until midnight, having drinks in one of the
hotel's bars. We were dazzled by them, and they wanted to know
all about us. Cortázar, kind and straightforward; Vargas Llosa,
serene and observant; Nicanor Parra, very nice; Cela, intolerable
and droll; Allen, stinking, deluded, and playing the "typical innocent American."

It was a memorable night; I have something written about that
encounter around here. When it came time to say goodbye, Allen
made Manolito and me accompany him to the door of his room,
playing a Hebrew psalmody on a little bell, accompanying it
with his peculiar and enveloping chant, "Come, come" (in English). He was saying it to Manolito—he was acting childlike—
so that he would come into his room. I had to tear Manolito away
from there to safety.] (Tr. Emma Claggett and Linda Howe)

The fact that Ginsberg was a well-known and openly gay poet with a
hankering for bad behavior presented problems for Ballagas and Mario,
who spent the most time with him. Later, Mario and Ballagas were
picked up by security police and questioned about their activities with
Ginsberg. They said that they had wanted to meet the poet and to show
him Ballagas's partial translations of his famous poems "Kaddish" and
"Howl" but that they had also enjoyed social time with him. Ginsberg

befriended the young men and heard their stories of official repression of gays. Later, he vociferously protested to authorities about officially sanctioned discrimination against homosexuals. Although authorities temporarily released the young men after they were apprehended, their problems were compounded by events at Casa de las Américas. Ginsberg pinched the director Haydée Santamaría's behind and made a flippant remark about wanting to sleep with Ché. Angered officials kicked Ginsberg out of Cuba for his irreverent behavior and scatological play (Ginsberg 25–30).[8]

Other incidents led to official disapproval of José Mario and to El Puente's demise. Manuel Ballagas claims that officials shut down the publishing house because someone gave the galleys that he had submitted to it for publication to Fidel Castro (interview with the author, Miami, 1996). In "Allen Ginsberg en La Habana" José Mario writes that Rodríguez Rivera witnessed the event (52). Ballagas explains that the text was a collection of fantastic stories influenced by Kafka. The book was never published because, according to Ballagas, Castro, in a speech at the University of Havana, criticized the corrupt and counterrevolutionary bent in his story "Con temor" (With fear). Allegedly, Castro condemned the story as a veiled parody of military service and the revolutionary government. The story goes that he criticized El Puente for its promotion of such decadent material. Ballagas says that, although the story (which was published in Casa de las Américas in 1963) wasn't necessarily controversial, the subject matter was sufficiently irreverent to supply a pretext for eliminating El Puente (interview with the author, Miami, 1996).

In the midst of the excitement generated by the revolution, the origins of Ediciones El Puente were humble. After the revolution there was an explosion of publications; the Cuban writer Alejo Carpentier returned to Cuba from Paris to become head editor of the National Publishing House, and there was extraordinary effervescence on the cultural scene. In 1960 José Mario began to publish young writers like Ana María Simo, Nancy Morejón, Gerardo Fulleda León, Miguel Barnet, and Georgina Herrera with the help of funds from his father's small family business. The young writers also funded their own publications. Gerardo Fulleda León says that, from the outset, José Mario named the publishing house El Puente (The bridge) because he wanted to create a space for political and artistic dialogue. Nancy Morejón met Mario through a mutual friend. He chased her around the University of Havana, insisting on publishing her work. He published one of her poems in his first anthology when she was only seventeen years old, and later he published a book of her poems in 1962.

In an interview with the author, Morejón, who was reluctant to provide details about the intrigue and underhanded maneuvers that destroyed El Puente, describes the idealism and enthusiasm of the group:

> N. M.: Se tejieron mucho, hubo mucha intriga o sea lo que es la mezquindad, la rivalidad literaria. Y con todo eso se trataron de crear problemas políticos donde no los había y el resultado fue un gran descalabro, que sus directores, dos escritores jóvenes fueron al exilio: Ana María Simo y José Mario. Y no se publicaba más. Había muchos matices que, pero entrar en detalles . . . no creo que en estos momentos valdría la pena. Lo que sí te digo es que fue una experiencia valiosa. . . . Él [José Mario] trata de publicar a la gente más joven. Sin embargo, publicó José Ramón Brene, Martínez Furé (que no era tan joven), Lina de Feria. En fin, teníamos una revista. Fue un momento bonito, cada cual tenía su personalidad, su manera de ver las cosas.
>
> L. H.: ¿No les afectó la nueva estética socialista en aquel momento?
>
> N. M: No hubo influencia. Se respetaba la poesía de cada quien. No había que escribir para El Puente. Sí tú eras un buen escritor y tenías un buen libro publicabas en El Puente. No es que ellos te exigieran algo.
>
> . . . No es que tenías que escribir de determinada manera ni con determinada estética. Había mucha variedad, incluso muchas contradicciones. Por ejemplo, ahí se publicó *Poesía yoruba* de [Rogelio] Martínez Furé, se publicaba una obra de teatro, *Santa Camila de La Habana Vieja* (José Ramón Brene) y un libro mío.
>
> . . . Me pareció José Mario el primer editor desinteresado. Él costeó la edición. Y nunca me pidió nada, ni ninguna manipulación de su parte. Siempre él estimuló a que yo siguiera escribiendo . . . y hacía libros y nunca se prostituyó. Él publicaba lo que él quería, lo que él entendía así. . . . Era una empresa privada. (interview with the author, Havana, 16 July 1994)

∞

> [N. M.: There was a lot of lying and intrigue or, rather, what's known as pettiness, literary rivalry. Furthermore, they tried to create political problems where there were none, and the result was a huge disaster. The directors, two young writers, Ana María Simo and José Mario, went into exile. And nothing more was published. There were many nuances that—but to go into detail . . . I don't think it would be worth it right now. What I will tell you is that it was a valuable experience. . . . He [José Mario] tried to publish the youngest people. He also published José Ramón

Brene, [Rogelio] Martínez Furé (who wasn't so young), Lina de
Feria. In short, we had a journal. It was a lovely moment, each
person had his/her own personality and way of seeing things.
    L. H.: Didn't the new socialist aesthetic affect you at that time?
    N. M.: There was no influence. Each person's poetry was re-
spected. One didn't have to write for El Puente. If you were a
good writer and had a good book, you published in El Puente.
It's not as if they were demanding something from you. . . . It's
not as if you had to write in a certain way or with a certain aesthetic. There was a lot of variety, even many contradictions. For
example, *Poesía yoruba* by Martínez Furé was published, a work
of theater was published, *Santa Camila de la Habana Vieja* [José
Ramón Brene], and a book of mine.
    . . . José Mario seemed to me to be the first disinterested edi-
tor. He paid for the publication and never asked me for anything,
nor was there any manipulation on his part. He always encouraged me to continue writing . . . and he . . . never prostituted
himself. He published what he wanted. . . . It was a private business.] (Tr. Emma Claggett and Linda Howe)

When Morejón refers to Mario as one of the few "disinterested" editors, one who did not adhere to any particular aesthetic, she emphasizes
the short-lived freedom that she and others experienced. José Mario
founded El Puente spontaneously, without any explicit manifesto.

In an interview with the author, the playwright and theater director
Gerardo Fulleda León described the activities of El Puente members.
They had published several authors' individual works and published
Novísima poesía cubana in 1962. Other works, including an anthology of
theatrical and a second anthology of poetry, were in the makings. There
were music and poetry performances at the club El gato tuerto and debates about theater and film. He said that the members were too naïvely
revolutionary in their desire to produce independent and ground-
breaking works on their own:

    G. F. L: Editamos los libros en una imprenta particular . . . y
    de allí salieron nuestros primeros libros: uno de José Mario, uno
    de Silvia Barros, el primero de Nancy Morejón. . . . Ana María
    Simo, Nancy, Eugenio Hernández Espinosa y yo (en el teatro)
    éramos como los asesores de libros a publicar. En un momento
    se llegó hasta la idea insólita, por el momento, de crear una re-
    vista de la cual se prepararon dos números y que estaban ya en
    imprenta al borde de salir cuando El Puente desapareció.
    L. H.: ¿Qué hacían ustedes como grupo en aquella época?
    G. F. L: Empezamos a dar recitales de poesía. Hay dos re-
    citales que se dieron en *El gato tuerto,* aquel cabaret nocturno en

donde leímos algunos de los jóvenes poetas y al cual nos ligamos de alguna forma.

También era la música que en aquel momento para nosotros significaba mucho. Por ejemplo, el movimiento de filin[9] con sus mejores exponentes, los cantantes de filing como Elena Burke, Bola de Nieve, Omara [Portuondo], Moraima, Doris de la Torre y el joven Pablo Milanés y compositores como Marta Valdés, José Antonio Méndez y Ela O'Farril, como César Portillo, y otros más. . . . Recuerdo que pasábamos la vida prestándonos libros. Además de eso participábamos mucho en el cine, los debates literarios que había en aquellos momentos y en las funciones del teatro.

L. H.: ¿Principalmente qué tipo de literatura publicaron?

G. F. L.: Se publicaron tres libros de teatro, uno de José Ramón Brene, *Mamico Omí Omó* de José Milián y un tomo con tres obras de Nicolás Door que era una revelación en aquel momento porque a los quince años hizo su primera obra. También publicamos poetas como Georgina Herrera, como Ana Justina. . . . algo de Mercedes Cortázar, como Santiago Ruiz, como Manuel Granados y un libro de poemas míos, un error de adolescencia, publicado como pecado de juventud. Pensábamos hacer una antología de teatro, ya la teníamos hecha por Eugenio Hernández [Espinosa] y por mí que también estaba en edición para que saliera con doce autores entre los que estábamos José Milián, José Brene, Tomás González, Eugenio Hernández Espinosa y yo entre otros más. Pero, principalmente lo que más se publicó fue poesía.

Ya en la revista, sí teníamos intenciones de publicar por ejemplo un poema de Allen Ginsberg, "Aullido," y cosas de Borges, y de diferentes poetas y narradores y de personas poco conocidas. Se pretendía darle salida a la última hornada de jóvenes creadores sin ver ningún tipo de tendencia. (interview with the author, Havana, 28 July 1992)

[G. F. L.: We published our first books privately: one by José Mario, one by Silvia Barros, the first one from Nancy Morejón. . . . Ana María Simo, Nancy, Eugenio Hernández Espinosa, and I (theater works) were like advisers on which books to publish. At one time, we even came to the unusual idea, momentarily, of creating a magazine, for which we prepared two issues. They were about to be published, when El Puente disappeared.

L. H.: What did you do as a group in those days?

G. F. L.: We started having poetry readings. There were two readings in El gato tuerto, that nightclub where we—some of the young poets—read. We bonded in that way. Music meant a lot to us in those days. For example, the *El filin* movement with its best exponents, singers like Elena Burke, Bola de Nieve, Omara [Portuondo], Moraima, Doris de la Torre, and the young Pablo Milanés, and composers like Marta Valdés, José Antonio Méndez, and Ela O'Farril, like César Portillo, and others. . . .

I remember that we spent our time lending books to each other. We also went to films, to literary debates . . . and to the theater.

L. H.: What kind of literature did you publish?

G. F. L.: Three books of theater were published: one by José Ramón Brene [Santa Camila de la Habana Vieja]; *Mamico Omí Omó* by José Milián, and one of three volumes of works by Nicolás Door, which was a revelation in those days, because he wrote his first work at age fifteen. We also published poets like Georgina Herrera, Ana Justina . . . Mercedes Cortázar, Santiago Ruiz, Manuel Granados, and a book of my poems—an adolescent error, published as a youthful sin. We were thinking of creating a theater anthology; Eugenio Hernández [Espinosa] and I had already been prepared one, which was in press. It comprised twelve authors, including José Milián, José Brene, Tomás González, Eugenio Hernández Espinosa, and myself, among others. But poetry was the main thing we had published.

For the journal, we did intend to publish, for example, a poem by Allen Ginsberg, "Howl," and works by Borges, various poets and prose fiction writers, and lesser-known people. Our intention was to introduce the latest wave of young authors without focusing on one particular [aesthetic] tendency]. (Tr. Emma Claggett and Linda Howe)

Mario, Fulleda León, and others collaborated to provide a space for young people to express themselves and to publish without needing entrenched editors' nods of approval. *Novísima poesía cubana*, the first and only poetry anthology that El Puente published, introduced an array of poets that included Nancy Morejón, Francisco Díaz Triana, Georgina Herrera, Joaquín G. Santana, José Mario, Ana Justina, Isel, Miguel Barnet, Mercedes Cortázar, Belkis Cuza Malé, Santiago Ruíz, and Reinaldo Felipe.

In "Notas para un prólogo" to the anthology, Ana María Simo and Reinaldo Felipe hypothesize an ideal poetry for the times, one that does not reflect extreme aesthetic and political positions. They invoke José Lezama Lima, Virgilio Piñera, and Rolando Escardó to expound on the influence of the seminal 1940s literary journal *Orígenes*, in which Lezama Lima exhibited his aesthetics, his chaotic exuberance, and his obsession with metaphors. Simo and Felipe say that although Piñera's poetry appeared during the apogee of *Orígenes*, he enriched his poems with

Kafkian preoccupations, existentialist angst, and absurdism that were absent in *Orígenes*. Likewise, they suggest that Rolando Escardó's poetry exhibits the same anxiety of influence as Piñera's works but that his themes include the overwhelming experience of the Cuban revolution. Escardó represents the antithesis to *Orígenes* aesthetics because of the social themes and personal style that mitigate against the use of fuzzy and disordered metaphors. Simo and Felipe compare and contrast styles featured in the anthology and endorse a poetry that maintains an equilibrium between content and form. They advise against excessive and exclusive focus on two particularly polarized poetic styles, which they allege would lead Cuban poetry to sterile extremes:

> 1)—una poesía vuelta hacia si misma que renuncia a toda comunicación a la más leve objetividad, produciendo como reacción.
> 2)—una poesía propagandística, de ocasión.
> Ambos extremos son ajenos al hombre, lo desconocen. El último porque lo despersonaliza, porque considera las circunstancias y no el individuo; el primero porque lo despoja de sus relaciones, porque considera al individuo sin sus circunstancias.
> De todo lo que antecede deben tener conciencia los jóvenes poetas si aspiran a una poesía que refleje al hombre en lo que tiene en común con los otros hombres, y en sus contradicciones; al hombre que existe, imagina y razona. (13)

> [1]—a self-referential poetry, focused on itself, which renounces all communication, the slightest objectivity, producing itself as a reaction
> 2)—a propagandistic, secondhand poetry
> Both extremes are alien to man; they misrepresent him. The first strips man of his relationships, because it conceives of the individual without his circumstances. The second depersonalizes him, because it deals with circumstances and not the individual.
> Young poets should be conscious of the preceding [pitfalls] if they aspire to a poetry that reflects man in all his commonality and contradictions from others: the man who exists, imagines, and reasons.] (Tr. Emma Claggett and Linda Howe)

It is interesting to look at the role the revolution plays in Simo and Felipe's aesthetic judgment. The reader is drawn into what seems like an intense debate on culture. The editors contrast the advent of a socially and politically committed poetry that could become mere pamphleteering (but is never art) and the dawn of a formal, neo-*Orígenes* verse that is tiresomely self-reflexive and hermetic. They add that some poets have adopted the neo-*Orígenes* style to compensate for the thematic vacuum, change of values, and invalidation of all previous experiences because of the overwhelming phenomenon of revolution (12–13). Simo and Felipe's rejection of either mere pamphleteering or hermetic vacuity, with its exotic and extraneous content, is passionate. Their proposal does two things: it hints of kowtowing to official rhetoric that calls for adherence to revolutionary ideals and, at the same time, it admonishes against propagandizing. Their statement that digressive and timorous neohermetic poetry may not be the most adequate way to express oneself seems disingenuous. Paradoxically, the editors become the defenders of perpetual innovation in poetry even as they give priority to the revolutionary experience, perhaps against their better aesthetic judgment. Faced with the task of reconciling the artist's need for creative freedom with cultural officials' demands for unconditional submission, Simo and Felipe fudge and equivocate.

"Notas" is perhaps best understood as a cautious attempt to build a precarious bridge between the aesthetic extremes that it describes. In spite of the editors' disclaimers, the anthology defies the trend of postrevolutionary Cuban poetry because it gives space to eclectic and cosmopolitan styles. El Puente editors wanted to create trends in different genres and to acquire an influence comparable to that which had been achieved by journals published by young people in other Latin American countries: *El Corno Plumado* (Mexico), *El Pecho de la Ballena* (Venezuela), and *Los Nadaístas* (Colombia). Transcending national politics, they attempted to create neo-panamericanist cultural and political links.

As Ballagas notes, the government had control of most presses and publishing houses by 1965 (interview with the author, Miami, 1996). Authorities assigned El Puente editors to choose a certain number of titles for the year as part of the quotas for UNEAC publications. Even though the editors selected the books, the government provided the paper and did the printing. This procedure completely changed the situation for José Mario. He would no longer be able to publish whatever he wanted. Ballagas emphasizes that, although no official censor was present at the time of publication, either someone at the printers would scrutinize the texts or government bureaucrats would periodically check to see what people were planning to publish. El Puente's first attempt to publish under stricter government control resulted in failure because officials found sufficient, albeit vague, reasons to shut it down.[10] Fulleda León points out that the group's sense of independence and the belief that it could publish almost anything caused political problems:

"Principalmente éramos demasiado revolucionarios en el mejor sentido de la palabra; en lo personal y en lo intelectual. Era una postura que, para algunos, pudiera ser demasiado liberalista, demasiado excéntrica, demasiado escandalosa. Tratamos de expresarnos en todos los sentidos y las peculiaridades personales de algunos de nosotros se pusieron en juego. En algún sentido se confundió, por gente de afuera, el manifestarse personal con las manifestaciones sociales que a veces entran en contradicciones" (interview with the author, Havana, 28 July 1992). [Basically, we were too revolutionary, in the best sense of the word, in the personal and in the intellectual. It was a posture that, for some, could have been too liberal, too eccentric, too scandalous. We tried to express ourselves in every sense and some of our personal peculiarities came into play. In a way, people on the outside confused personal lifestyle with social expression, elements which are often contradictory (tr. Emma Claggett and Linda Howe).]

Unfortunately, in spite of the enthusiasm they generated and the variety of material El Puente published, its contributors were unable to circumvent criticism and to avoid accusations about some individuals' sexual orientation. Rival groups labeled the contributors "los disolutos" (libertines) and accused their editors of scabrous humor, insolence, and deviant social behavior. In reality, some of the group members were homosexuals; many shared ideas, cultural interests, and friendships; and all contributed to El Puente publications. The entire group became vulnerable to vicious attacks on their character.[11] In the confusing and competitive times, the accusations about homosexuality were compounded by the charges of "inappropriate" literary styles and esoteric metaphysical language.

Not surprisingly, the group's enthusiasm for experimental and tentative themes and styles drew sharp criticism from rival groups that found—or affected to find—their works offensive. Jesús Díaz, who became founder and editor of *El Caimán Barbudo*, accused El Puente members of producing "pure" and inane literature and personally singled out particular members (Mario, "Allen Ginsberg en La Habana" 52). Other young writers also challenged El Puente's "decadent" works and drafted "Nos Pronunciamos," a manifesto published in *El Caimán Barbudo* (January 1966) to reprimand El Puente for its alleged apolitical, antirevolutionary aesthetics. This group claimed that the revolution had formed them and that, without it, they could not define themselves. Dramatic oppositions were played out in the manifesto, and the authors established a link between the targets of their attack and their own identities, which were always inscribed in Cuba's cultural tradition of under-development but within the context of a victorious nation that was moving toward authenticity. To paraphrase, the all-encompassing collective "we" claimed that Cuba was following the path to communism through the struggle to become a free nation; Cuban poetry must emanate from the revolutionary experience. Literature cannot be apologetic; rather, it must confront issues. After other pronouncements about the need to create a social poetry of popular language and culture, the authors re-nounced "bad" poetry that takes refuge in poetic words impregnated with "second-hand" metaphysics. The authors claimed that "bad" po-etry alienates man from his circumstances and concluded that "poetry should be a terrible testimony of happiness, sadness, and hope for Cuba's permanency in the world; otherwise, there is nothing."

The inchoate manifesto juxtaposes atemporal ideas about the nineteenth-century writer José Martí's natural man (the particular his-torical and social circumstances of Latin America) and Gramsci's organic intellectual (the intellectual's dedication to the revolutionary cause and to the betterment of society). Because of the sociohistorical and materi-alist point of view, "Nos Pronunciamos" is a culturally specific attack on Cuba's vanguardist trends (1920s–1950s), which was the tradition that El Puente writers wanted to perpetuate. The bellicose language of "Nos Pronunciamos" also had utopic overtones. Modeling themselves on Martí (and backed by the power of the communist state), the young Cubans attempted to imagine an embattled nation through literature that reflects the autochthonous rebellious struggle and new beginnings.

Manuel Díaz Martínez underscores that the document reflects the attitudes of the 1960s, when youths launched their ideas in the name of all new Cuban writers and artists who rejected exhausted formulas and what they saw as pretentious "poetic" words. Echoing the official rhet-oric of Otero, Marinello, and Portuondo, the young authors of the "Nos Pronunciamos" proposed a new and audacious literature, without avant-garde pretensions. They rejected "populist" literature that falsely intellectualized everything and masked "intellectual vacillations," and they singled out El Puente members as perpetrators of decadent litera-ture ("Poesía cubana" 116–17).

The Cuban literary critic Víctor Casaus explains that he and others reproved the individuals allied with El Puente for their insistence on "escapist" poetry: "En términos generales realizaban una poesía meta-física, practicando escapismo de segunda mano (o de tercera: esto era en 1962), y—asombradamente—mantuvieron la edición (a veces autoedición) durante años" (10). [In general terms, they created a meta-physical poetry, a second or third-hand escapism and—amazingly—they maintained the publication (at times self published) for ten years.]

According to Casaus, Jesús Díaz sustained a polemic against the aesthetics that characterized these writers' works. In the journal *La Gaceta de Cuba*, Díaz reiterated the need to eliminate "hysterical-liberalist" thought from Cuban literature and urged—rather ominously—that all young writers be held accountable for their works (10). Casal underscores that the overzealous effort of Díaz to establish himself in cultural affairs and to engage in conflicts with others was another reason for the demise of El Puente; he labeled members of El Puente "terrorist dogmatic" and "hysterical-liberal." Casal says that the group was "rejected ostensibly because of the 'metaphysical' and 'escapist' nature of their poetry. But the 'hysterical-liberal' label implies the origins of the rejection: "they are seen as being afflicted by individualism and liberalism, two unforgivable sins for a true revolutionary." Casal lists Diaz's countless conflicts, labeling them as "Díaz against Jesús Orta and the populist poets as well as Díaz against 'El puente,'" and so on ("Literature and Society" 451).

Presumably, Díaz and others considered their own perspectives as exclusively appropriate for revolutionary expression; Díaz titled his last article condemning the independent publishing house "El últímo puente" (The last bridge). El Puente members attempted to assert themselves during the antagonistic barrage of insults and opportunistic denunciations. In *La Gaceta*, Ana María Simo rejoined Díaz's indictment and attempted to rebut his histrionic generalizations, but to no avail; the handwriting was on the wall for the young intellectuals affiliated with the independent publishing house. Nancy Morejón and Miguel Barnet, who later became successful Cuban writers, were asked to sign the manifesto and refused to do so. On separate occasions, Barnet (*Autógrafas* 42) and Morejón (Bianchi Ross, "Nancy Morejón" 32) stated that they did not feel compelled to subscribe to the manifesto. Although Casaus claims that Barnet and Morejón were not part of the "antirevolutionary trends," they were not spared during the debates. In an interview with Ciro Bianchi Ross, Morejón attests to the professional envy that "despertó odio, recelo y resquemores" [awakened hate, foreboding, and divisions] and contributed to the group's downfall (32). Morejón went twelve years without having any collections of poetry published in Cuba. Nicolás Guillén, who was director of UNEAC at the time, protected Morejón somewhat, and she continued to find work. However, those twelve years of silence seriously affected her cultural output. In her interview with Bianchi Ross, Morejón talks of the repercussions of the El Puente incident: "Nosotros aglutinábamos en 'El Puente.' Pero ni constituíamos un grupo ni jamás subscribimos un manifiesto. . . . Hay gente que nunca nos ha visto bien. No nos vio bien entonces, ni después" (32). [We bonded in El Puente. We neither constituted a group nor did we ever subscribe to a manifesto. . . . Some people have never liked us. They didn't like us then, or afterward.]

Morejón adds that some of the writers from the group who live in exile have spoken out against the Castro government. After the El Puente scandal broke, José Mario was sent to UMAP, and Ana María Simo was taken to a mental institution (with her mother's permission because, purportedly, she feared that Ana María was "turning gay"). Nancy Morejón, Eugenio Hernández Espinosa, and Gerardo Fulleda León did not publish for a long time, until they had ostensibly "reformed" themselves. These young intellectuals found themselves at odds with former allies in spite of their previous symbiotic relations, and all the members found themselves under official scrutiny. José Mario, Ana María Simo, and Manuel Ballagas chose exile (Casal, "Literature and Society" 450–51). Both José Mario and Ana María Simo appeared in the controversial documentary film *Improper Conduct*, in which they criticized official treatment of El Puente members. Castro's intellectual supporters continue to link those dissident voices with former El Puente members who remained in Cuba.

When asked by Bianchi Ross about her long period of poetic "silence," Morejón says that she paid a price for her involvement:

> C. B. R: Ese libro [*Richard trajo su flauta y otros argumentos*] se publicó en 1967. Usted no dio a conocer otro poemario hasta '79, *Parajes de una época*. ¿Qué pasó en esos años?
>
> N. M: Ni yo misma lo sé. Lo único cierto es que nadie quería publicar mi poesía. Se me cerraban todas las puertas. No sufrí humillaciones, pero de poemarios, nada. Hay que recordar que en esos años di a conocer *Lengua de pájaro*, '69, un testimonio escrito en colaboración con Carmen Gonce, y una recopilación de textos sobre Nicolás Guillén que Casa de las Américas incluyó en 1974 en un Serie editorial de Valoración Múltiple.
>
> C. B. R: ¿La melló ese silencio?
>
> N. M.: Sí, me melló. En estos años trabajé como correctora de pruebas, era dirigente sindical. Estaba dispuesta a estar en el lugar donde más se me necesitara. Y quería comprender lo que sucedía conmigo. ¿Qué había hecho yo? Pronto supe que a un escritor se le mide por su obra, y alguna gente quiso pasarme la

cuenta por lo que publiqué en "El Puente". Una poesía que ellos tacharon de hermética. Una acusación que me convirtió en una poeta lezamiana, cuando todavía yo no había leído a Lezama Lima. Imagínese, acusar de herméticos a versos escritos antes de los quince años. Lo que sucedió es que hubo mala fe y mucho misterio y contra eso una no puede hacer nada. (33)

~

[C. B. R.: That book [*Richard trajo su flauta y otros argumentos*] was published in 1967. You didn't publish another collection of poems until '79, *Parajes de una época*. What happened during those years?

N. M.: I don't even know myself. The only certain thing is that no one wanted to publish my poetry. All the doors were closed to me. I didn't suffer humiliations, but as far as collections of poetry, nothing. You must remember that during those years I did publish *Lengua de pájaro* in '69, a testimonial piece in collaboration with Carmen Gonce, and a compilation of texts on Nicolás Guillén, which Casa de las Américas included in a 1974 editor's series called Evaluación Múltiple.

C. B. R.: Did that silence upset you?

N. M.: Yes, it upset me. During those years, I worked as a proofreader and I was a union leader. I was prepared to be wherever I was most needed. And I wanted to understand what was happening with me. What had I done? Soon I found out that a writer is measured by her work, and some people wanted me to pay a price for what I had published in "El Puente." They said the poetry was hermetic, an accusation that turned me into a Lezamian poet, when I had not read Lezama Lima yet. Imagine, labeling verses, that I had written before I was fifteen as hermetic. There was negative intrigue and a lot of mystery; when faced with all that, you can't do anything.] (Tr. Emma Claggett and Linda Howe)

As a consequence, Morejón went to the countryside and dedicated her energies to a testimonial on Nicaro's industrial working conditions. As she noted, she also collaborated with Carmen Gonce on *Lengua de pájaro*. As Morejón says, she did everything possible to reform her image.

After the scandal, not only Morejón but also Barnet shifted away from poetry and concentrated on testimonial writing to emphasize officially approved genres and themes. However, it is important to point out that Barnet was already producing ethnographic works and preparing his interview with Esteban Montejo, the protagonist in *Biografía de un cimarrón*, before the scandal occurred.[12] As the El Puente incident illustrated, artists and writers like Morejón and Barnet complied with the official cultural rules because they did not want to lose the opportunity to publish and to receive literary prestige and prizes. Although Morejón and Barnet later adopted other styles, conversationalism remains a hallmark of their poetic work. Their decisions to remain in Cuba and to seek an accommodation with the new government eventually persuaded the authorities to "forgive" them for the company they had kept.

After the initial surge of committed political poetry, however, new generations of poets in the 1970s deemed exteriorist and conversational style poetry insufficient to fill the gap produced by the suppression of Cuba's hermetic tradition and the prerevolutionary exteriorist traditions from the 1950s. As the Cuban literary critic Victor Fowler Calzada suggests, young poets began producing poetry in a variety of styles, eliminating the socialist-realist style. By the late 1980s, critics and writers conjured the ghosts of avant-garde writing. In Fowler's view, the 1990s were characterized by the resurgence of a neohermetic aesthetic and by the sudden prominence of a new cluster of themes: gays and AIDS, the antiheroes of Castro's "internationalist" wars (particularly Angola), the disaffected youth culture of the "freakies," and intimate, deliberately nonpolitical verse (interview with the author, Havana, August 1996). As Cubans plunged into the Special Period, communist poetry became merely one of many aesthetic styles.

Orphaned Cuban Aesthetics: Poetic In/Justice and Out/Rage

By the early 1990s the Cold War was over, and the Cuban government's Soviet patrons had abandoned the scene not with a bang but with a whimper. Once a subsidized geopolitical bone of contention between boxing superpowers, unexpectedly, the island now had to fend for itself and to lick its utopian wounds on its own. By the dawning of the new millennium, Cuba was approaching the ten-year mark of the Special Period. Economic and political instability had forced the country to overcome one obstacle after another. Like the unfortunate young Elián González, who floated across shark-infested waters from Cuba (economic instability and political entrenchment) to Little Havana in Miami (media-orchestrated political divisiveness, nostalgia, and patriotic histrionics) and back, the island dog-paddled in all directions to stay afloat. Faced with the necessity of saving the government (and quite conceivably their own necks), the authorities no longer had the time or energy to scrutinize every single aspect of Cuban cultural or "moral" affairs.

In the face of potential economic disaster, Castro's government cranked up the rhetoric of national integrity and mobilized the masses to solve food crunches, transportation crises, and power outages. Authorities concentrated on social and economic projects and political marches; they had no time to censure defiant (or merely "decadent") intellectuals. Art to art's fate!

Artists and writers used little cash and lots of ingenuity to paste together cultural output; a simulacrum of Cuba's former lavishly financed art scene. Cultural production in the 1990s disclosed a gaunt state with few resources. Sensing that the critical situation had loosened the authorities' grip, the culturally "enfranchised" (show-business people, artists, and literati) responded with deliberate and unrestrained chastisement. Literature, dance, art, and theater revealed much that had been restrictive, abusive, and erroneous about the revolution. The bloodletting and bitching ranged from eloquent to grandiose. Some intellectuals, grandstanding in self-righteous tones, were wild to blame officials and others for Cuba's failures. Others simply depicted the almost forty years of purges and censorship, the squandering of resources, and the damage to personal integrity. The intelligentsia tallied the battles waged, the damage done, and the elephantine price paid. Works alluded to the demise of the Soviet Union, the loss of "discretionary" funds, the end of the island's chimerical status as a combatant in others' wars, and the unearthing of forbidden topics. Still others were critical of the "selling off" of the island to foreigners, in particular the rampant, Thai-style sex tourism. (Given the government's constant boasting about having put a stop to the prostitution that had flourished under Batista, the communist authorities' eagerness to profit from the sex trade struck many Cubans as particularly grotesque and hypocritical.) Simultaneously appalled, amused, and outraged by the communists' new pragmatism regarding world markets and venture capitalism, artists also were fascinated by the inherent contradictions of their predicament.

At first, officials feigned indifference to the writers' and artists' creative faultfinding. However, by the year 2000, cultural authorities responded more vociferously. They deemed Cuban culture—with its obsessive themes of former official decadence, abuse, and destruction of culture and society—regressive, clichéd, and unquestionably passé. An official persecuting spirit of value formation resurfaced, but there was a hubbub in the art world, perhaps somewhat attenuated by the everyday wait in the breadlines and at bus stops where semi trucks converted into oversized buses, *camellos* (camel-buses), arrived infrequently.

Production stumbled along. Some examples of plays staged in the 1990s provide insight into how the playwrights realistically described contemporary Cuban society's most complex problems and obsessions. Artists conveyed visions of social indignity with audacious creativity. The plays' protagonists' personal circumstances reflect the nation's economic and ideological predicaments, which are constantly placed in contrasted with idyllic revolutionary fervor; hysteria and anarchy are placed in contrast with the stifling ranting of the political old guard. The result is chilling; the audience witnesses the unraveling of the social fabric; the mordant perspectives epitomize a ragtag tarnished, semimoribund Cuba.

The Ministry of Culture loosened the reins on the organization and hierarchy of Cuban theater, and Havana's theater directors immediately transformed production and reshaped the content of plays. For example, the theater directors Flora Lauten, Victor Varela, and Carlos Díaz experimented with innovative forms and distinct themes. Flauten's original version of *La emboscada*, Varela's *La cuarta pared* (with its cacophonic, manic gestures), and Díaz's innovative staging of the classic plays *The Glass Menagerie*, *Tea and Sympathy*, and *A Streetcar Named Desire* instilled fresh blood into the formal features and the actual process of production. With his theater company, Teatro Público, Díaz freely interpreted modes of productions and distinct themes in other staged works like *Caligula*, *The Crucible*, and *La Celestina* to defy audiences' expectations. He juxtaposed cabaret, circus-like elements, and performance art to create engaging and bawdy works that both appalled and titillated audiences and redefined the parameters of Cuban theater.[13]

Likewise, artists who had flourished in Flora Lauten's Teatro Buendía later excelled as directors of their own theater companies. Both Nelda Castillo (El Ciervo Encantado) and Carlos Celdrán (Teatro Argos) took bold steps in different directions to produce beautifully eccentric theatrical works. Castillo's abstract works prioritize gesture and painterly image rather than verbal expression. *Las ruinas circulares* (1992)—a rereading of the "conquest" of Latin America, based on works by Borges and Cervante's *Don Quixote de la Mancha*—is an intellectual wonder of plasticity and metaphor. Castillo also transformed Cuban writer Severo Sarduy's novels into a series of ingenious and colorful images created by the actors' elaborate physical movement and intricate costumes. She injected aspects of cabaret and musical theater in *De donde son los cantantes* (1990). Her brilliant interpretation of *Pájaros de la playa* (2001), Sarduy's posthumous novel, is a complex visual spectacle of disturbing gesticulation and noise. Seminaked and bandaged actors, donning hospital tubes and wrapped in huge pieces of transparent plastic, not only represent states of illness (AIDS) and the illusion of returning to health, but also the agony of imminent death for all human beings.

Celdrán's symbolic and lyrical *Safo* (1991), based on Marguerite Yourcenar's short story "Sappho or Suicide," and the realist psychological thriller *Roberto Zucco* (1995), a play by De Bernard-Marie Koltès based on a criminal's true life story, are masterpieces. *Safo* is a poetic and esoteric play with minimalist staging. Celdrán juxtaposed precious images and prose from Yourcenar's story to portray Sappho's lesbian desire, the ambiguities of sex and gender, and the artists' creative struggle with eternal questions about death and suicide. *Roberto Zucco* is tense, emotional, and critical. Celdrán emphasizes not only the moral ambiguity of his young assassin, but also of the society as a whole. On stage Zucco has unexpected appeal as a modern tragic antihero who resembles Hamlet, paralyzed by alienation, crossed with a preplunge Icarus on a crime spree. The hyperbolic references to a miserable immoral context may be a metaphor for the generalized delinquency of Cuban society since the economic and ethical plunge of the 1990s. Zucco reacts to a spiritually dead world without moral codes; like others in his society, he is a bizarre compendium of victimization, helplessness, and rebellious violence.

Bold thematic changes also occurred; Eugenio Hernández Espinoso's play *Alto riesgo* (staged in 1993) criticizes the lewd and lascivious tourist scene and slings indirect denunciations at society's corruption. Alberto Pedro's play *Manteca* (1993) presents the dilemma that confronts a family that is raising a pig in the bathtub of its city home. When the ill-fated pig grows into a cuddly pet, the family struggles with need to slaughter a loved one to put food on the table during harsh economic times. The thought of devouring the beloved pet torments the family. A microcosm of Cuban society, the family members are forced to abandon their lofty sentiments and to adjust to the deteriorating quality of life. Need and hunger beat them down and numb their common sense.

Grupo Teatro Rita Montaner performed foreign plays about repressive systems, with several symbolic references to corrupt politics and the demoralization of a society. In 1993 Juan Carlos Maurén directed *Dos perdidos en una noche sucia,* by the Brazilian Plínio Marcos, to foreground problematic sexual politics, and in 1995 Gerardo Fulleda León directed

Noche del satín regio, by the Venezuelan José Gabriel Núñez, which exposes the ills of prostitution and draws parallels with Cuba's circumstances. Fulleda León also staged *Dos semanas con la reina* (1995), by the Australian Mary Thompson, which deals with themes of homosexuality and AIDS (Santos Moray 5). Likewise, in 1994, the director Carlos Díaz and his company produced Federico García Lorca's "gay" play *El público* at the Hubert de Blanck theater.

Cuban playwrights also traveled to New York and Miami to expand the theater scene that was evolving in Havana. Ester Suarez's *Baños públicos* and Abelardo Estorino's *El baile o el collar* were staged in New York City in 1999 (Repertorio Español, Gramercy Arts Theater) and Raúl Martín's adaptation of Abilio Estévez's monologue *El enano en la botella* appeared in Miami (3 May 2001, Theater Festival, University of Miami) before it was staged at Repertorio Español at New York's Gramercy Arts Theater. *Baños* emphasizes the Cuban people's spiritual impoverishment and the government's measures to prohibit individual entrepreneurship. The two characters wrestle with each other and with the contradictions produced by the influx of capitalism in a socialist system. The play symbolizes the backyard invasion of private enterprise and the persistence of the black market in every neighborhood on the island. Remnants of the past and numerous worn-out clichés clash with a frightening and new order of things; practically everything is up for sale, and everyone is selling something.

Similarly, in *El baile o el collar,* directed by Estorino, we see the tension mount between what went before the Special Period and the present state of affairs. The seventy-five-year-old Nina roams about in a grand old house of ghosts. Unfortunately, since the present is bleak, she must sell her precious pearl necklace, a family heirloom, to survive. Estorino alludes to Cuba's dire economic straits, and Nina serves as a metaphor for a decrepit system that clings to expired glory as a limited response to the current crisis.

In Estévez's *El enano en la botella* (adapted and directed by Raúl Martín), a dwarf lives a deprived life in a bottle and waxes philosophical and positivistic with regard to his incarcerated fate. When he entertains thoughts of escape from the bottle, he justifies his need to remain within the confines of his lonely prison. Even though the boundaries of his reality oppress and restrict, he succumbs to the only environment he knows. With distressing resignation, he embraces his mentally, physically, and symbolically dwarfed condition and forgoes freedom, adventure, and the opportunity to discover other realities. A metaphor for the universal triumph of mediocrity and the conformity of an inured impoverished existence over personal liberty, the dwarf is a pathetic character, at odds with his own condition but unwilling to change it. Like Goethe's Homunculus in *Faust*, Estevez's dwarf looks to the sea for the source of life; he symbolizes both the human desire for a rebirth and the dwarfed spirit that chooses not to become alive. For many Cubans, after forty years under the rule of a paternalistic government that has restricted freedoms, the idea of radical transformation instills fear and triggers self-censorship; many have acquiesced in the paucity of options and internalized restrictions on expression.

Theatrical adaptations of Senel Paz's novella *El lobo, el bosque y el hombre nuevo*, which deals with the relationship between a gay man and a blinkered, *machista* communist ideologue, became very popular in several theaters in the mid-1990s. The first version was staged in 1991 under the same title as the novella and was directed by Rafael González. Another version, staged that same year and titled *La catedral de helado* was presented as a one-man show in Havana's Teatro Bertolt Brecht, directed by Sarah María. Later that same year, Tony Díaz directed yet another version of the novella, titled *Para comerte mejor* at the El Sótano theater before the play was made into the famous movie *Fresa y chocolate*. Roughly at the same time, some Cuban intellectuals used the medium of documentary film to explore hitherto clandestine Afro-Cuban religious practices, which grew enormously in popularity during the Special Period. The documentaries dealing with this subject matter include Tato Quiñones's *Nganga Kiyangala*; Elio Ruíz's *¿Quién baila aquí?*; Gloria Rolando's *Oggún*; and Lázaro Buria's *Los dioses del futuro*. The films showed that many ordinary Cubans belonged to Afro-Cuban religious societies and participated in religious ceremonies that the government had previously attempted to suppress.

Cultural officials' decision to embrace certain of the cultural manifestations that it had formerly persecuted sometimes took on a comic tinge. For instance, the Afro-Cuban poet Eloy Machado, who had been arrested during one of the boisterous poetry slams and rumba jams that he held in his Cayo Hueso neighborhood, was suddenly invited to perform in the devoutly communist halls of UNEAC, which in the 1960s and 1970s had shown itself so eager to denounce ethnic "microfactionalism." Since 1994, his performances have consisted of readings of his "Afro-Cuban" social protest poetry, accompanied by Afro-Cuban music (Stubbs and Pérez-Sarduy, *Afro Cuba* 18–19).

Writers and artists quickly took advantage of this latest semitolerance.

They joined newly formed cultural foundations, semi-independent institutions that served as alternatives to the state's monopolized institutions (Evenson 21). The painter Tomás Sánchez and the singer/songwriter Pablo Milanés are examples of artists who attempted to create alternative venues for artists to promote their works, although their projects were foiled due to bureaucratic hostility.

The intelligentsia also revived the legacy of previously marginalized writers such as Virgilio Piñera, José Lezama Lima, Calvert Casey, and Gastón Baquero with homages. Casa de las Américas invited the exiled novelist Severo Sarduy (who was dying of AIDS in France) to Havana for a retrospective celebration of his oeuvre, though Sarduy declined the honor. Would Cuban culture ever have to witness the tide turn back and to endure comparable repression? Slowly and tentatively, intellectuals began to feel freer to acknowledge openly that some of the artists and writers whom cultural bureaucrats had persecuted and driven into exile in fact deserved a place of honor in modern Cuban culture.

Some established writers began to write about the economic devastation of the island in the 1990s. In their works, Nancy Morejón and Miguel Barnet depict the abhorrent conditions of prostitution, poverty, and social desperation. In her poem "Marina," from *Paisaje célebre,* Morejón describes a thin horse that wanders in a metaphorical landscape of dilapidated buildings, decaying streets, and zombie-like figures under dire circumstances. The emaciated horse can be viewed as a synecdoche for the devastating physical and psychological state of the Cuban condition. In Barnet's poem "Hijo de obrero," he portrays a young Cuban man's hellish descent into prostitution on the Havana streets. His willingness to sell himself for material goods, his moral degradation, and his imminent death from AIDS symbolize the appalling predicament that young Cubans faced in the demoralizing atmosphere of the 1990s.

Controversies and provocative works also characterized artists' response to the faltering economic and social circumstances. Some cultural bureaucrats who were intolerant of bohemian lifestyles and of certain themes for art limited the exposure and activities of talented artists, including the painter Tomás Sánchez and the Afro-Cuban painter, performing artist, and sculptor Manuel Mendive. Sánchez suffered a serious setback in the 1990s when officials quelled his attempt to create a semiprivate cultural foundation. He angrily left Cuba for the United States. Manuel Mendive never chose exile; his growing international fame was only enhanced when zealots in Miami burned one of his paintings at a 1999 exhibition in Coral Gables.

According to the art critic Gerardo Mosquera, Cuban painting was already aggressive, critical, and irreverent by the 1980s. He reminds us that the official Bolshevik motto "Art: An Arm of the Revolution" and exhibitions with such themes and titles as "Art and Cattle Raising" had by that time all but disappeared from the Cuban art connoisseurs' collective memory ("Introduction" 25). The painters José Bedia and Juan Francisco Elso and the photographers Marta María Pérez and René Peña, who photographed their own bodies to illustrate sexual and religious taboos, exhibited images and symbols of Afro-Cuban culture and religions in their works.[14] Irreverent, humorous, scatological, parodic, and carnivalesque works also characterized the art of Tonel, Grupo Arte Calle, José Ángel Toirac, and Grupo Puré in the mid-1980s. Apparently, these artists overstepped the bounds of official tolerance, because several of their patrons in the cultural bureaucracy were subsequently fired. However, many artists took advantage of the less restrictive climate of the 1990s to venture into heretofore forbidden territory with innovative performance techniques or by employing previously prohibited or ignored styles and subjects in their painting (Mosquera, "Introduction" 28). Others unique artists such as Kcho, Sandra Ramos, Aimé García, Roberto Fabelo, Carlos Estévez, Douglas Pérez, Rolando Estévez, Pedro Pablo Olivia, Carlos Guzmán, Rocío García, Ibrahim Miranda, Carlos Garaicoa, Zaida del Río, Elsa Mora, and José Ángel Vincench traveled abroad to promote and to sell their works, while maintaining residency in Cuba.

Several talented artists of all ages reflect the creative verve of the period, albeit with contradictions and predicaments. Cultural officials promoted the work of the iconoclastic painter Olympya [Olimpia Ortiz Porcegué] in the 1980s and early 1990s, but she later made only intermittent appearances on the official exhibition circuit. The Afro-Cuban graphic artist Belkis Ayón, who committed suicide in 1999, stunned the Cuban art world when she symbolically invaded the secret all-male religious society the Abakuá by drawing female imagery alongside images of male Abakuá figures performing sacred ceremonies. Her graphic prints intrigued the art world but appeared to offend religious leaders and followers. Since the Abakuá society absolutely barred women from any knowledge of or participation in the organization, Ayón's creative evocation that women could invade this all-male world appeared to be sacrilegious and offensive. The installation/performance artist Tania Bruguera produced a newspaper/artwork that was quashed by cultural bureaucrats because it expressed the unauthorized and independent

views of several artists. Moreover, officials saw it as an illegal act to produce an independent publication. Sandra Ceballos and Ezequiel Súarez
challenged the official monopoly on exhibition space by organizing independent exhibitions in a home (with the support of the renowned
Cuban artist Fabelo), a practice widely adopted by later artists.

OLYMPYA

Somewhat snubbed by officials when she was omitted from significant
exhibitions of contemporary Cuban art for more than a decade, the hermetic painter Olympya rose from the ashes to become one of the Cuban
intelligentsia's favorite bohemian painters.[15] Neither the trendy texts
on contemporary Cuban art nor *Artecubano*, the authorative journal on
Cuban visual art, featured her works.

Olympya's paintings transform her living quarters in a cramped
apartment in the Vedado district of Havana into a gallery of nightmar-
ish and fascinatingly tawdry motifs. The resultant scene would cause
most middle-class suburban art collectors and finicky art dealers to con-
tort the face à la Munch and buy everything in the place. Intertextual
references to classic paintings abound; Olympya loots the classic pieces
of the great museums and incongruously fragments them through the
prism of her corrosive and ironic metagaze. She adapts Michelangelo's
depiction of hell in *The Last Judgment,* Goya's *Caprichos,* portraits by
Velázquez and Rembrandt, and Greek and medieval images of Ganymede. She paints a recognizable classic image and provides new interpretations within a Cuban context.

Olympya's renderings lend themselves to creative elucidations. The
Greek image of Ganymede, cupbearer to the gods, has a long, quasi-
religious association with homosexuality. If Olympya approaches any
recognizable interpretation of sacred buggery, it is without Classical or
Renaissance artists' idealized brushstrokes that bestow exceptional
beauty upon Ganymede. By contrast, Olympya's figures, like the
neutered and disconcerted youth whom Jupiter cunningly despoils,
pose among a dizzying display of syncretic Santería and Christian para-
phernalia: crosses, horns, cauldrons for Ogún, sacred beads and candles,
rosaries, sheaths of cowrie shells, coconut renderings of Eleggúa, and
Christ's crown of thorns.

The genius of several paintings and sketches lies in the artist's intertextual, amorphous takes on classic Greek admiration of the male body;
hermaphrodite monsters with sagging breasts, effeminate figures, and

caricaturized vaginas share space with priapic monuments. The attractions of ideal male and female beauty are distorted and filtered through a Dantesque seventh circle of sexual consciousness. In one piece, two satyrs with twisted torsos and full, globular chests and buttocks embrace each other. Some paintings and sketches are variations on a Florentine marble relief that depicts a goat-footed Pan, his well-endowed and stiff member in plain view, pursuing Olympus.[16] Yet other works that distort Renaissance depictions of hell and temptation appear to represent Havana's underworld. For example, in one painting, Olympya illustrates Havana's hours of darkness and the imminent perils of sex and corruption for a woman dressed in a white robe with a hood. Perhaps, Olympya makes a painterly allusion to an allegorical figure like "Purity," but one suspects she also represents a succubus. The cathedral of Old Havana looms on the canvas swathed in lugubrious grays, ominous blues, and sullied whites. A gang of miniature winged monsters hovers over the female figure dressed in a hoary cloth. The monsters portray temptation and evil spirits that attempt to seduce "Purity" as she "innocuously" reclines in the lower half of the canvas. Her apparent innocence is clouded by the sinister, diminutive fiends of avarice and mischief that emanate from the canvas.

In another example of Olympya's political analysis or allegorical repertoire, eerie cupids, dwarfs, deformed angels, and other phantasmagoric masked figures skulk on the canvas. They vaguely recall specters from Goya's *Caprichos* who have emerged to reign over Havana's Bacchanalia. A hodgepodge of bacchantes and statuesque male bodies congregate alongside colorful coconuts, papayas, and flaming-red hearts that, like a pentimento of the mind's eye, accentuate a hidden and multilayered world of eroticism, desire, violence, and seduction.

Still other canvases have painted-on fragments of frames that break up the painterly narratives. Individuals seemed trapped and/or protected by pieces of frames that also serve as demarcations between contradictory religious and sacrilegious practices. Do these works of art represent protection from temptation or repression? Or do they simply comment on how humans succumb to taboo sexual yearnings and religious practices? Olympya executes these impressionistic, partially framed vignettes to create a canvas-as-mask that constantly unmasks traditional imagery in unconventional ways; she cuts a wide swath to evoke paranoia and repression in a mêlée with rapacious cravings and distressing bliss. These harrowing scenes perturb the apparent order of things on and off the canvas.

Olympya's steadfast production, although not considered popular with official Cuban art galleries, is an intrinsically Cuban synthesis: the exogenous elements—an intertextual mix of traditional European styles, cultural elements, and themes—are juxtaposed with local elements drawn from Cuban art and society. Like great twentieth-century Cuban painters such as Wifredo Lam, Amelia Peláez, and Mariano Rodríguez, Olympya inserts herself in well-established traditions, but with innovative irreverence.

TANIA BRUGUERA

While Olympya seldom travels and always paints in her tiny, claustrophobic apartment in Cuba, Tania Bruguera is a globetrotting performance artist who lives and works in the United States and Cuba. Her work—for example, she currently straps animal carcasses to her body—shocks and provokes. Bruguera's body art is reminiscent of the work of the great Cuban performance artist Ana Mendieta. Bruguera's body-as-animal-carcass, like Mendieta's beheading-a-chicken-while-naked performance, constructs what Gloria Moure describes as "a recovery of the mystic and magic sense of life" through archaic and religious iconography (33). Both artists achieve a unique synthesis by linking their own bodies to esoteric symbols of nature, ritual, and sacrifice to defy what is conventionally considered artistic.

In the early 1990s, Bruguera also challenged the protective shield of official Cuban cultural politics when she published an independent renegade art newspaper. According to Eugenio Valdés Figueroa, Bruguera's clandestine newspaper/artwork, titled *Memoria de la postguerra* (Postwar memory), "was a fleeting attempt to fill that space for encounter, debate, and coherence—an attempt to recharge a dynamic that has been extinguished in the Cuban art world" (18–19). Although only two issues of the outlawed work made it to press, Bruguera's bravado gave memorable voice to the artistic and spiritual angst of the Special Period. Her defiant performance gained notoriety in the Cuban cultural milieu, as well as on the international circuit.

BELKIS AYÓN

In the Cuban art world and on the streets of Havana, some Cubans feared that Belkis Ayón's artistic invasion of the African-based secret and exclusively male religious society, the Abakuá, would bring her bad luck. Although many others believed that such ideas were superstitious nonsense, Ayón's suicide in 1999 sent shock waves through the art community. She was an innovator in the official art world and demonstrated overt insolence toward patriarchal Afro-Cuban religious ceremonies when she artistically crossed over into a prohibited and misogynistic religious world. Ayón explores taboos on several levels where race, gender, and religion intersect when she inserts female figures into her portrayal of the Abakuá rituals and ceremonies. She is one of only a few Afro-Cuban women to win recognition as a major artist in Cuba, and her works call into question well-established patriarchal traditions by which women are usually excluded from the hierarchy in most African-based religious societies and are absolutely excluded from the Abakuá organization.

Ayón's suicide cut short a brilliant and creative process in which a young black female artist challenged established norms on several fronts.

CEBALLOS AND SÚAREZ

Irreverence toward tradition and standards was a prevalent artistic motif in the 1990s. In 1994 Sandra Ceballos and Ezequiel Súarez founded Espacio Aglutinador, an unofficial, intimate venue outside the officially sanctioned space for art exhibitions (Valdés Figueroa 20). Upon declaring in their manifesto that "every house is a gallery," the founders of Aglutinador provided a place for young artists to express themselves freely and shielded them from their own skepticism.[17] Several artists came to feel that they were wasting their lives on mere survival tactics in the 1990s, especially since they had no place to exhibit their work. Ceballos and Suarez provided them with a personal art space that offered a reprieve from the stifling officialdom and hierarchical institutions that excluded them.

While several Cuban artists made a reputation for themselves on the national art scene, others carried their portfolios with them wherever they ventured to travel. The exodus of Cuban artists created a new export—talent.

Mosquera compares the artist's life to that of a fisherman: "they make a living offshore but always return to port." He describes the artist's relation to changing demographics and to diasporic production in terms of a nomadic peddler who sells abroad: "A possible taxonomy could be defined as follows: those who remain (islanders); those who left, pay their taxes (dis-islanders); those who stay but are eager to leave (involuntary islanders); those who left, pay their taxes, and come back on vacation (low-intensity exiles); and those who come and go, called 'papinization' types (referring to Los Papines, a group of globe-trotting drummers). Today, art is principally an export product" ("Introduction" 28).

Cuban artists communicate their spiritual exhaustion and disillusionment with abstract freedoms through social perspectives derived from the fall of utopian ideals. They have witnessed Cuba's contradictions where "Hispano-American *caudillismo* is joined with 'socialist' orthodoxy and with opening up to foreign capitalism and where the authoritarian system is joined with mercantilism and sexual tourism" (Mosquera, "Introduction" 28).

While some artists and writers seemed unquestionably earnest in their criticisms of the government's worst depredations, in some cases a certain self-serving hypocrisy made its appearance. For example, the smash hit *Fresa y chocolate* won the top award at the 1993 Havana Film Festival. Interestingly, the film itself has become a commodity well marketed by the same bureaucrats who once wavered between tolerance and repression of cultural expression but who have always remained deftly in step with official decrees. Dopico Black reminds us that the only constant during three decades of contradictions in intellectuals' relations with the government is "the dependence of artistic policy on Cuba's prevailing political climate" (107). Facts about those who determine what, if anything, can be criticized at all are hidden away in cultural officials' mysterious vaults.

By the time the Special Period was no longer special, several Cubans had lost their fear of expressing previously censured ideas. Like impatient children whose reverence for paternal care and authority unexpectedly gives way to rebellion and sassiness, the artistic community reacted with critical interpretations of "socialist reality." The cultural elite surfaced to express the general malaise and the bitterness of the oxymoronic Special Period, more eternal than special and, ironically, with no end in sight.

Everyone in Cuba appeared to be exhausted and hungry but with a persistent thirst for the revolutionary past. Nevertheless, the young (and not so young) artists wanted to have their say about the autumn of the patriarchal relationship. Under often-contradictory circumstances, affairs, and nasty breakups, Cuban artists and writers chewed at the official hand that rationed their appetite for production. Some artists refined pathological mirroring and satirized the loss of their privileged status. The wide range of themes and images conveyed a dismal collective vision.

"I Have Always Depended on the Kindness of Strangers"

Enter Blanche DuBois, the tragic heroine of Tennessee Williams's *A Streetcar Named Desire* (1947). She clings to her former beauty but is exposed as a tawdry sex goddess fading into madness. Marianela Boán, a celebrated Cuban choreographer and the director of DanzAbierta, has adopted the persona of Blanche DuBois for her modern dance performance entitled *Blanche,* which premiered at the National Theater in Havana (18 February 2000).[18]

Boán insists on telling Blanche's story of regrets, lurid desires, unfulfilled dreams, and frustrations. More vulnerable than voluptuous, Blanche wears signs of sinister erotica and pathetic psychosexuality all over her breasts, thighs, and groin. Boán recites and sings some of Blanche's lines from *A Streetcar Named Desire* and dances her way through a metaphorical journey of physical and moral decay in the Cuban context of flag waving and erotic, reverent devotion to chimerical utopian causes. Boán's Blanche, as a worn-out militia girl, mocks a nation's unbridled nationalism and perpetual calls for sacrifice.

Equally striking is Blanche's bitterness over her tiny pension, the miniscule return received in exchange for so great a labor of love. Boán's depressing, enervating, and erotically charged salute to a "glorious" past dovetails with Williams's message that Blanche's remembrance is not truly of things past. Williams's text starkly highlights the contradiction between Blanche's elegant, genteel life on the plantation Belle Rêve (Beautiful dream) and her squalid encounters with drunken soldiers and with patrons of the seedy Flamingo Hotel. Blanche struggles to confirm a romanticized version of her past and tries to erase the ugliness of life with booze, long, hot baths, and the hope of starting afresh with a new beau in New Orleans.

Unfortunately, Boan's Blanche has aged, her pension has shrunk, and her sex appeal has all but evaporated. Momentarily undaunted, she pays her respects to patriotism. At one point in the performance, we witness Blanche, dressed in the delicate (and grossly misleading) white robe of a virgin. She lies face up on a clothes trunk with a flagpole between her legs, breathing heavily against the emptiness of the stage. Boán simulates the sexual act as Blanche desperately gyrates against the flagpole, repeatedly thrusting her middle-aged body at the hard rod. In Blanche's imaginary world, the power of pleasure segues into an exquisite masturbatory show of solidarity with the flag. Her appetite for eternal youth and her feigned mawkishness overpower her energetic drive. Blanche's flagpole humping is a perfunctory last stand. Subsequently, she collapses, crushed by the weight of the trunk and the years of philandering.

At the beginning of the performance, Blanche emerged from the trunk with great difficulty to begin her dance of madness. As if to express a simple physiological reaction, she releases a reluctant homage to her own moral and physical decadence, inadvertently alluding to some apocalypse. We sense the demise of the *monstres sacrés* of her former world; delusions of grandeur mesh with blind nationalism to create virtual reality legacies: a juxtaposition of whoring to save Belle Rêve and to save herself from the ravages of time. Clenched fists punch out the performance; Blanche is victimized by her insistence on the glory of bygone days. Her genteel dreams and erotic frustrations resurface like cancer cells after failed chemotherapy.

Although the gist of the performance stands in sharp contrast to Williams's text, Boán represents the burden of Cuba's current predicament. Many in-house references convey urgent and disheveled impressions of the revolution. We find Blanche either trapped within the trunk or propped up by it or pinned underneath it. The boxy chamber that preserves and protects her is ultimately her tomb.

Blanche's desire to prolong her tattered and pathetic image beyond her years is finally consumed by madness. A wasted life of debauchery? False courage and dedication to haughty survival? Boán recounts the Cuban condition through a dilapidated body and spirit; she brilliantly portrays Blanche's erotically charged prancing as an antithesis to unrestrained nationalism. Measured against epithets from famous Cuban poems—"Beautiful Cuba" and "Pearl of the Sea"—Blanche weighs in as a degenerate and smudged barnacle. She does not seem to have a grip on what is happening to her.

Boán's delirious, feverishly erotomaniacal demimondaine is a shocking but curiously apt symbol for late socialist Cuba. Blanche's pleas bitingly mimic the billboards festooned around Havana in 2000, where the once-proud slogan "Viva Cuba" (Long live Cuba) has been replaced with the comically nervous reassurance that "Cuba vive"—that is, that the old girl is still hanging on. With theatrical boldness and uncanny movement, Boán lifts Blanche's voice from the ashes of rock-bottom luck. Her agonized facial expressions and contorted gestures convey strong narcissistic and paranoid tendencies; Blanche's impending insanity is a tragicomedy. Echoes of "Cuba vive" hauntingly float through the musty and stifling air of the theater. We focus on Blanche's ultimate distorted mask of former ecstasy and present agony.

The Eternal Return, Again

In contrast to Boán's performance as a diminished antiheroine, the Cuban theater director Raúl Martín, in his version of Virgilio Piñera's *Los siervos,* depicts one of Cuban theater's most recent heroes, Nicleto (played by Dexter Pérez Cápiro, formerly an actor with Martín's Teatro de la luna troupe). Nicleto sanely and deliberately declares himself a slave to the state; he ensures his own martyrdom by exposing the hypocrisy of the "egalitarian" system. The apparatchiks, perplexed by his appeal, want to uphold themselves as the exclusive, perpetual heroes of their political system without deferring to Nicleto's passive protest and against the inequalities of the system. Nevertheless, when the antihero insists on his servitude as a way of mocking the status quo, the leaders are reluctantly compelled to eliminate him.

Los siervos was never staged during Piñera's lifetime. Not surprisingly, it was also not included in the edition of Piñera's "complete" works for theater, published in 1961. In Piñera's original text, published in the journal *Ciclón* in 1955, the characters have Russian names, and, according to the stage directions, portraits of Lenin and Stalin hang on the walls of the sets. When Martín produced the first successful opening of the play in Havana, in September 1999, he substituted "neutral" names for the Russian ones, expunged verbal references to communism, and purged Russian revolutionary iconography from the production. Since most Cubans have no access to the original text, perhaps the "subtle" extraction of Russia, communism, and Lenin was a deliberate attempt to repoliticize the work. Martín manipulates the text and Piñera's juxtaposition of philosophical approaches that criticize a Stalinist government, which piques our curiosity. Does the erasure of Stalinist content actually confirm Piñera's thesis in Cuba's contemporary context? In a blurb from the performance program, Martín claims that the play is about a futuristic society but emphasizes the party's abuse of power and its leaders' corruption.

Restrictions on free will and repression of "deviance" underscore the performance. Throughout the play, the apparatchiks deliver convoluted speeches with empty phrasing and incessantly plot among themselves. Martín's production shows a baneful world in which being earnest is naïve, laughable, and politically precarious. The leaders build up Nicleto to study his political charisma and to help him achieve fame and glory as the paragon of revolutionary ideals. All the while, they scornfully plot his doom. As the sun falls on the fictitious empire, our hero dances himself into a trance of ecstasy and eventual paroxysm like a whirling dervish. The narrative winds up and then down; the hero anxiously contemplates his role. Like Joan of Arc, he is a victim of his own mystic qualities and prey to the bureaucracy and the ideological battles that uphold him. He foresees his ill-fated end and vows to die for his independence and freethinking. As a martyr, he beats the establishment at its game, since the leaders are overcome with hatred and must quash him. Even though they fear that his death will destroy their political system, they feel that he must die for having revealed the true hierarchy of the master/slave system. With a vengeance, they snuff out the iconoclast hero. As predicted, more "slaves" appear to take his place, indicating the cyclical struggle with unsullied players. The eternal return of Piñera's defiant "siervo," whose sacrifice produces thousands more "siervos," underscores a defiance that transcends time. Likewise, Piñera's appropriation of Nietzsche's skepticism undermines romantic revolutionary ideals of progress and revolution. Here, a universal message about the repetition of cycles disturbs the apparent order of things.

Martín's strategies are in keeping with Piñera's critical tendencies. Piñera was a well-known Cuban playwright, poet, and a significant figure of absurdist literature of the 1940s and 1950s. After the revolution, he continued to publish stories and to write plays until his death in 1969. Unfortunately, his personal battles with government officials, his flamboyant and witty personality, and his controversial gay lifestyle made for a thorny life in Cuba.

Although Piñera died in a state of official disgrace, he appears to have passed the iconoclast wand on to Martín, who is one of the most promising young theater directors in Havana. Martín scrupulously pushes the envelope as far as he can to criticize officialdom. He goes beyond Piñera's mockery of the status quo, superimposing Piñera's cynicism onto current revolutionary myth and the infrastructure of the state. Staging potentially explosive plays in an officially "controlled" atmosphere is a brilliant stoke of bravado. In productions of other Piñera plays, such as *The Wedding* and *Electra Garrigó*, Martín successfully draws out their humor but adds his own burlesque references to popular Cuban music, dance, and the media. In these campy performances, Martín manages to circumvent direct attacks on official propaganda, while exposing the contradictory morality of authoritative rhetoric with Piñera's absurd double-speak. Although *Los siervos* does not share the humor of Pinera's other plays, Martín directs a risky performance within potentially hostile territory.

Unlike Boán's Blanche, Martín's Nicleto performs ceremonious dance to prepare for his death at the hands of the authorities. He reaches heights of well-planned beatific fastidiousness when he chooses to sacrifice himself to bring down the system. Both Martín and Boán portray subversive individuals who do not survive in decadent systems. Nicleto's sacrifice differs from that of Blanche; sadly, her flame simply expires, but the laborious measures required to destroy Nicleto leave the spectator exhausted but with the hope for transformation.

Not surprisingly, Martín's and Boan's daring productions are extremely popular among young Havana intellectuals. Their performances are well staged and intelligently produced, using some of the best youthful talent in the business. Frankly, these artists profit little from their loyal but elitist following, and, up until now, they have avoided censorship in spite of the fact that some official criticism has been directed at their works. Part of their success lies in their ability to deny what is meant and to use double entendres and ambiguous, often humorous gesticulations to make critical points. Interestingly, in a parallel way, in communist Poland of the early sixties, Claudius in *Hamlet* was often portrayed as a vicious communist. The producers made their point but preserved deniability.

Martín and Boán juxtapose various historical periods, revolutionary rhetoric, and a variety of extraneous cultural texts. Intertextual flashbacks and freeze-framing of scenes and characters from Williams's and Piñera's works become Boán's and Martín's layered and embellished commentaries on Cuba's contemporary circumstances. These artists provide Blanche DuBois and Nicleto with new contexts; each protagonist's downfall is a thinly disguised critique of a failing political system.

The two artists share symbolic systems and have created projects together; Martín collaborated with Boán on the choreography for the Blanche DuBois performance, and the two have teamed up on other dance and theater performances. They are esteemed and intrepid artists who question "revolutionary truths" and shake up the ideological rigidity that has often been a barrier to cultural invention.

Retractors of the Revolutionary Period:
Bad Boys, Bad Girls

Within the context of the Special Period, Cubans with fresh perspectives assess the cultural and political events that have thrust artists and writers into controversial polemics since the 1960s. Several works depict authorities' battles to restrain writers and artists, to marginalize them, or to eliminate them. And yet these are not altogether new themes for Cuban culture. Wronged, tragic, and pathetic heroes have always struggled with decadent and corrupt political and social systems. Numerous artists have defied the moral self-righteousness of the government to point out the repression and trauma that pervaded the artistic and literary worlds. More often than not, these writers and artists have eventually left Cuba.

One such case is the late Cuban writer Reinaldo Arenas. He, along with other exiled artists and writers, thoroughly scrutinized Cuba's institutional repression long before the economic plunge of the 1990s. In several works, none of which could be published in Cuba, he criticized official repression with intertextual references and pseudohistorical data. In 1980, during the Mariel exodus, Arenas left Cuba and arrived in the United States. In 1991 he committed suicide while in the final stages of physical deterioration due to AIDS. Among other work, he left a trail of literary testimony and exposés on the art of gay seduction in Cuba. According to Arenas, sexual inveiglement was a skill in the clandestine, bisexual, macho world that he had experienced as a youth.

In Arena's hilarious and distressing novel *El mundo alucinante*, authorities relentlessly pursue, imprison, and torture the protagonist, Fray Servando Teresa de Mier (1763–1827), after he argues against Spanish officialdom's version of the legend of the Virgin of Guadalupe in a sermon in 1794. His heretical theory that the Virgin first appeared on Quetzalcóatl's cape undermines Spain's claim to have introduced Christianity to the New World. The narrative depicts an individual's struggle against the gray, bureaucratic power of the Inquisition. Fray Servando's story also can be viewed as a melodramatic, bombastic, and picaresque portrayal of oppression, with all the caustic barbs aimed at the Cuban government's policies.

Although the novel ostensibly deals with the tribulations of an independence-era Mexican liberal, there is little doubt that in reality it is an allegory of Cuban authorities' repression of culture under Fidel

Castro. Fray Servando's life of misfortune occurs in an atmosphere of ter-
ror parallel to that of the Cuban cultural milieu during the period of the
UMAP camps. Unwittingly, the camps became a precedent for the infamous *quinquenio gris* (1970–75), when scholars, writers, and artists were
systematically purged. Many critics claim that officials deliberately un-
derestimate the length and scope of the repression.

Thinly disguised semiautobiographical details of Arenas's life frame
dreamlike sequences of Fray Servando's misadventures. We witness a
series of acerbic vignettes, each disclosing subtle aspects of the protagonist's political and personal calamities due to official censorship, subjugation, and persecution. There are evident analogies with the Cuban
government's random and acrimonious treatment of some irreverent
souls and "scandalous personalities" like Arenas. Arenas lived a picaresque life, fleeing from authorities to avoid arrest and stashing his manuscripts in hiding places or smuggling them out of the country to get
them published.

Curiously, an overview of his works reveals a trajectory that deliberately moves from parables of official repression to depictions of capri-
cious sexual aberration in a homophobic world. Later on, with the cu-
mulative experiences of exile and sexual promiscuity and a penchant for
high productivity, Arenas produced several more creative and somewhat rabid texts. His literary output peaked with his autobiography,
Antes que anochezca, which includes vignettes of several phases of his life.
At first, we witness stories of an *enfant sauvage* who eats dirt in the
Cuban countryside and sodomizes animals. Later, the picaresque antihero, who resembles a ravenous Lazarillo de Tormes and a seductive
Tom Jones, scandalizes the city with his sexual adventures before becoming a writer—not just any writer, but a brash Cuban homosexual
bad-boy writer who escapes to the United States. Soon, he experiences
ennui in the American "gay" world of predictable bar scenarios and
tedious cultural events. Finally, we witness him as an ill man whose suicide brings closure to his political rage and biting tongue.

Most of the wild behavior described in *Antes que anochezca* is a scatological response to Cuban intellectuals' lack of freedom and to the
Cuban authorities' ludicrously obsessive determination to banish
homosexuals and other "undesirables" from official artistic life. Published posthumously, this text can be viewed both as one of Arenas's
ferocious, scurrilous frenzies and as a masterpiece à la Jean Genet. He
slams one ignominious metaphor after another down the reader's throat,
performing character assassination on practically everyone involved in

the cultural milieu of the times. In fragmented doses, he illustrates the zeitgeist of three decades (1960s–1980s), sparing no luxury of detail, except for bits and pieces of his own painful past.

When one mentions the name Zoé Valdés or her novel *La nada cotidiana*, published outside Cuba during the Special Period, in 1992, Cuban intellectuals on the island tend to cringe. They have nicknamed her "Soez" Valdés (the word means "vile" or "coarse"), and they protest that her work is cheap, opportunistic trash. It is true that Valdés's erotic and gaudy themes of discontent embody the trendy bitching that has become cliché par excellence in Cuban cultural production in the diaspora and in Cuba since the early 1990s. Her caustic tone seems less rabid than Arenas's and comes at a later stage of the revolutionary system, when "rationing" meant the equal distribution of a diminishing number of goods and when the black market was no longer an outlet for luxury items, like canned Russian meat, but an absolute necessity if you wanted to eat. Likewise, sex was no longer an adventure or a curiosity. Rather, as many Cubans have said, it was the only satisfying and affordable activity a Cuban could experience without having to wait in long lines or use the official socialist rationing card.[19]

Whereas Arenas strikes back at the dictatorship that harassed him and confiscated his texts, Valdés chews and spits out the revolution that nurtured her to adulthood. She suggests that fornication characterizes the official duty of revolutionary idealists. Caustically, she delights in descriptions of sexual acts and ridiculously humiliating erotic exploits. She depicts a young Cuban woman's struggle with relentless hassles and a meaningless life in economically strapped and politically compromised Cuba. The female protagonist's encounters either with the overblown ego of an established and cynical intellectual who takes advantage of her naiveté or with the underflated ego of the nihilist, symbolize Cuba's bravado and impotence when faced with insurmountable historical challenges.

Valdés portrays the revolution as a retrogressive and worn-out residual self-image. Her scathing narrative does not cut the Cuban bureaucracy any slack. Her deliberate "bad" writing seems to be synonymous with the modus operandi she portrays. Even when Cuban critics describe *La nada cotidiana* as trivial and poorly written, they acknowledge the tremendous impact the work has had on European literary circles, especially in France, Spain, and Germany. The fact that Cuban officials condemned Valdés's book as a compilation of tawdry lies confirms that they found it significant enough to complain about. In spite of the

criticism, Valdés's humor and mockery of Cuban sensibility share ground
with many works produced in and out of Cuba during the Special
Period. Since Valdés published *La nada cotidiana*, several other authors
have written exhibitionistic sexual narratives or depicted characters
ridden with philosophical angst and social alienation. Among the best
known are Chely Lima's *Triángulas mágicas*; Daína Chaviano's *El hombre, la hembra y el hambre*; the tetralogy *Las cuatro estaciones*, by Leonardo
Padura Fuentes (*Máscaras, Paisaje de otoño, Pasado perfecto*, and *Vientos
de cuaresma*); the chilling testimonial *Dulces guerreros cubanos*, by Nor-
berto Fuentes; Pedro Juan Gutiérrez's *Dirty Havana Trilogy*; and *Livadia*,
by José Manuel Prieto. Chaviano's and Lima's work share characteristics with that of Valdés; the authors all use first-person narrators who
lead lives chock full of humorous calamities and constant hunger. Likewise, Fuentes, Prieto, and Padura Fuentes reveal the corruption and ar-
bitrariness of the political and social system, using a range of styles. For
example, Prieto's first-person narrator journeys in and out of reality
between the lush and the seedy, but always with alluring prose. In
Gutiérrez's *Dirty Havana Trilogy*, we watch a former journalist engage
in untroubled multiple sexual encounters and unbridled drug use. First-
person musings betray a mind coping with the exigencies of day-to-
day survival through a blissful cloud of rum and marijuana. Richard
Bernstein describes the novel's "Sadean" versions of hedonistic lives
and its Bukowski-like "prolo-macho" narratives that depict raw street
life (Bernstein). The text also suggests a Célinesque journey to the end
of the revolution. Washed-up, innocent, and self-destructive characters
are sheltered by sex, drugs, delusions of grandeur, and scabrous ni-
hilism. In one case, Berta, a seventy-six-year-old woman, consummates
an unlikely union with a young hustler named Omar, because, frankly,
sex is good. Under mysterious circumstances, she dies before the ink
dries on her newly drawn-up will in which she bequeaths everything
to Omar. For his part, Omar filches what little remains of Berta's dignity, as well as her money. Gutiérrez's picaresque narratives illustrate
the defiant, loose, and "dirty" spirit of the streets of Havana.[20]

Many characters in these works question their own banal, hand-to-
mouth existences. Some suffer and endure, while others hope and de-
lude themselves, fabricating surreal and magical "realities" that do not
endure. A subdued counterpoint to the creative bitching and revision-
ist questioning of Cuban history and identity can be found in the works
of the writers Abilio Estévez and Ena Lucía Portela. Although poignant
portraits of a depraved society, Estevez's *Tuyo es el reino* and Portela's

El pájaro: pincel y tinta china and *La sombra del caminante* are poetic works that give priority to style and form. Unlike other Cuban writers who vividly portray the peeling and crumbling of their country's socialist façade and infrastructure, Estévez and Portela distance themselves from the realist narratives to explore interior worlds.

In one way or another, several works critical of the Cuban government or society reflect on the personal consequences of political experiences. In light of Reinaldo Arenas's horrendous experiences with government officials and the more recent revelations about bureaucratic repression and purges of artists and writers, we may ask what purpose such works serve. Is Arenas's caustic babbling just a frivolous bad boy's much ado about nothing? Are his furious ad hominem attacks on his fellow Cuban writers just poetic license, linking something conspicuously nefarious to his unsuspecting enemies? Are the woman's sexual experiences, sometimes humiliating, at other times titillating, in Valdés's novel gratuitous smut or clever and telling metaphors for a well-deserved psychosexual spanking on the aging and wrinkled *trasero* (behind) of the revolution? It might be possible for some to argue that Martín's and Boán's portrayals of fragile heroes and ideals crushed by totalitarian systems are opportunistic gestures in the post-Soviet era of cultural production. Supporters of the Castro government would maintain that Arenas's and Valdés' writings, Martín's reproductions of Piñera's plays, Boán's acidic dance performances, and the different artistic and iconoclast works by Bruguera, Olympya, and Ceballos are nothing more than "bourgeois decadence," the work of status-hungry opportunists. After all, these critics argue, it is unfair to pick on Cuba, considering the sociohistorical circumstances under which the revolutionary government was to survive after 1959.

Viewed differently, these artists' jabberwocky voices the muffled roar of long-forgotten works that offended stodgy and moralistic officials. Justification or disregard for these works does not neatly dismiss the veiled repression and the subsequent damage to the human spirit; they merely insinuate that something flagrant took place. Perhaps the works of the 1990s and the early 2000s pay homage to those artists and writers who never fit in; to those who simply went mad or are soon to be mad; to the ones who left; and to those whose integrity was sacrificed for rash political causes.[21]

2

Revolutionary Politics, Cultural Production, and Afro-Cuban Intellectuals
The Elusive Afro-Cuban

While Cuban scholars have linked historical forms of racial oppression to discrimination in the first half of the twentieth century, criticizing paternalistic governments, segregationist policies, the 1912 "race war," and limited Afro-Cuban cultural representation, they have largely avoided examining Afro-Cuban expression itself after 1959. Sociological works on contemporary conditions published after the revolution are scarce because authorities argued that they produced contradictions for a socialist state. The Cuban journalist Gisela Arandia, who writes on Cuban racial and sexual relations, attributes this phenomenon to the government's assertion that only capitalist societies produce racism and that, therefore, only they require sociological scrutiny: "Yo creo que esto se debe a que, en general, en los países socialistas la sociología ha sido una ciencia bastante preterida, hasta olvidada, porque esta ciencia se vió como algo que podría hacer, ¿cómo decir?, podría crear contradicciones en ciertos niveles políticos" (interview with the author, Havana, 5 August 1992). [I think this attitude is a result of the fact that, in general, in socialist countries, sociology has been a generally ignored, even a forgotten, science, because it was seen as something that could—how to explain it?—could create contradictions on certain political levels (tr. Linda Howe).]

The historians and writers Jean Stubbs, Pedro Pérez Sarduy, Frank Taylor, Wyatt MacGaffey, and Clifford R. Barnett agree that authorities discouraged studies of blacks, claiming that institutional eradication of racism had resolved racial discrimination.[1] At a time when the United States was threatening Cuba's unification and independence, dividing the country over racial or other microfactional issues meant weakening the struggle against counterrevolutionary forces. Research on Afro-Cubans is limited to historiography, anthropology and folklore; folklore scholars conceive black culture as consisting of purely "popular" elements in Cuban society (F. Taylor 22–24).[2]

Outside Cuba, studies on Afro-Cuban expression are marred by the authors' implicit condemnation or defense of Fidel Castro's racial policies. For example, Jean Stubb's and Pedro Pérez Sarduy's *Afro Cuba* is a substantive compilation of writings about blacks, but their decision not to discuss Afro-Cuban politics, coupled with their expressed doubts that anyone can surmise which writers are black, inadvertently whitewash racial relations after 1959. Carlos Moore's *Castro, the Blacks, and Africa* is an illuminating probe into the government's racial policies, but it is encumbered by undisclosed sources, passionate anti-Castro diatribes, and distortion of events. Eugenio Matibag's *Afro-Cuban Religious Experience: Cultural Reflections in Narrative* depends largely on Moore's statements about official repression of Afro-Cuban culture. Matibag glosses over the complex political and social changes that blacks experienced after 1959, opting to concentrate on officials' attempts to eliminate Afro-Cuban religions and the labor groups associated with these religions.[3]

For the allied and competing factions that sought to foment a culture appropriate to the revolutionary society—Afro-Cubans, independent intellectual and artists' groups, and others supported by official institutions—just what was essential to Cuban society, how it should develop, and who should control the cultural agenda were the subject of polemical debates. During the first years of the revolution, neither writer nor party member could predict with certainty the character and obligations of Cuban revolutionary cultural production.

Soon, official policies and actions limited blacks' political activity and circumscribed scholarly output on any contemporary black expression that departed from officially sanctioned views of black politics as an integral aspect of Cuban national identity. The Afro-Cuban intellectuals and artists Sara Gómez, Nancy Morejón, Tomás Fernández Robaina, Inés María Martiatu Terry, Walterio Carbonell, Tomás

González, Eloy Machado (El Ambia), Alberto Pedro, Rogelio Martínez Furé, Pedro Pérez Sarduy, Gerardo Fulleda León, Eugenio Hernández Espinosa, and others have promoted Afro-Cuban culture in their works and lives since the revolution. They have received official support and awards as long as their works conformed to official prescriptions and did not contest the status quo on cultural production or racial relations. However, when their pro-Afro-Cuban politics have gone beyond the party line, Cuban authorities have reproached them (Menton 141; Bethell 119–20). For example, in the 1960s, when Afro-Cubans attempted to join the African American Black Panther leader Eldridge Cleaver's Panther chapter in Cuba or when Afro-Cuban intellectuals and artists gathered to discuss black issues, Malcolm X, Frantz Fanon, and their own works, officials quelled their meetings. Authorities would not tolerate unofficial, controversial, or putatively separatist Afro-Cuban expression.[4] As a consequence of this official silencing, little is known about what happened to Afro-Cubans who expressed black pride and promoted black issues during the turbulent 1960s and 1970s. However, militant African Americans visited or escaped to Cuba, expressing solidarity with the government's anti-imperialist, antiracist, pro–Black Power rhetoric.

Does cultural production in Cuba reflect the reality of blacks' societal integration, or does it merely mimic revolutionary rhetoric on ideal racial harmony? Did official promotion of folkloric aspects of black culture eclipse black "separatist" politics, thereby neutralizing Afro-Cuban cultural and political expression? If officials restrained black intellectual and artistic expression, how did this affect Afro-Cuban women's voices, since both gender and racial barriers influence cultural production? The paucity of debate and hard statistics on blacks' social reality renders the study of black women's specific problems virtually impossible. It has been well documented that during the period of slavery, black women suffered triple oppression due to racism in general and the sexism of black male slaves and white masters (Bush, Morrisey, Scott, Kutzinski).[5] Black and mulatto women continued to experience varying degrees of prejudice after 1959. Although officials would argue that the revolution's progress must be measured against black women's equality, it is important to ask how postrevolutionary cultural production has reconstructed the Afro-Cuban woman's image.[6] Smith and Padula argue that, in general, it is difficult to discern the role of sex and gender in Cuba as a result of the "much debated issue in current feminist thought—

whether or not feminist concerns transcend cultural boundaries" (149). One aspect of the problem stems from politics:

> Yet the issue here takes on decidedly political overtones given the charged atmosphere of U.S.-Cuban relations. . . . The bizarre notion that there are "culturally inappropriate questions" can be seen as a euphemism for self-censorship—that is, a veiled admonition not to pose embarrassing questions, not to report, or instead to attempt to rationalize, information that could be awkward for a politically embattled Revolution. It is a common phenomenon in the study of Cuban women. (149–50)

The problem for Afro-Cuban women is further complicated by the erasure of color. By avoiding debate on Afro-Cuban politics, cultural officials nullified the border between white and black production. They unwittingly smoothed over black issues with egalitarian rhetoric that did not correspond to the reality of prevalent racism and its negative effect on cultural production (Amaro and Mesa-Lago 350–53).

Have Afro-Cuban women's intellectual and artistic contributions received attention in an ostensibly colorless society? Vera Kutzinski has noted that "there are, of course, exceptions, but how many published nonwhite women writers are there in today's Cuba in addition to [the poet] Nancy Morejón? How many were there before her?" Kutzinski says that this "raises of course the fundamental question of a discursive site that might be occupied by a nonwhite female writer in a country such as Cuba" (16). In Cuba, the fact that theoretical attention to contemporary racial issues is practically nonexistent further compounds the quandary facing those who would do research on the artistic production of Afro-Cuban women.

Given that Cuban scholars have tended to overlook issues involving blacks' cultural participation, it is not surprising that they have ignored black intellectuals' ambiguous and polemical relationship with government officials. The myth of a racism-free Cuba as a black haven resulted from the fact that few Afro-Cubans have left Cuba since the 1960s; by deduction, they must be unconditionally loyal to the revolutionary government's racial policies. Cuba supported the Black Power movement in the United States and provided sanctuary for American blacks who were dissatisfied with the racial tension and impasses they encountered. As a result, most critics have underscored the revolutionary zeal of Afro-Cuban intellectuals and artists, assuming the straightforwardness of their works, without questioning the official folklorization of Afro-Cuban expression to the exclusion of meaningful black politics or alternative voices.

The Official Position

In the first months of the new regime (March 1959), Fidel Castro, in a public address, warned Cubans that the divisive nature of racial politics would endanger the nation. Castro's call for solidarity was a political effort to avoid a split among different factions and to resist persistent U.S. intervention in Cuban affairs. Castro's rhetoric demonstrates continuity with Cuba's nineteenth-century thinker, poet, and hero of independence wars José Martí. Martí defended blacks' dignity and claimed that Cuban identity went beyond the stratification of skin color. He made a humanist appeal for cultural unity to mitigate racial tensions (Martí 84–94, 306–14). Many Cuban Creoles and plantation owners feared that there would be a black takeover if independence was achieved. This panic was partly a reaction to the Haitian revolution (1791–1804), in which blacks defeated the French and Creoles who ruled the island, and partly a response to Spanish propaganda against Afro-Cubans disseminated as part of a strategy to convince Cuban Creoles that independence from Spain would leave them at the mercy of Afro-Cuban military and political leaders. The black scare was permanently etched in the Caribbean psyche as an exhortation to whites that black contributions to independence could lead to their subjugation (Helg, Pérez Jr., Graham, Paquette).

Another historical factor that contributed to racial conflict in Cuba was the so-called race war of 1912, which Helg labels "a black massacre"; officials killed many black political and military leaders in a struggle over Afro-Cuban political representation. Following the race war, in the 1930s and 1940s, officials purged the secret Abakuá societies that controlled labor on the Havana docks. After the revolution, in the 1960s, officials again attempted to extirpate the Abakuá organizations from society, purportedly linking the secret sects to delinquency and atavistic behavior (Ziegler 339–59; Domínguez 225).

While Cuban revolutionary officials sought to eliminate Afro-Cuban religions and to discourage political organizations that presumably posed a threat to national unity, Castro, faced with hostile, racist whites who did not want to share power with blacks, reiterated Martí's convictions that Cuban blacks were not separatists, thereby reassuring whites that blacks had no intention of wrenching power from them. Castro re-

lied on Martí's humanistic rhetoric to ask Afro-Cubans to identify themselves as part of a harmonious, rather than a racially divided, nation; the
erasure of skin color implies whitewashing racial differences and downplaying the legacy of slavery, racial discrimination, and residual racism.

Many intellectuals supported Castro's appropriation of Martí's humanistic approach to racial issues. In 1965 the Haitian intellectual René
Depestre, who lived in Cuba and published in official Cuban journals,
reiterated the official revolutionary position by comparing the nation's
positive racial relations to those existing under the racist governments
of the United States, South Africa, and Rhodesia. Citing Martí, he proclaimed that all Cubans are born first of all Cubans, and not blacks and
whites; the humanization and liberation of both races were obligatory
tasks of the revolutionary process. He believed that it was absurd to
think that promoting one particular race would benefit a nation; he
cautioned that black leadership was also capable of abhorrent political
corruption: "Los negros también, a causa de la alienación . . . pueden
ser envidiosos, sinverguenzas, tiranos, criminales, oscurantistas, etc. . . .
Qué se vuelva, en estos días, hacia mi país, Haití. ¡y verá de lo que son
capaces también los negros, lo que los negros pueden hacer con el poder
político, cuando el sistema dominante es un instrumento de deshu-
manización de la vida!" (60). [Blacks also, due to alienation . . . can be
envious, shameless, tyrannical, criminal, obscurantist, etc. . . . Look at
my country, these days, this applies to Haiti! It remains to be seen what
blacks too are capable of, what blacks can do with political power, when
the dominant system is an instrument of dehumanization! (tr. Linda
Howe).]

Depestre's arguments, coupled with examples of the dehumanizing
tactics of Papa Doc's black Haitian regime, preclude Afro-Cubans'
scrutiny of their own nation's contemporary racial problems. In contrast,
Enrique Patterson argues that, in Cuba, identity politics, reduced to
paternalistic humanism, eliminates and effaces Afro-Cubans' legacy of
slavery and their specific historical, economic, and social circumstances.
Martí's humanism was a necessary criticism of Cuban racist thinkers
like Saco and Arango; the theory represents progressive thought on
racial relations and conceptualizes blacks as human beings. However,
Patterson believes that misuse of the theory underestimates Afro-
Cubans as historical subjects and erases their specific social and historical problems. According to the logic of humanist philosophy, simply not
discussing specific contemporary Cuban racial relations becomes the
solution to racial problems: "La mejor forma de resolver el problema

desde esta perspectiva, es no hablar de él. Es imposible que un grupo social afectado no abogue y luche en pro de sus reivindicaciones; desde los esquemas del discurso de la negación—al adaptar los negros la actitud reivindicativa—sobre éstos, más que sobre la sociedad, caerá el calificativo de racistas" (54). [The best way to solve the problem from this perspective is not to talk about it. It is impossible that an oppressed social group would not defend itself [against discrimination] and fight for its rights; from the frameworks of the discourse of denial—once blacks adopt a righteous attitude—the racist label, rather than being applied to society, will be applied to them (tr. Linda Howe).]

Patterson asks how it is possible that a group so assailed by history would not struggle to recover its history. He suggests that fear and concern about the stigma of being called separatist and racist have discouraged Afro-Cubans from procuring a political position to emphasize their own controversial history.

However enthusiastic and far-reaching the government's original programs were for Afro-Cubans, over time, these projects inadvertently displaced contemporary black political expression. The Afro-Cubans Eugenio Hernández Espinosa, Rogelio Martínez Furé, Tomás González, Alberto Pedro, and Sara Gómez extrapolated the idealism of the American Black Power movement to radicalize Cuban racial politics, perhaps misinterpreting authorities' position on black activism or simply desiring to push beyond official limits. Afro-Cubans had to contend with the revolution's hegemonic utopian representations: a homogeneous nationalism politicizing the aesthetic, fusing the political, ideological, and cultural in an attempt to do away with imperialism, religious tradition, and entrenched racism.

Several factors created a chasm between Afro-Cuban intellectuals and artists' idealism and reality. For the most part, the Afro-Cuban working class was grateful for the material benefits the revolution provided them and had little knowledge of black intellectuals' call for shifts in cultural and political power. Since the majority of the black population had been illiterate and poor before the revolution, there was no established link between the black masses and the Afro-Cuban intelligentsia, who read Malcolm X and envisioned a black revolution-within-the-revolution to unite Afro-Cubans from diverse socioeconomic and political backgrounds. In Cuba a politically motivated movement of black consciousness on a grand scale did not occur, and Cuba had no black leaders like Martin Luther King, who brought together black people from distinct socioeconomic and political backgrounds to organize peaceful mass protests. Clearly, in the United States, King's assassination prompted some American blacks to take more radical measures.

Another factor that impeded the development of a civil rights or Black Power movement in Cuba was that, historically, Afro-Cuban intellectuals and politicians have often been divided among themselves over black politics. The scholars Tomás Fernández Robaina, Louis Pérez Jr., and Aline Helg have shown that, since the nineteenth century, different black political factions had debated the validity of separate political parties based on race. Evidence of such struggle was the establishment of the Independent Party of Color in the early twentieth century; Afro-Cubans vehemently argued about whether to alienate themselves from white power. By the 1930s several Afro-Cubans had joined the Communist Party, with the faith that the party's programs would benefit Afro-Cuban society in the class struggle since blacks ranked the lowest in the socioeconomic and political hierarchies.

After the revolution, Cuban authorities began correcting racial inequalities with concrete social programs that provided housing and food for indigent blacks. According to Sheldon B. Liss, although officials abolished all social and political organizations based on race, "they established National Organization of Orientation and Integration, composed of prominent Black and White professionals" (159).

On the cultural scene, officials created institutions that promoted aestheticized versions of Afro-Cuban cultural manifestations. After 1959 the Department of National Theatrical Folklore, directed by the well-known scholar and folklorist Argeliers León, produced several studies on Afro-Cuban culture. León developed a Department of Folkloric Research as a division of Havana's National Theater. The organization founded a Folkloric Seminar, at which prominent scholars and artists such as the ethnologist Alberto Pedro, the writer Miguel Barnet, the filmmaker Sara Gómez, and the theater critic Inés María Martiatu Terry developed their talents. Parallel to the birth of the folklore seminar was the creation of a theater seminar that was instrumental in the growth of Cuban playwrights. Among those who participated were José Triana, José Brene, Eugenio Hernández Espinosa, Maité Vera, Gerardo Fulleda León, and Tomás González.

Cultural figureheads from both seminars produced dance performances and theatrical displays of Afro-Cuban cultural and religious elements that had never been presented before in Cuba. Cuban artists and writers modernized stagnant Afro-Cuban stereotypes and aesthetics.

The modern Cuban dance director Ramiro Guerra and, later, the ethnologist Rogelio Martínez Furé and the Mexican choreographer Rodolfo Reyes incorporated into traditional theater and dance "unprofessional" artists like Jesús Pérez, Trinidad Torregosa, and Nieves Fresnada, who were popular street artists from diverse communities within Cuban society. The Cuban ethnologist Rogelio Martínez Furé underscores the fruits of the efforts of León, Guerra, Martínez Furé, and others to create highly original hybrid works. For his part, Ramiro Guerra commingled Martha Graham's modern dance approach with Lucumí legend, making possible syncretic performances of traditional religious dance reinterpreted through experimental dance theory and choreography. Artists used diverse techniques, traditional religious ceremony, and avant-garde aesthetics to erase the border between the purely secular presentation and sacred practices popular among Afro-Cuban religious communities. Hermetic and clandestine religious elements of Cuban society were brought to the forefront as aesthetic manifestations of Cuban nationalism (interview with the author, Havana, 10 March 1998).

These creators defied the dichotomy of high and low culture and called into question the binary opposition of art and folklore. Afro-Cuban culture, ethnological in orientation, became artistically sophisticated culture (aestheticized and "modernized") as an integral aspect of revolutionary national culture.

At the same time that choreographers reinterpreted traditional consecrated ritual with the new language of modern dance, playwrights from the theater seminar produced works that synthesized avant-garde technique and stylized interpretations of Afro-Cuban religious experience. However, Martínez Furé makes clear that, for example, although a successful play that brought popular religious beliefs into the limelight, *Santa Camila de la Habana Vieja* reflects a didactic version of official cultural production insofar as it discourages Afro-Cuban religious practice; the protagonist performs the most improbable act and eliminates the *orishas* (Afro-Cuban gods) from her life. Cultural institutions not only produce a formal representation of religion; they add a tinge of socialist realism to the works, encouraging Cubans to eliminate their prerevolutionary "atavistic" religious practices. Afro-Cuban religious experience—traditionally and historically viewed as a culture of resistance for slave communities—is depoliticized and aesthetically homogenized.

The revolution's scheme to rewrite black history and culture has its antecedent in Cuban cultural history. During the past two centuries, various plastic, performing, and literary artists have endeavored to shape the black aesthetic. From Placido, the nineteenth-century mulatto poet assassinated for his alleged participation in the Ladder conspiracy, to Nicolás Guillén, twentieth-century Cuba's most celebrated poet, whose concept of *mestizaje* brought the Afro-Cuban aesthetic in line with the rhetoric of a racially mixed nation's united struggle against imperialism, writers' and artists' attempts to define Afro-Cuban culture have been met with the dominant culture's imposing aesthetics.

Moreover, the resultant overlapping aesthetic is fraught with distortion and a sense of alienation for Afro-Cubans. A frequently tormented consciousness has plagued Cuban writers and artists caught between traditions and paradoxical efforts to determine a black aesthetic. For example, in the nineteenth century, Domingo Del Monte created a literary salon to support writings by and about Afro-Cubans, which made possible the advent of antislavery narratives and poetry. Several works from the period romanticized the slave experience and racial relations. Gertrudis Gómez de Avellaneda (who wrote in Spain) and Cirilo Villaverde, in their respective antislavery novels *Sab* and *Cecilia Valdés*, used similar literary themes to expose the cruelty of slave exploitation. Nevertheless, their efforts were undermined by their own idyllic nation-building literary discourse and by their notions of ideal miscegenation.[7]

In the twentieth century, Nicolás Guillén and other poets of the Latin American Negrismo movement and the writers and ethnographers Fernando Ortiz, Lydia Cabrera, and Alejo Carpentier inherited and reinterpreted the European avant-garde's folkloric and anthropological perspective on black art as ontologically exotic and primitive. They created a radically different sense of the black aesthetic, focusing on the shared and positive value of African-based culture, as well as exposing the imperious racism of the era. Since slavery, Afro-Cuban writers and artists have had few ideological choices for their cultural production: (1) to succumb to and to perpetuate romantic and exotic notions of their submissive relationship to the dominant powers; (2) to express an aesthetic perspective slightly critical of the dominant culture that still reasserts dimensions of that culture; (3) to provoke change. The first possibility led to the development of a nineteenth-century black romantic aesthetic and a twentieth-century revolutionary vision of racial harmony with limited critical focus. The second aestheticizes black culture and proposes (especially after the revolution) a Marxist humanist approach to racism, by means of, first and foremost, the class struggle. The third insinuates a radical black aesthetic that fuses separatist rhetoric inspired by the Negritude and Black Power movements with traditional African-based cultural or religious expression to produce a racially politicizing art that goes beyond the limits of Cuban national rhetoric and the dominant cultural stereotypes of black articulation.

The Cuban writer Manolo Granados emphasizes how a Marxist perspective on historical and literary influences, such as the Haitian revolution, Caribbean Negritude, Surrealism and U.S. racial strife during the Cold War mitigated potentially radical Afro-Cuban expression (interview with the author, Paris, 9 June 1996). Granados says that, in the thirties, bourgeois Creoles folklorized black aesthetics by presenting "primitive" aspects of Afro-Cuban culture in surrealist imagery. Thirty years later, he argues, the Cold War transformed and revolutionized the African American and the Afro-Cuban predicaments. On the one hand, Marxist rhetoric about the dictatorship of the proletariat includes blacks and the eventual resolution of the race problem. This proposition appealed to blacks, since Marxist thought positioned racism as a product of class conflict and an element of the superstructure of the capitalist system. On the other hand, blacks viewed racism couched in Marxist terms as a necessary concession; they are recognized in Marxist thought as human beings who participate in a national struggle of liberation even though their goal to eradicate racism is subordinated to the class conflict; the black battle in socialist terms requires a precarious assumption of delayed progress, since the white left or right is never likely to cede power to blacks.

In the revolutionary period, the government promoted a rewriting of Cuban history that included black history, breaking with tradition and scrutinizing a colonized perspective of Cuban history. Nevertheless, as both Granados and Patterson emphasize, the humanist and socialist projects, later wedded to Marxist rhetoric in the revolution, were limited inasmuch as officials rendered black politics secondary or already obsolete.

Black Power: Yanquí Sí, Cuba No

In the early 1960s some Afro-Cuban intellectuals fell out of grace with the Castro government for conceiving a so-called Black Power movement. Many Afro-Cuban intellectuals prefer not to use the term "Black Power" to define those gatherings since the stigma implied microfactional, antirevolutionary politics. Tomás Fernández Robaina elucidates how this movement—which he also labels "movimiento de la negritud en Cuba"—developed:

> "Se produce un fenómeno que algunos han llamado el movi-
> miento de la negritud en Cuba . . . donde un grupo de negros
> comenzaron a redescubrir a una Cuba de valores éticos y estéti-
> cos negros. . . . Cabe preguntar ahora si este movimiento de la
> Negritud surgió por una deficiencia en este supuesto programa
> o proyecto revolucionario, donde algunos de los negros vieron
> que no se estaba estudiando la cultura negra en la forma más
> correcta." (interview with the author, Havana, 16 July 1994)

≈

> [A phenomenon that some have called the Negritude movement
> [Fernandez Robaina and other black intellectuals use the eu-
> phemism "Negritude" to downplay and association between the
> radical Afro-Cubans and the U.S. Black Power movement] in
> Cuba emerges . . . a group of blacks began to rediscover a Cuba
> of [white] aesthetic values and another Cuba of black values and
> aesthetics. . . . One might ask whether this Negritude movement
> arose because of a deficiency in the putatively revolutionary pro-
> gram or project, when some blacks realized that black culture
> was not being studied in the most appropriate way]. (Tr. Emma
> Claggett and Linda Howe)

If, as Fernández Robaina suggests, a movement developed as a result of deficiencies in the revolution's proposed solutions to racism, how was it defined, and what were the ramifications? Black intellectuals' gatherings to read Malcolm X and Frantz Fanon and to celebrate black consciousness did not actually constitute a Black Power movement in Cuba, although the connection between the radical black politics in the United States and in Cuba was solidly forged. Van Gosse argues that, in 1959 and the early 1960s, Castro received support not only from the U.S. pro-Cuba "fair play movement," which encompassed the icons of New Left theorists, including I. F. Stone, and celebrated Beats, such as Allen Ginsberg and Lawrence Ferlinghetti, but also from many key black radicals and early nationalists, among them Amiri Baraka [LeRoi Jones] and Malcolm X (3). Gosse says that Castro's week-long stay in a Harlem hotel in September 1960 united him with black America and adds that from "Joe Louis on, the Cubans' notably successful wooing of black celebrities, tourists and radicals has been similar to Fidel's September 1960 Harlem sojourn" (152). On 4 July 1960, the Cuban literary magazine *Lunes de revolución* came out with a special issue, *Los negros en U.S.A.*

Produced in collaboration with U.S. blacks, it included contributions from Baraka, Langston Hughes, and James Baldwin (148).

Unity between some North American and Cuban blacks continued when the "Black Panther leader Eldridge Cleaver and Assata Shakur, founder of the Black Liberation Army, were among the prominent black exiles given sanctuary in Cuba; Stokely Carmichael and Angela Davis made well-publicized trips there at the height of their fame" (154). Government officials invited U.S. Black Panther members and politically controversial African American figures, treating them as persecuted heroes.

In the United States, Richard Gibson was instrumental in involving African Americans in the defense of the Cuban revolution. As leader of the Fair Play for Cuba Committee, he was also executive secretary of the New York–based Liberation Committee for Africa. Gibson was able to engage national liberation struggles with U.S. black politics. Gibson's political duality, together with the Cuban revolution, had a hand in combining black nationalism with what he called a "Fanonist expression of solidarity" with Cuba, a politics in which, at times, even the dichotomy of communism and anticommunism gave way to national struggles (147).

Afro-Cubans also witnessed Robert Williams's flight from a local race war in Monroe, North Carolina, and his subsequent asylum in Cuba. Williams, who was considered by U.S. black radicals (as well as by the white right) to be the "black Fidel Castro of the South," promoted racial desegregation early on; as a result, he was accused of backing revolutionary Cuba (153). Cuba harbored the black radical William Lee Brent when he hijacked a plane to Cuba after escaping arrest for his involvement in a shoot-out between Black Panthers and the police. The regime also issued invitations to Huey Newton, John Clytus, Eldridge Cleaver, and other well-known black radicals. Gosse also notes that the "long-term Cuban solidarity in the form of aid, technicians, and troops to beleaguered African revolutions from 1965 on, when Che Guevara fought in the Congo, through the South African army's decisive defeat at Cuito Carnivale in southern Angola in 1988," gave Cuba prestige in many sectors of the black community (154). These black causes generated mutual admiration between some African Americans and Cubans. Cold War politics and the American Black Panthers' self-proclaimed battle against imperialism, capitalism, and racism created cohesion between the more radical political sector of African American society and the Cuban government.

Collaboration between a cross-section of American black society, including Panther members, and Cubans is also evident in articles and interviews published in Cuban journals and newspapers in the 1960s. For example, in an interview, the Black Panther party member George Ware alluded to imagined, more than real, political goals for American blacks and for Cubans when he suggested the Black Panther internal struggle would extend to Latin American nationalist liberation movements. Ware added that the way to fight imperialism is by gradually eliminating interventionist troops and suggested that the Panthers might be able to relinquish Guantánamo to the Cubans (C. M. Gutiérrez 18).

However fanciful Ware's assertion that the Black Panthers could remove U.S. interventionist troops from Cuba may appear, his statements illustrate an internationalist rhetoric of national liberation beyond U.S. borders. Both the Black Panthers' anti-imperialist mission and Third World politics proposed to obliterate the "evils of capitalism" throughout the world. Carlos María Gutiérrez, who interviewed Ware and other Student Nonviolent Coordinating Committee (SNCC) members, states that no true liberation of blacks is possible without the acquisition of political power and the destruction of capitalist structures; one fight is intimately related to the other (16).

A united front between Panther members and the Cuban nation did not evolve into an internal structure for promoting Afro-Cuban politics and for scrutinizing national racial discrimination. Rather, Cuban officials envisioned the North American Black Power movement as a platform from which to espouse anti-imperialist and pro–Third World rhetoric. Cuban officials' encouraging African American radicals to seek refuge and their simultaneous discouraging of their own blacks' radical racial politics perplexed Afro-Cubans. Apparently, the U.S. Black Power movement encumbered Afro-Cuban cultural and political activity in Havana, because of the difference between the Cuban government's position on the limits of racial politics and individual Afro-Cubans' interpretations of the Black Power movement's value and purpose.

The dilemma inadvertently exposed the Cuban government's double standard toward Afro-Cubans when they manifested black pride and gathered to discuss racism and black solidarity. Incongruously, Cuban authorities harassed Afro-Cubans on the basis of their alleged ideological association with African American radicals and their agenda. The paradox was especially striking for the playwright and theater director Tomás González, who says that his unofficial title as leader of the Cuban

Black Power movement persuaded officials that he was a principal player and a racist promoting separatist politics in Havana (interview with the author, Canary Islands, Spain, 16 May 1996). González, the anthropologist Alberto Pedro, the film director Sara Gómez, and others found themselves at the center of controversy over the legitimacy of a Black Power movement. They had envisioned themselves at the cutting edge of the revolutionary moment, poised at the brink of an epoch of radical change, as the representatives of Black Power and an emerging new black aesthetic in Cuba. In spite of the fact that some Cuban blacks had contact with Black Panther party members, it is difficult to determine what constituted black "activism" in Cuba.

The postrevolutionary discussion over racism and the legitimacy of black solidarity in a country with nationalist interests at stake is evident in Cuban literary and political journals of the 1960s. Disagreements among intellectuals about racism in Cuba and how to deal with it are also reflected in a debate between Carlos Moore (a.k.a. More) and the Haitian René Depestre. Moore challenges the notion of a racist-free Cuba in "Le peuple noir a-t-il sa place dans la Révolution cubaine?" The gist of Moore's article is that there was never a true Cuban revolution because Afro-Cubans did not benefit in social or political terms. Depestre contests the charges in "Carta de Cuba sobre el imperialismo de la mala fé," an acerbic essay defending the revolution's racial policies.

According to Depestre, Cuban officials recognize capitalism's racism, a residue of the consciousness inherited from slavery and colonial systems but manifesting itself in relatively autonomous terms. Racial prejudice cannot be simply eliminated by law as one might dissolve large landed estates. Rather, racism is a sum of human consciousness, which comprises layers upon layers of monopolies and large landed estates. The type of racism Depestre describes exists in socialist Cuba, long after the historical and capitalist structures that produced it have been destroyed. In an appeal to Engels's logic of "reciprocal action," Depestre explains that those who claim that revolutionary Cuba is racist erroneously treat racial dogma as an independent phenomenon detached from economic and political factors. When one society transforms into another, certain ideological values belonging to the old social structures survive; the fight against these values and the goal of obliterating them should come about through dynamic dialectical analysis and not according to mechanistic norms extraneous to current historical contradictions ("Carta" 57).

Depestre's ideas reflect Cuban officials' position on racism and reveal the dogma that challenged black activism and any critique of the system, since such action was purportedly divorced from historical and political processes and, therefore, erroneous. Depestre's defense of the revolution's "successful" campaign to eradicate racism compiles an inventory of contemporary historians who exposed Cuba's racist versions of black history. In a gesture that approximates "tokenism," he cites positive statements by Afro-Cubans (the political leader Blas Roca and the national poet Nicolás Guillén) about historical black contributions. Depestre emphasizes the improvements produced by the revolution in the economic, educational, medical, and political lives of blacks, practical measures and not simply dogma. He quotes Guillén, stating that the revolution's accomplishments merit nothing less than revolutionary loyalty and professional effectiveness (36). He reiterates that if it weren't for the revolution, he himself wouldn't be able to freely criticize Cuba's erroneous versions of black history.

Depestre validates a "scientific approach" that he believes appropriately questions capitalist racist myths and permits change of Cuban national history (39). He also encourages whites to raise their level of racial consciousness, to renounce their false concepts of blacks, and to relinquish their privileged positions in the work place (42). Depestre exposes unfair critiques of the indefatigable racism in the revolutionary period as imperialist schemes to destroy the revolution and declares Cuba the vanguard of national liberation for the "Second Independence of the Latin American People" (57). The patriotic call for unconditional support for internationalist and anti-imperialist solidarity grants blacks a space in the revolution (57–58).

Depestre's rhetorical strategies to bring Afro-Cubans into the mainstream of revolutionary society crystallizes the predicament for blacks: how to justify "separatist" activities, since they are allegedly divorced, a priori, from historical and political processes. This paradox is evident in Afro-Cubans' defense of their activities in the 1960s. Afro-Cuban activists, such as the poet and black activist Eloy Machado (El Ambia), exonerate their activism in the 1960s by invoking a self-contradictory position reaffirming their loyalty to the Cuban revolution as a necessary defense mechanism. Machado told me that officials misconstrued Afro-Cuban protest even though blacks believed that their activities were within the parameters of the revolution: "Nada era fuera del marco, pero los blancos del poder empiezan a formar campaña de que había un movimiento de Black Power. Pero no había nada" (interview with the author, Havana, 15 June 1996). [Nothing that we did went beyond the parameters of the revolution, but the whites in power started a campaign against us by saying that we were part of a Black Power movement. There was no such thing (tr. Linda Howe).] During these years of strife, blacks continued to meet, although officials persecuted them.

In the 1970s officials eliminated other Afro-Cuban study groups, a loose network of young people who shared black music, literature, and discussion of racial problems. Cuban authorities also thwarted their attempt to create separate cultural organizations (Moore, *Castro* 309–12). This meant that for two decades, officials supported neither cultural nor political organizations for blacks. These limits dictated unspoken racial policies that black intellectuals understood but did not completely obey.

Georgina Dopico Black explains that the First National Congress of Culture and Education, in 1971, included discussion on black activism and Afro-Cuban issues. Congress participants affirmed a trend that had begun shortly after the revolution; they mandated that cultural officials attack and ferret out counterrevolutionary sentiment. The Congress's proponents underscored the need to maintain a "monolithic ideological unity" and to battle all forms of deviant behavior: "'Snobbism, extravagance, homosexuality, and other social aberrations' are taboo themes in Cuban literature. It is also considered subversive to write Afro-Cuban literature that is autonomous from regime-sponsored, stylized Afro-Cuban art. 'Intellectual . . . societies of and for blacks . . . have been banned' and 'Afro-Cuban writers have fallen into disfavor'" (118–19).

The synthesis of limits on cultural expression, combining bourgeois, gay, and black elements under the negative rubric "social aberration," reflects official paranoia as well as a strategy to crush any challenge to the homogeneous Cuban identity and the folkloric concept of Afro-Cuban society. Officials airbrushed these undesirable images from the ideal utopian concept of national identity and culture to promote a hegemonic notion of a unified culture. Did officials want to recover sovereignty without relinquishing power to separatist groups? By eliminating the black threat and other "subversive" activities, did authorities succeed in encroaching upon Cuba's African-based legacy with nationalistic rhetoric about rescued traditions of culture? Perhaps the revolution's folkloric and anthropological lenses allowed its officials to focus on nationalism and national culture as "retrieved." They maintained prerevolutionary prejudicial divisions in hierarchical form; a predominantly white "high" culture and a revived black heritage stripped of "atavistic" religious and menacing political overtones.

What Is Afro-Cuba?

A combination of Marxist idealism that predicts that class struggle will eradicate racism, the egalitarian concept of the proletariat in racial terms, and Martí's humanism transmogrified the term "Afro-Cuban" into a contradiction. Fernández Robaina elucidates the dilemma for Afro-Cubans, stating that some thinkers believe that Cuban culture already comprehends African-based elements because of its syncretic nature. He also remarks that Cubans still differentiate between "high" (hispanized) art and Afro-Cuban folklore. Arguments in favor of an egalitarian concept of Cuban culture or identity as an all-encompassing term are utopian. Negative stereotypes of Afro-Cuban society prevail, and Cuba remains a biracial society or, at least, a society measured by stratification of color.

Cuban poet Nancy Morejón underscores the exclusiveness of the term and mentions the danger of commercializing folkloric Afro-Cuban cultural elements. Evidently, Morejón is not against the use of the term "Afro-Cuban culture": she urges that it be understood historically in relation to Hispanic culture and that scholars contextualize its evolution and preservation mainly through religious manifestations and as a center of black resistance. Unfortunately, as Morejón, and Walterio Carbonell before her, stated, successive Cuban governments have often permitted the financially profitable aspects of Afro-Cuban society to manifest themselves: music, divination, organized carnival, and so on. The subtle racism inherent in such contradictory projects merits reflection. At any rate, Cuba's rapidly changing reality makes it difficult to determine identity based on any racial theory or economic or social environment. Admittedly, accepting Cuban culture as a symbiosis of cultures does carry the risk of neutralizing the context in which that culture is produced. Afro-Cubans' history and cultural production are a struggle to define *cubanidad* against a Eurocentric cultural ideal. As Morejón states, African-based religion and cultural activities have always constituted a history of insurgency against total obliteration.

Efforts to define black culture constitute a search for more decentralized notions of culture and have never been carried out in an impartial context, but in one of domination. As Tomás Fernández Robaina asserts, couching the black legacy in scant folkloric terms denies various, and possibly more critical, versions of history. The Cuban art critic Gerardo Mosquera also scrutinizes egalitarian concepts that characterize Cuban culture in democratic and syncretic terms. *Mestizaje* (a mixing of cultures and races that synthesizes a new race) is "based on ethnocultural identity" and is "tainted by ontological aftertaste" that "runs the risk of being an all-encompassing term with which to blur differences, power relationships, and conflicts of interest" (*Beyond the Fantastic* 14).

The debate over power relationships inherent in social, racial, and cultural terms that either promote the syncretic or individual nature of distinct cultural aspects is evident in the clash between revolutionary egalitarian rhetoric and separate black politics. In the revolutionary period, the disparity between a political concept of blacks as an integral part of national politics and the reality of the defiant Afro-Cuban intellectual upset by racial imbalance caused an official backlash. Racial strife was evident in several realms of cultural production. For example, after the revolution, Afro-Cubans complained that there were no black actors in the Institute of Radio and Television. To fill the gap, authorities allowed the production of *The War of Palmares*, a television adventure series. All the actors in the show were Afro-Cubans. However, shortly after the series began, some whites, who resented sharing cultural space with blacks, complained that it was an all-black show. Fernández Robaina suggests that this exposed the contradiction inherent in government policy. Value given black representation contradicted Cuban society's racist attitudes. This substantiated the persistent character of racial prejudice in Cuban society: "How is one to reconcile the objective fact of the existence of prejudice against things of black origin with the undeniable fact that there is a preoccupation with preserving the values of black culture?" ("Struggle" 51). Black culture was paradoxically contained by a racial policy oriented toward a predictable curriculum of production. This policy contradicted socialist realism's tenets and severed black politics—that is, substantive issues such as racism—from cultural expression. As a result, authorities muted Afro-Cuban culture with a certain kind of aesthetic resonance.

For the most part, Afro-Cubans' essayistic writings during the revolutionary period use Marxist rhetoric to discuss black heritage, current Afro-Cuban cultural manifestations, and/or racial discrimination and integration. Clearly, Afro-Cuban critical and literary production is not homogeneous; Afro-Cuban scholars and artists reveal a plethora of distinct and conflicting interpretations and perspectives. For example, Pedro Serviat's text on blacks and revolutionary politics, Martínez Furé's essays on folklore, and the ethnologist Alberto Pedro's articles on Marxism and black politics elaborate on racial politics and black culture in diverse ways.

In *El problema del negro en Cuba y su solución definitiva,* Serviat utilizes a Marxist-Leninist theoretical paradigm to propose the absorption of blacks into the socialist system; he rejects Afro-Cuban "traditional" cultural and religious elements as atavistic and believes that they impede the progress of black integration into the new revolutionary society. On the other hand, Martínez Furé, in *Diálogos imaginarios,* chooses an Afrocentric theoretical framework to underscore the significance of African-based folklore (e.g., myth, art, dance, rituals) as one of Cuban society's fundamental elements opposing "the official" or "the institutional" (258). Although Martínez Furé does not follow the party line as closely as Serviat, his treatment of black culture—culling specific "positive" components for revolutionary society to appreciate and juxtaposing them with materialist thought—illustrates the complex political situation that many Afro-Cuban intellectuals encountered when promoting Afro-Cuban culture. Perhaps what is most striking about *Diálogos imaginarios* is that Martínez Furé underscores the importance of African-based traditions at a specific historical moment, using Marxism-Leninism to write between the lines—a discursive tactical maneuver to illustrate the importance of Afro-Cuban heritage.

The ethnologist Alberto Pedro's work is an example of an assimilationist, rather than a radical black separatist, rhetoric. Pedro was initially active in the Cuban Black Power movement, and his writings from the 1960s reflect ideas contrary to those that characterize radical black politics. In "El Tercer Mundo exige una dramática decisión de los intelectuales," Pedro differentiates between intellectuals whose aesthetic choices favor the dominant bourgeois "decadent" aesthetics and those who recognize their obligations to the "new guerrilla morality" in Cuba. The new morality obligates intellectuals to participate in Cuban society's reconstruction and development; their responsibility goes far beyond national boundaries, since Cuba's culture may well serve as a moral example for all Latin American cultures (44). Pedro concludes that the new guerrilla revolutionary culture is inevitably linked to intellectuals' historical and social roles and is dictated by the urgency of Cuba's revolutionary transformation (45–46).

Pedro's ideas of guerrilla culture express a humanist concept of Afro-Cuban history and culture. In a review of Stokely Carmichael's *Black Power,* he maps out the history of the U.S. black struggle, explaining how

Western culture has imported black culture and how blacks have resorted to their African roots to legitimize their histories, recovering the remote past to ameliorate historical alienation. Pedro suggests that this strategy negates true national consciousness; black intellectuals should discover and interpret black reality from within their respective nations' histories, recovering their "true" history and rebellious traditions and emphasizing the negative and positive aspects of customs, folklore, and cultural character of the most humble classes ("Poder negro" 141). Pedro concludes that American Black Power movement's goal of eliminating imperialism, capitalism, and racism is parallel to the Cuban revolution's humanist objectives, thereby precluding the need for black activism in Cuba.

Although Pedro was a key figure in the defunct Cuban Black Power movement, his less strident objectives indicate how blacks adapted to revolutionary rhetoric after political strife with officials. Martínez Furé's use of purely formal elements to detach Afro-Cuban culture from its religious connotations and Serviat's Marxist solutions that obliterate race problems with the discursive rhetoric of class struggle expose the difficulties inherent in expressing Afro-Cuban culture's complexities.

The works of the Afro-Cuban scholars Serviat, Martínez Furé, and Pedro illustrate how blacks carved out a discursive space for Afro-Cuban thought under socialism through materialist rhetoric; this meant conforming to Cuban institutions' attempts to smooth over racial conflicts, opting for an assimilationist style and themes that corresponded to hegemonic rhetoric on national unity (Casal, *Revolution* 4–5). Although Afro-Cubans' works are replete with contradictions, they provide sustenance for Afro-Cuban culture. These works reveal how scholars of black cultural production attempted to consolidate Afro-Cuban production into the revolution's cultural, political, and intellectual framework, making what was specifically black unequivocally national. This is also evident in the seminal works of the historians Pedro DesChamps Chapeaux and Manuel Moreno Fraginals, among others, whose significant contributions to the rewriting of black history focus on slave systems in the colonial period. Criticism of Cuba's racist society was retrospective and concentrated on historical, rather than contemporary, issues.

As for Afro-Cuban artists and writers themselves, some of their particular writings and performances slipped the reins of officialdom, at least for a brief period, to make a mark on the coetaneous cultural scene. Although the government's suppression of black politics and control of

cultural expression affected some of its most loyal Afro-Cuban con-
stituents, renegade voices prevailed in contemporary Afro-Cuban
cultural production. What is most revealing is not the production of
these works so much as their *reception* and revolutionary cultural officialdom's reaction.

A particularly complex case is Walterio Carbonell's personal contribution to black activism before and after the revolution. The historian
Hugh Thomas says that Carbonell, a party member who defended Castro's 1953 attack on the Moncada Barracks to the disapproving Cuban
Communist orthodoxy, ended up in a rehabilitation camp after the revolution because, among other alleged reasons, officials believed his
"folkloric investigations had racist overtones" (*Cuban Revolution* 655).
Pisani declares that Carbonell's book, *Crítica, cómo surgió la cultura
nacional* (1963), was removed from circulation shortly after it was published and the author destined to oblivion (8). Thomas claims that Carbonell was sent to a UMAP camp (*Cuba* 685). According to Moore, in 1968
Carbonell was picked up by the secret police and taken off to a labor
camp in Camaguey; this was not one of the UMAP camps (Moore, *Castro* 309–10; Luis, *Literary Bondage* 255 n. 63). Carbonell corroborated this
information in an unpublished interview with me (Havana, 16 July
1992). Authorities imprisoned him not only because of his book but also
because of his participation in drafting a document that asked for more
black representation. In addition, his disagreements with officials
(namely the Minister of Education José Llanusa Globels) over black
artists' and intellectuals' lack of freedom further endangered his position (Moore, *Castro* 310). He was unable to publish for several years. By
the 1990s he was "working" at the José Martí National Library as a con-
sultant. Afro-Cuban intellectuals describe Carbonell as a pitiable victim
of the conflict between black politics and official race policies.

Whether or not officials actually pulled the text from circulation has
been debated, but, without a doubt, Carbonell's problack politics were
not popular with Cuban authorities, either before or after the revolution.
Furthermore, the confusion over Carbonell's predicament as an Afro-
Cuban revolutionary intellectual results from a combination of personal
tragedy and political dissension. While it is true that his contributions
to Afro-Cuban history were controversial, his iconoclastic Marxist teach-
ings and writings, his personal friendship with Castro, and his tragic car
accident in Tunis, which produced a diplomatic break between that
country and Cuba, reveal Carbonell's complex history.

According to my interviews with Carbonell, Tomás González, and

Tomás Fernández Robaina, Carbonell was Castro's intimate friend during their university days before the revolution. He was a member of the Biracial University Committee against Racial Discrimination. Carbonell went into exile in Paris during the Batista regime. When the revolution occurred, Castro purportedly asked him to return to become a government official. Carbonell was appointed ambassador to Tunis. Both González and Fernández Robaina state that Carbonell's mysterious and tragic car accident in that country, in which someone was killed, was a serious blemish on his political career. Unlike Tomás González and Sara Gómez, Carbonell was an established member of revolutionary officialdom.

Carbonell's participation in Afro-Cuban political thought began with newspaper articles from the first years of the revolution and the text *Evolución de la cultura cubana,* in which he clarifies and emphasizes the importance of African-based elements in Cuban culture. Seen within the context of Marx's and Fanon's writings and the international Negritude and the Latin American Negrismo movements, Carbonell's work creates a discursive space for black intellectual thought in Cuba; with a materialist approach, he attempts to rescue hitherto undervalued Afro-Cuban cultural and political manifestations.

Sara Gómez was another distinct case. She was an ardent revolutionary, outspoken about black politics and in constant conflict with cultural officials. This antagonism is not immediately apparent from her cultural production. In her famous documentary, *De cierta manera* (1974–78), she characterizes the black struggle in revolutionary terms but also offers a complex interpretation of gender and race issues in Cuba. As Zuzana Pick explains, Gómez was critical of prevailing racist attitudes toward "marginals." Gómez "chose to approach marginality through the historical conditions that generated it. She revealed how social relations in underdeveloped countries are distorted by inequality and discrimination" (131). In Gomez's film, Mario, a young black man who contemplates becoming a member of the secret Abakuá society, learns to give up his traditional Afro-Cuban religious beliefs and joins others to work toward building a socialist society. Pick says that Gómez "linked deviant forms of behavior (such as male chauvinism and delinquency) to poverty and social alienation" and focused on "the conditions that prevent the integration of blacks and mulattos into the revolutionary process" (131, 137).

Perhaps Pick's interpretation is a myopic explanation of Gómez's perspective on the secret Abakuá societies. Gómez had already made several short films on Afro-Cuban society, recording the everyday lives and struggles of blacks. According to Inés María Martiatu Terry, some of these short films have never been shown in public because they express controversial aspects of racism, sexism, and religion for revolutionary society. Her full-length film is an extension of her celebration of black vitality in Cuba, with a particularly moral revolutionary message. Conversely, Gomez's fictionalized sociological study of an Afro-Cuban's struggle to integrate himself into revolutionary society unwittingly exposes the strength of underground religious practices. Government officials had specifically attached the label of "delinquency" to the Afro-Cuban secret Abakuá societies and discouraged any religious practice. The official campaign to eliminate religious organizations was also linked to power struggles between the State and independent unions on the Havana docks controlled by the Abakuá societies; eradicating "backward" African-based societies was part of the government's drive to control part of the labor force (Thomas, *Cuban Revolution* 55). In this matter, the revolutionary government perpetuated the historical image of black criminality—the renowned anthropologist Fernando Ortiz's first work on Afro-Cuban society was a study on black criminality—when it arrested many *babalaos* (Afro-Cuban high priests) in an attempt to derail Afro-Cuban organizations. One interpretation of Gómez's film is that it devalues and calls for the elimination of the secret Abakuá religious societies. Another may be, paradoxically, that, even after several years of harassment, tenacious Afro-Cuban religious organizations prevail. Was it controversial for Gómez to assert the existence of something the government claimed had been eradicated? In some of her earlier short documentaries, she had interspersed images of Afro-Cuban religion without comment, presenting them as integral aspects of Afro-Cuban society. In contrast to the positive, matter-of-fact perspective in the short films, the full-length one projects religious imagery clashing with images of "progress" toward building a revolutionary society: people learning to be revolutionaries in their jobs, attempting to abandon religious practices and organizations. How could Cubans still be practicing religion and clinging to "obsolete" social and cultural traditions years after the revolution had occurred?

Gómez died before she finished editing the film. Motives for the film's delayed production and debut remain a mystery. However, no matter what obstacles may have been responsible for the procrastination, Chanan explains that the content and completion of the film caused conflict and suspicion among Cuban intellectuals.

Gómez also earned her reputation as a black activist and a trouble-maker by participating in several black protests. She was among the young black intellectuals whom government officials had accused of writing the "Black Manifesto" (1968). She allegedly planned, along with Carbonell, Eugenio Hernández Espinosa, and Rogelio Martínez Furé, to present the document containing black grievances at the opening of the World Cultural Congress in January 1968 (Moore, *Castro* 310). The Manifesto's authors were called before the Minister of Education, José Llanusa Globels, and asked to express their complaints. After everyone had spoken, they were told that they would not be allowed to go to the Congress. The government was unwilling to tolerate divisive black politics in Cuba.

Another example of controversy and conflict between blacks and government officials was the production of Eugenio Hernández's play, *María Antonia* (1967). Apparently, many whites were insulted by the strong black characters and specifically black themes, which broke with traditional images, dating back to the era of the Bufo theater, of blacks as mere simpletons. However, the theater critic Inés María Martiatu Terry linked historical factors with contemporary revolutionary politics in order to elucidate the play's complicated fate. She explained that, historically, the black image was that of the buffoon: someone whose manner of speech, thoughts, and actions were always material for theatrical comedy. In addition, Afro-Cuban women's stereotypical sexual and sensual image is called into question when the protagonist, María Antonia, breaks the female mold and defies a world dominated by paternalism and racism. She is a rebellious figure who defies even the Afro-Cuban gods (interview with the author, Havana, 15 August 1996).

Even though people waited in long lines to see the play, performances were suspended. Officials' negative reaction to *María Antonia* had grave personal consequences for Hernández Espinosa, as well. Gerardo Fulleda León explains that Hernández Espinosa's problems developed, partly because the play's first performances coincided with the U.S. Black Power movement and the Afro-Cuban gatherings that emulated U.S. activism, and authorities feared that a racial conflict like the one in the United States might develop. Moreover, perhaps Hernández Espinosa's use of a complex black woman's image of strength and rebellion piqued petty bourgeois sensibility and exposed revolutionary officials' double standard of morality toward Afro-Cubans (interview with the author, Havana, 20 July 1994). Authorities excoriated Hernández Espinosa for his association with Afro-Cuban religious practices and accused him of moral depravity, depriving him of work for at least two years.

Cuban officialdom's racist backlash against Hernández Espinosa's play illustrates that contradictions existed in revolutionary rhetoric over aesthetics, which proved to be exclusionary. The government wanted to promote black culture in a limited formal, aesthetic, and folkloric manner that had little appeal to the black masses that went to see *María Antonia.*

Initially, several Afro-Cuban cultural manifestations were produced. However, although Hernández's play and Carbonell's text appeared, officials did detect "danger" and feared unexpected ramifications. In both cases, they responded with repression. They shelved Hernández's play and punished the author with intimidation and "silence" for two years; Carbonell was imprisoned and excluded from employment for several years.

Perhaps these lessons, involving blatant discrimination and official reprisals, also ultimately contributed to blacks' internalizing repression. Rather than risk officials' negative response, many Afro-Cubans simply chose not to publish. Self-censorship is not peculiar to black production. Rather, as Dopico Black explains, the mechanisms of "internal repression" permeate Cuba's cultural production: "Indirect repression of freedom of expression emerges from the same norms as direct repression; the difference is one of degrees. At the direct, external level, a certain message is transmitted through a public act: the censorship of a book, the imprisonment of a writer. A line is drawn. At the private level, that 'line' is interpreted as a boundary across which it is dangerous to trespass; the message is internalized" (132).

A case in point that reveals the extent of the private level of repression is Fernández Robaina's missing last chapter from *El Negro en Cuba.* In the published text about black struggle in Cuba, history ends in 1959 because Fernández Robaina chose to omit chapter 13, entitled "The Struggle."

In interviews, I asked both Fernández Robaina and Tomás González why they have not published much of what they have written. Fernández Robaina responded that he believed he practiced self-repression and commented that self-censorship has always existed for Cuban writers (interview with the author, Havana, 12 July 1996). González responded by using the former Cuban Black Power activist Alberto Pedro as an example of an Afro-Cuban intellectual who suffered repression and subsequently chose to be mute. As for his own lack of publications, he claimed that he knew officials wouldn't publish his works, so he did not submit them, adding that they were too politically controversial (interview with the author, Canary Islands, Spain, 16 May 1996).

The fact that Fernández Robaina omitted chapter 13, which examines contemporary problems for blacks, and the cases of González and Pedro, who were key members of defunct Afro-Cuban political activist groups, may confirm what Dopico Black has said: "Often, uncertainty breeds silence" (133). Although it is presumptuous to declare Fernández Robaina's clear-cut case of self-censorship a pattern for all black intellectuals, Afro-Cubans experienced overt "lessons" that may have later encouraged their "voluntary" silence. In an interview with Magdalena García-Pinto, Pedro Pérez Sarduy, another former member of the Cuban Black Power movement, also conceded that he used to think that his own timidity impeded him from publishing; he came to believe that it was a combination of self-censorship and official censorship. When asked what was behind the official disapproval of his works, Pérez Sarduy replied that officials did not approve of his approach to literature at that particular historical, political, and social moment in Cuba, preferring the style known as socialist realism, a style he never used. As a consequence, his work was not published for years: "Fueron diez años durante los que no me publicaron un solo poema en Cuba, concretamente entre 1969 y 1979" (29). [Those were difficult years, between 1969 and 1979, when I could not get a single poem published (tr. Linda Howe).]

Clearly, Pedro Pérez Sarduy, Fernández Robaina, Martínez Furé, Tomás González, and others either could not publish works with themes of black activism or simply did not want to be suspected of antirevolutionary activities by manifesting "separatist" black politics or labeling as racist Cuban revolutionary society. "Self-censorship," explains César Leante, a Cuban writer, "consists of assuming the fallacy that any criticism of the system is a way of helping the enemy, and, therefore, the temptation must be repressed" (Dopico Black 132).

The relationship between Afro-Cubans and the revolutionary government is characterized by mutual fear and misinterpretation. Censorship and punishment are realities that have bred suspicion and self-censorship among Afro-Cubans and other intellectuals who include Afro-Cuban themes in their works. According to Dopico Black, with the 1980s institutionalization of cultural policy, "repression has incorporated itself into daily Cuban reality. In the intellectual arena, freedom of expression is reduced for the sake of political control" (138). All too often, in an effort to contain black politics, the government chooses repressive measures that make it extremely difficult to find concrete evidence of censorship or to identify social protest themes in Afro-Cubans' works without their own extrinsic corroboration. Furthermore, the Cuban government has never officially acknowledged controversies raised by Afro-Cubans as real occurrences in Cuban history or that blacks have struggled with authorities in the revolutionary period. There is no accessible, specific information written to date by Cuban scholars living in Cuba concerning the controversies blacks experienced with the Castro government.[8]

The Castro government managed to impose limits on pro–Afro-Cuban political expression to discourage black activism and to restrict studies of Afro-Cuban society, whether in scholarship, literature, films, or theater. The fear of being stigmatized as an "antirevolutionary" activist may have led to a nationwide denial of race heritage among Afro-Cubans. The question remains: If the revolution created institutional racial equality, why are so few Afro-Cuban writers represented in the literary canon?

3

Nancy Morejón's Precarious Wings

"Pure" Poetry, Revolutionary Aesthetics, and Fragile Abstractions

In the first and final verses of the poem "Paisaje célebre," Nancy Morejón alludes to the Flemish artist Pieter Brueghel's sixteenth-century painting *Landscape with the Fall of Icarus* and muses: "Ver la caída de Ícaro desde la bahía de / azules y verdes de Alamar / / Es el atardecer y necesito las alas de Ícaro" (*Paisaje célebre* 54).

On Brueghel's canvas we see peasants, ships, and even nature (personified) go about their business while, almost unseen, Icarus plunges to his death. One can barely find the boy's legs sticking out of the sea because they are off to one side of the canvas.

In Morejón's poem, as afternoon falls, the poet enigmatically wishes for Icarus's wings. It is in Morejón's craving for wings that we can recognize her commentary on the question of the poet's obligations to society. Since it is by nature an ill-fated journey, introspection merely leads to indignity. More lyric than expository, the poem depicts the quandary of the poet, who, as antihero or fool, is settling accounts with the powers that be, out of either desperation or self-criticism. On the other hand, perhaps the poet situates herself in the tradition of Renaissance moralists who believed that Icarus's fate taught us about the dangers of going to extremes and the virtues of moderation. Or perhaps, as others thought, the youth's adventure symbolizes the pursuit of intellect spirit.

Almost forty years after the Cuban revolution, the image of Icarus surfaces again with ironic nuances. The poet and antihero mockingly accepts, as did Huidobro's antipoet and magician in his famous poem "Altazor," the extended fall (but without a parachute) into an abstract landscape of disillusionment. Like the poetic voice of Huidobro's poem, Morejón's speaker also is painfully aware that the world is indifferent to the artists' calamitous trajectory.[1] However, both Huidobro's antipoet / magician and Morejón's antihero / poet see the absolute necessity to embark on the journey.

Perhaps Morejón wraps her poem with the re-creation of Icarus's mythical and perilous journey to probe inward about a particular Cuban conjuncture in history in the 1990s. Since the breakup of the Soviet Union and the beginning of Cuba's so-called Special Period, Cubans have experienced severe economic and political measures as they manage their lives with a scarcity of goods. Cuban intellectuals have taken advantage of the circumstances to produce works critical of the government's repression of artists and writers and of cultural officials' attempts to make them socially useful (theater and dance have been at the forefront of this significant critique). As we shall see later in this chapter, Morejón also examines her country's dilemma and portrays the Cuban condition in this recent poetry.

As a poet and essayist, Morejón has lived through extraordinary times; from the Cuban revolution to the Special Period, she has managed to juggle aesthetics and politics in a skillful game of cultural production. She began her career as a poet when the private publishing house El Puente brought out her collections *Mutismos* (1962) and *Amor, ciudad atribuída* (1964) immediately after the revolution. She went on to publish several more poetry collections, among them *Richard trajo su flauta y otros argumentos* (1967), *Parajes de una época* (1979), *Cuaderno de Granada* (1984), and *Piedra pulida* (1986). Her most recent poems appear in *Paisaje célebre* (1993), *El río de Martín Pérez y otros poemas* (1996), *Botella al mar* (1996), and *La quinta de los molinos* (2000).

Morejón's changing attitudes toward poetic style, feminism, and the situation of blacks in Cuba clearly bear the marks of the political and institutional milieu in which she has produced her oeuvre. Like all writers and artists in post-1959 Cuba, she has had to pay close attention to the limits placed on literary and political expression. While she has remained steadfast in her commitment to the ideals of the revolution, she has also worked to extend those boundaries and to open up the official discourse from within. Her efforts have been marked by contradictions and painful reversals and at times by limited success. Surveying

Morejón's more than four-decade-long career, one can discern an ongoing struggle to reconcile the demands of her poetic sensibility with the government's demands for a didactic, highly politicized literature.

Indeed, Morejón has produced a variety of styles and themes within official limits. She has concentrated on the Cuban revolution, Caribbean history, and the Third World agenda and also has emphasized race and gender issues. Although she altered her early literary style from metaphysical and "pure" to transparent, conversational poetry, she has never completely abandoned symbolist-style aesthetics.

Immediately after authorities imprisoned and ostracized some intellectuals, such as José Mario and Ana María Simo, who were associated with El Puente, Morejón dedicated her energies to more politically committed and substantive texts that corresponded to the official policies on aesthetics. She was able to cope with successive abrupt changes in cultural policy and learned from her experiences with the El Puente scandal. Since she was unable to publish actual texts of poetry in Cuba for twelve years, she de-emphasized the putatively "decadent" symbolist aesthetics that characterize the earlier works published by El Puente. At one point, she even left Havana to work on a sociohistorical study of industrial workers in Nicaro (*Lengua de pájaro* 1971) and participated in several local political activities.[2]

In an unpublished interview with the author, Morejón explains her "silence" and alludes to subsequent aesthetic "corrections" in her poetry. She attributes the so-called silence to Cuban publishers' whims. It is significant that the decision not to publish her work was official since there were no longer any independent publishers in Havana; they had all been eclipsed by official institutions by the early 1960s. Their "unwillingness" to publish her works was a major factor in her hiatus from publishing and attributed to some lapse in her own creative process:

> N. M: Son dos cosas distintas. Una cosa es que escribas y otra es que publiques. Esos fueron los años en que escribí mucho, pero mi poesía no fue del gusto de las capillas que manejaban tanto las revistas de aquel momento como las editoriales. Lo cual, hasta hoy, es un misterio. Hay factores estéticos, quizás factores políticos, factores de enemistad, son cosas que siempre quedan en una nebulosa . . . no sé. . . . Entonces, esos son los años en que yo realmente no publiqué y es esa circunstancia la que establece la relación de un poeta con su público. Esa relación se afecta porque tú dejas de existir y cuando dejas de existir—por las razones que fueran; porque no gusta lo que tú hagas o porque no hay papel, es lo mismo, ¿no?—hay un vacío.

Es necesario publicar en el mundo moderno. Yo te digo que no se concibe que alguien que tiene cosas que decir, que las dice relativamente bien, se tenga que conformar con no existir literariamente, con no tener ese intercambio incluso con otros movimientos literarios en otras lenguas. Yo creo que el mundo moderno tiene que asimilar esta lección de estos ostracismos que por lo general son estériles, inútiles. ¿Qué voy a hacer con mi pobre poemita que un editor rechazó porque estaba aludiendo a un problema circunstancial que no le convenía al presupuesto de su revista? Yo creo que tenemos que ir saliendo de estas cosas; sin embargo te digo que, hoy por hoy, estoy un poco indiferente hacia el hecho de publicar un libro o no publicarlo. Te hablo con absoluta sinceridad porque mi poesía, yo creo, siempre ha sido esperada y eso es algo. A pesar de todos esos vacíos y a pesar de esos momentos en que yo no he existido literariamente, mi poesía ha sido esperada, ha circulado de alguna manera. . . . ¿Por qué escribo poemas? Siempre se ha acercado alguien a decirme qué quiso decir usted aquí, esto lo hizo por tal razón, independientemente de que yo no tenga una difusión. Mi difusión, por ejemplo, con *Richard trajo su flauta* tuvo una edición de tres mil ejemplares, en muchos casos eran 1,500, 2 mil, no eran más. Fue un libro que le gustó a la gente y esas cosas a mí me hacen muy feliz. Ahora, hay una Nancy Morejón hasta *Richard trajo su flauta* (desde *Mutismos*). En *Richard trajo su flauta* hay una gran diferencia, hay más o menos un puente ahí, ¿verdad? Para esta época, hay un cambio; naturalmente hay un cambio que yo creo que se debe a ese silencio, a esos años en donde, además, trato de tocar temas que aparentaban estar prohibidos para mí. Es decir, haberme dicho que yo no hacía poesía política (me puso a mí a pensar, no?) me hizo a mí querer escribir poesía política. . . . Ya te vas a encontrar para esta época con una poesía más abierta, con una poesía de la ciudad, de la gente, de todo eso, pero con una marcada preocupación de latitudes con fenómenos políticos que no tienen que ver exactamente con Cuba sino con el descubrimiento de la noción del "Tercer Mundo." Aparecen entonces los poemas al movimiento negro norteamericano y otros temas que están en este libro, *Parajes de una época* (1979), que es un sencillo cuaderno. (interview with the author, Havana, 16 July 1994)

[N. M: It's one thing to write and another to have your work published. Those were the years in which I wrote a lot, but my poetry wasn't accepted by the circles that controlled the journals as well as the publishing houses . . . which is a mystery, even today. There are aesthetic factors, perhaps also politics and enmity; they are factors that always remain nebulous. . . . I don't know. . . . So, those are the years in which I really didn't get

published, and that circumstance establishes the relationship of
a poet with her public . . . because you cease to exist, and when
you cease to exist—for whatever reasons, because no one liked
what you did, or because there's no paper; it's all the same,
right?—there is an emptiness. It's necessary to publish in the
modern world. I would say that it is difficult to imagine that
someone who has things to say and says them relatively well
should have to concede to not exist literarily, to not even have an
exchange with other literary movements in other languages. I
think the modern world has to heed the lesson of these os-
tracisms that are generally fruitless and ineffectual. What am I
going to do with my poor little poem that an editor rejected because it alluded to a circumstance that didn't suit the objectives
of his journal? I think we have to overcome these matters; nevertheless, I would say that, today, I am slightly indifferent to
whether or not I publish a book. I say this with absolute sincer-
ity, because I believe that my poetry has always been eagerly
awaited, and that's something. In spite of all the gaps and in
spite of those times when I haven't existed literarily, my poetry
has been . . . circulated in some way. . . .

Why do I write poems? Someone has always approached me
to ask, "What did you want to say here? You did this for such and
such a reason," independently of whether my work was circulated. My circulation, for example, with *Richard trajo su flauta* was
three thousand copies; in many other cases, there were 1,500,
2,000 copies, no more. *Richard* was a book that people liked, and
that makes me very happy. Now, there is a Nancy Morejón up until *trajo su flauta* [beginning with *Mutismos*]. In *Richard trajo su
flauta*, there is a big difference—there's more or less a transition
there, right? During this period, there is a change that I think is
due to that silence, to those years when I tried to treat themes that,
apparently, were forbidden to me. That is, when I was told that I
didn't write political poetry, that made me think, didn't I? That
made me want to write political poetry. . . . Now, in this period,
you'll find a more open poetry, a poetry of the city, of the people
. . . but with a marked preoccupation with political phenomena
that don't exactly have to do with Cuba but rather with the notion of the "Third World." During that time, my poems referred
to American black activists and other themes that appear in . . .
Parajes de una época (1979), which is a mere notebook.] (Tr. Emma
Claggett and Linda Howe)

Morejón claims that she began to create more politically committed
poetry because she felt personally challenged to experiment with that
particular style. However, she offers a disclaimer; the underlying motive
for the changes was to have her work published once again. She also

states that she began to manifest her increasing consciousness and engagement in political issues on a national scale.

As Morejón refocused her writing, she contended with other factors as well. While Cuban officials' demands on writers and the impact of the Cuban revolution on Latin American politics (and vice versa) influenced Morejón's choices, she also experienced the popularity of Latin American "exteriorista" poetry.

According to Steven F. White, the Nicaraguan poet Ernesto Cardenal actually coined the term "exteriorism," relating it to the specific situation of Nicaraguan post-avant-garde poetry. Cardenal's concept of exteriorism was particularly influenced by Pound's Imagism, but Cardenal reshaped the notions of objectivity as "giving form to a political history revolving around the American continent" (*Modern Nicaraguan Poetry* 169).

Cardenal's artifice of objectification is critical to the formation of a "moral position"; the poet insists on politicizing literature to encompass Nicaraguan history and politics (White, *Modern Nicaraguan Poetry* 168). Cardenal opposed what he defined as "interiorista" language, the language of poetry removed from everyday experience and disengaged from social realities (González and Treece 289). In an interview, Cardenal also emphasizes the need to make everything that exists in life fit in a poem: "Todo lo que se puede decir en un cuento, o en un ensayo, o en una novela, puede también decirse en un poema. En un poema caben datos estadísticos, fragmentos de cartas, editoriales de un periódico . . . cosas que antes eran consideradas como elementos propios de la prosa y no de la poesía" (Benedetti, *Los poetas* 87). [Everything that can be said in a story, or in an essay, or in a novel, can also be said in a poem. In a poem even statistical information, fragments of letters, newspaper editorials, can be included . . . things that previously were considered elements particular to prose and not to poetry (tr. Linda Howe).]

Exteriorist poetry was significant in Nicaragua and in other countries like Cuba, where political strife, repression, and possible rebellion were constants. Another obvious influence on Morejón was the "antipoetry" of the Chilean Nicanor Parra. Like Cardenal, Parra embraced a matter-of-fact presentation of everyday life and used prosaic poetry to convey his ideas.

Objective descriptions of events and life from one's social, political, and economic reality were crucial for the perpetuation of the Cuban revolution. Cultural officials gladly embraced exteriorism as an official poetic style because it politicized literature to reflect Cuba's specific sociohistorical situation and state of affairs (Merino vi–xiv). Even though conversationalist poetry already existed in Cuba in the 1940s and 1950s, some Cuban poets of the 1960s and 1970s converted this incipient style into an official one and put their work to the task of raising historical consciousness. Themes of Cuban exteriorism consisted of, for example, descriptions of the struggle in the Sierra Maestra against Batista's troops; the triumph of the Cuban revolution; the exaltation of the guerrilla fighter (especially the image of Che Guevara, a hero of the Cuban revolution who lost his life attempting to create a new guerrilla front in rural Bolivia); criticism of the ills of capitalism; and the promotion of popular culture (Rodríguez Nuñez 21–22).

Evidently, in contrast to her former hermetic poetry of ambiguity, Morejón's prudent invocation of revolutionary imagery produced a quiescent conversational style that corresponded to officially promoted aesthetics.

In the highly politicized climate of cultural production, Morejón created a juncture between Latin American exteriorist poetry and her own poetry, thereby joining the ranks of her generation (e.g., Miguel Barnet, Luis Rogelio Nogueras, Victor Casaus) to establish what Fernández Retamar called Cuban revolutionary poetry (*Para una teoría* 86–88). However, in contrast to Morejón's eventual use of conversational-style poetry, her first poems published with Ediciones El Puente, *Mutismos* and *Amor, ciudad atribuída,* are marked by the influence of the Latin American modernista poets who appropriated French symbolism to forge their own movement.

Morejón's admiration for Baudelaire, Rimbaud, Mallarmé, and Breton is quite apparent in her early works of "pure" poetry. Replete with haunting metaphors of the city, her poems represent psychological states of consciousness. The inchoate but elevated and formalized style also has its roots in the tradition of Latin American symbolism. Typically associated with the nineteenth-century modernismo literary movement led by the Nicaraguan poet Rubén Darío (1867–1916), symbolism continued to be a prominent aspect of subsequent literary movements during distinct historical periods in the Hispanic world. In the late nineteenth century, Darío acted as intermediary between Paris and Latin America during the height of symbolism's influence in Spain and Latin America. Modernista poets were concerned principally with form and portrayed an exotic world of beautiful objects superior to the banality of everyday things.

As symbolism waned in the early twentieth century, many poets rebelled against abstract poetry. Others, like the Spaniard Federico García Lorca and the Latin Americans Octavio Paz and César Vallejo, rejuvenated and modernized symbolism. They infused their poetry with abstract images of decadent urban landscape to convey philosophic torment and spiritual states.

Cuban poets also inspired Morejón's creative perspective and choice of literary style. During the 1940s and 1950s, José Lezama Lima and Virgilio Piñera reigned as poets who exemplified a combination of experimental, symbolist, and neobaroque styles in Cuban letters. They also served as an aesthetic bridge between the period of the Batista regime and the Cuban revolution. Lezama's neobaroque style (characteristic of the works in the Cuban literary journal *Orígenes,* which he founded) was often obscure; his poetry projected irrational and sensory communication and intangible plights. After the revolution, cultural bureaucrats denounced Lezama's poetry for its "bourgeois individualism" and "decadence," arguing—no doubt correctly—that it did not qualify as "revolutionary" literature. Several young Cuban poets imitated his style and combined themes of spiritual decadence with conversational poetry, expressing conditions of restlessness and angst. Some Cuban critics even dubbed Morejón's poetry in *Mutismos* "neooorígenes," claiming that it was reminiscent of the Lezamian-style verses.

A Lezamian-style writer who also greatly affected Morejón's early poetry, and perhaps served as a bridge between Lezama's generation and Morejon's, was Rolando Escardó. He is an almost forgotten poet who died in an automobile accident in 1960 at the age of thirty-five. Born in Camaguey, he was an influential and multitalented figure of the 1950s cultural milieu; an impoverished intellectual who lived an agitated and mobile life that often verged on the picaresque. His first poetry collections, the posthumously published *Libro de Rolando* (1961), exudes the mood of the epoch. Escardó blends the nineteenth-century modernismo of the poet Julián del Casal (who translated Baudelaire's prose poems into Spanish) with Lezama's twentieth-century abstract metaphors. Virgilio Piñera describes Escardó as a spiritual beggar who evokes emotional states of despair and fear without precedent in Cuban letters ("Introduction" 23). In "Miedo" Escardó exhibits the quiet desperation of existence:

> Me ven así las gentes:
>   Como si estos pellejos que me cuelgan
> no tuvieran la forma
>   de ser algo que existe y es . . . (47)

∾

> [People see me this way:
>   as if this skin hanging on me
> did not have the shape
>   of something that exists and is . . .] (Tr. Linda Howe)

The poet describes an outcast; a mere amorphous figure without real presence, an everyman whose urban entrapment accentuates his bleakness. Piñera suggests that Escardó's pathos is reminiscent of that of city poets like Martínez Villena and Lezama, whose cities are, among other things, hyperbolic structures, erratic rhythms, human frenzy, and images of tumultuousness that permit the poet to waft though the multitudes (24). Escardó imparts a pathetic being in "Delirios": "Quiero estar un día con lo que no me dieron / y contar y reir por sólo un día . . ." (35). [One day, I want what I have never been given / And I want to sing and laugh for just one day . . .] And in "Salida," a modern drifter hunts living souls in the urgent search for a human pulse, a sign of vitality:

> Uno sale a la calle, así de pronto, y anda y
> pregunta y mira
> descender la tarde en la ciudad.
> Acechando ventanas, con un anhelo de hallar
> un latido, una voz,
> cuelga en la lengua pegajosa una pregunta
> ¿En dónde estás?
> ¿En cuál ventana o en qué puerta?
> El tiempo cruza y cruza, los ojos abiertos
> buscan en medio
> de la soledad en los días . . . (117)

∾

> [Suddenly, you go out on the street, walking,
> you look and ask questions and,
> watch the afternoon fall on the city,
> spying in windows, yearning to catch
> a heartbeat, a voice
> a single question stuck to your tongue
> Where are you?
> In which window or door?
> Time runs on and on; wide-open eyes
> search in the midst
> of the loneliness of days.] (Tr. Linda Howe)

The "I" lurks among elements of the metropolis to spy in windows and doors; the poet suffers in desperation and solitude.

Escardó's vulnerable and tormented voice has an unmistakable affinity with Morejón's pensive one in *Mutismos*. Her metaphors often convey similar hermetic, romantic, and passionate visions of the sensorial, with topical references. For example, in Morejón's "Sofisma 4," the poetic speaker complains of anguished thoughts and conveys personalized wretchedness:

> . . . y logro apenas sentirlo dentro
> encima de mi cabeza
>   inquieta de angustias
> de lodos
>   de sombras
>   de colores
>   de miedo
> no afectada de otra cosa
> más que de castidades malditas y de locuras
> obscuras, inanimadas
> no cabe nada más en ella [la cabeza]
> no puedo. . . no puedo (51)
>
>   ⌒≈⌒
>
> [. . . and I hardly manage to feel it within
> above my head
>   troubled by anxieties
> of mud
>   of shadows
>   of colors
>   of fear
> not affected by another thing
> more than by cursed chastity and madness
> obscure, inanimate
> nothing more fits in it
> i can not . . . i can not] (Tr. H. Rosario Sievert)

Colors, shadows, and fear reign as the "I" pleads for reprieve from the onslaught of excessive tangibility and moody reflection. Several poems in *Mutismos* convey the confusion present in "Sofisma 4"; there are allusions to death and love; the poet conjures interior spaces and nebulous sensations that constitute the symbolic. Morejón verses reflect on the omnipresence of indeterminacy. In a resigned tone, the poetic voice declares that comprehension of the world is something always beyond our grasp.

In these verses, Morejón focuses on the dark and muddled side of the Cuban condition. Later, in *Amor, ciudad atribuída*, she turns from the gloom of her previous work to a poetry laden with correspondences of light and sound that exude alacrity, romanticism, and sensorial richness.

Notwithstanding, love themes continue to encompass the emotional spectrum, in accordance with the Cuban musical tradition called *filin*. *Filin* is a Spanish transliteration of "feeling," a musical style influenced by crooners such as Nat "King" Cole. In 1940s Cuba, the music of Angel Díaz, who regularly played gigs with other Cuban musicians at his now-famous home "el Callejón de Hammel," was the precursor to the "feeling" movement.[3] The music sets a mood with clever, satin lyricism, overstatement, and emotional color. Morejón brings out the taste of *filin*, skillfully showing the interplay between romanticism and defiant, suggestive sexuality. She translates well the vernacular in this poem, "Cuando":

> cuando te amo no conozco paredes ni trastes
> solamente comienzo a poseer mentiras y verdades
> Tú me surges de todo y esa hora tranquila en que escoges al viento
> naces para cada rasgo triste de mi vida
> Si este tiempo padece como una línea abierta
> quisiera batallarle
> para los que no quieren mirar a nuestros lechos
> Les ofrezco esta voz
> te amo

⤚≋⤙

> [When I'm loving, I don't know walls or dishes
> I simply begin to possess lies and truth
> You surge up completely and at that quiet moment when you
>   catch the wind
> you're born for every sad trace of my life
> If this moment suffers like an open line
> I would like to defy it,
> for those who do not want to see our beds
> I offer them these words
> I love you.] (Tr. Linda Howe)

Words flow like detailed melodies as Morejón, in the role of improvisational musician, produces candid verse as if she were performing a live gig. Numerous impressions come into play. Amorous appetite and bravado transgress imaginable barriers between lovers; there are no walls, no disorder; love is both truth and lies. The bed is the only invariable where the lovers unite to make their erotic bond. At the poem's climax, the naked declaration "I love you" exudes sensuality: pure, lucid, and youthful.

In this collection the tone is celebratory in some poems but continues to be vague and moody like the poetry of *Mutismos*. Gabriel Abudu notes that Morejón experiments with formal characteristics producing bold metaphors, such as "la calle es como 'un párpado común cerrado / en una gota espesa'" (71). [The street is like "a sealed eyelid / within a thick drip."] Throughout *Amor,* Morejón converts topographical features (sea, city, streets, parks, and neighborhoods) into symbolic landscapes that reflect psychological states (desperation, sadness, existential angst, and loneliness). Jacques Gilard points out the poet's "minuscule search" for order framed within the mystical geography of the street. In poems such as "El cerro viejo," "the spacial and essential model, the street embraced by observation, begins in that immense street that enlargens my pupils" (322). The poet invokes the images of love and despair through enumeration of language, dislocation of syntax, and ambiguous metaphors. Morejón's accumulation of formal elements draws the reader into the poetic speaker's emotional states. Her stylization is evident in "La ciudad expuesta":

> —lugar corroído en cimborios
> verjas y campanario—
> como pasa el hombre de piedra
> desnudando las puertas
> —de sinuoso sudor y ruido
> de frágil cántaro—
> como de nuevo el chirriar forzoso
> el olor a sorda casona
> en la ciudad (29)

> [—a place corroded by cimborium,
> iron railings, and tower bells—
> like the passing of the stone mason,
> who is stripping doors
> —sinuous sweat and noise
> from a fragile jug—
> like repeated forced squeaking
> the smell of a deaf home
> in the city] (Tr. Linda Howe)

Noises, grammatical ellipses, and split similes generate sensations of urban effects. Like the Italian futurist poets, who sought to capture the simultaneity of impression and expression, and thus to fuse the object and image, Morejón flashes several impressions of an entire city. The crippled grammatical forms simulate the visual and auditory starts and stops on the streets. The poem conjures a journey through a metropolitan spectacle and, at the work's finish, describes it only partially.

Synesthesia in the line "el olor a sorda casona" has us smelling deafness or silence. Similar to Federico García Lorca's manipulation of green-colored wind, "verde viento," in "Romance sonámbulo," Morejón's synesthesia "olor a sorda" asks the reader to imagine the aroma of silence or deafness. Morejón's free association of ideas and mixing of sensations distort the poem's verisimilitude and permit multiple interpretations. Is the poetic "I" referring to a thing, an emotional state, or an event? The use of silence and deafness can also be viewed as a commentary on poetics, an oxymoron that refers to silent poetry. In other words, the poet's inability to encompass the city's elements results in the creation of a poetry with mute words and ideas "unheard." Here, the poetic speaker not only conveys a city's visual and audial images from a multiangular perspective but also pushes the limits of poetic expression. The stunted metaphoric impressions point to the imperfect process of artistic creation.

The alliterative play and the intermittent "como" string together words like "corroído," "campanarios," "cántaro," and "casona" and others beginning with "ch" or soft "c," like "chirriar," "cimborrios," and "ciudad." The conglomeration of sounds produces cacophonies that do not mimic the actual sounds produced by the items named (such as tower bells and forced creaking) but imitates the sights, sounds, and smells of the city and therefore "yields" urbanness. We are caught up in the city's imprint on the poetic speaker's mind, the mental residues of the city, rather than the city itself.

Morejón manifests a propensity for metaphysical themes and seems obsessed with probing the limits of sensory perception. In these poems of formal experimentation, she portrays a vague, yet exuberant, spirit.[4] Her curious amalgam of graphically realistic allusions and incongruous images converts elements of the city into an immense, metonymic, surrealistic spiritual landscape. We discover the complexity of the Cuban condition in the montage of iconography.

It was not long after *Amor* was published, in 1965, that authorities shut down El Puente. One way to establish how official measures influenced Morejón is to observe her altered approach to poetics: metaphysics and surrealism gave way to social and political themes. Although it is certainly possible to attribute these alterations to the natural evolution of Morejón's poetics, it is also feasible to conjecture that Cuba's troublesome political climate affected her literary orientation. Her next poetry collection, *Richard trajo su flauta,* published in 1967, contains more politically committed poetry.

In such poems as "La razón del poema" and "Parque central, alguna gente," Morejón combines a Third World consciousness and revolutionary voluntarism with formal elements to create a politicized poetic vision. The verse is less obscure (with fewer abstract metaphors), making objects and themes more tangible and revealing the poet's adherence to the regime's values. For example, in "La razón del poema" (The poem's purpose), the poet uses the metaphor of a bed with sheets that no longer "fit" to discuss transformation: "a estas horas descubro el lecho árido / las sábanas no acostumbran mi cuerpo" (17). [At this hour, I discern the sterile bed / the sheets take no comfort in my body (tr. Linda Howe).]

Morejón contrasts a barren bed, a space symbolizing obsolete tradition, with significant revolutionary activity. The "I," who suffers isolation among abstract imagery, becomes immersed in concrete symbols of strength, production, and energy. Transparent images of the sugarcane harvest and Castro's hands intertwine with ordinary human activities such as going to the movies and taking literature classes:

> cada minuto es el tiempo que consume
> que deposita los ademanes diarios:
> la clase de literatura la guardia el reloj
> la conferencia el cine la zafra
> la exposición las manos de Fidel
> los grabados el canturreo pegajoso
> esta revolución ansiosa (17)
>
> ⤳
>
> [Every minute is time which consumes
> situates everyday gestures:
> the kind of literature the vigilance the clock
> the conference the movie theater the sugar harvest
> the exhibition Fidel's hands
> the engravings the captivating hum
> this anxious revolution] (Tr. Linda Howe)

The Castroist iconography usurps the poetic voice's murky metaphors. Morejón suppresses punctuation to symbolize that daily life and revolution are one and the same activity. The use of anaphora generates a positive rhythm, making the verses hum like a fine-tuned machine; all elements of life (power, action, and spirit) become enmeshed with Castro's hands and the harvest. The poem glorifies the "eager" revolution's energy and production.

Likewise, in "Parque central, alguna gente," Morejón describes the elderly people who spend their days sitting in Havana's central park next to a statue of the "apostle Martí" (José Martí, the nineteenth-century national hero and martyr of Cuba's independence wars with Spain). It is 1966, and the Cubans are about to commemorate the anniversary of their country's independence and to pay homage to its martyrs. To traverse the park—a space of light that represents the revolution—is to vehemently sacrifice one's life as a "comrade":

> ... tiene que suspirar
> y andar despacio y respirar
> y andar ligero y suspirar y respirar y andar despacio
> y dar toda la vida
> rabiosamente
> compañeros (51)

⤚⤙

> [... has to sigh
> and slowly walk and breathe
> and walk softly and breathe and walk slowly
> and give your life completely
> ravenously
> comrades] (Tr. Linda Howe)

Revolutionary dedication emanates from these verses; the rhythmic repetition of the infinitive verbs "to walk," "to breathe," and "to sigh" push toward crescendo and into full-blown action. The demand for "ravenous" dedication to the revolution is heightened by the word "comrades" at the poem's end. The poet reiterates the significance of collective radical deeds within a charged atmosphere of revolutionary effervescence. Morejón has adapted her creative energy to focus on revolutionary iconography.

Appropriately, significant historical phases and subsequent major events of the Cuban revolution manifest themselves as well in Morejón's symbols of the Cuban spirit. Metaphors of the city, the revolution, and anchored ships from three poems reveal her changed perspective on Cuban vitality. Confusing, surrealistic images of the city coincide with the euphoria, bewilderment, and aesthetic freedom of the beginning phase of the revolution. The lovely red lance of the revolution tokens institutional and political entrenchment for many intellectuals in the 1960s and 1970s. The anchored ships exemplify the phase after the collapse of the Soviet Union and the subsequent political, moral, and spiritual decay of Cuban society.

Morejón's newly politicized style is best exemplified in her revision of the poem "Amor, ciudad atribuída," which first appeared in *Amor*. In *Richard*, Morejón has rewritten the poem to accentuate a revolutionary voice (Luis, "Race" 88). The poet attached a dedication in the later version, "al lector, compañero." If we interpret "compañero" to mean comrade (a salutation often, but not exclusively, associated with socialist and communist countries), we must ask how the dedication sets the tone for the entire poem. Does addressing the reader as "comrade" require us to ask whom the poetic speaker designates as the audience? And what does labeling readers as comrades imply? Is Morejón indicating that she wants a broader audience, that her new poetry is accessible to all in socialist Cuba? This and other changes in the poem signal that Morejón's individual experimentation has given way to communicative, exteriorist poetry. Unlike the earlier version, here the poetic speaker openly embraces the revolution:

> la poesía viene sola con todo lo que dejo a mi paso: flor o demonio,
> la poesía viene sola como un pájaro
> (le doy un árbol rojo)
> y se posa muy fiera sobre mi cabeza, y come mi esclerótica;
> pero ahora no es tan sólo el
> cantar de los pájaros
> no es sólo la ciudad
> aquí diré las olas de la costa y la Revolución
> aquí la poesía llega con una lanza hermosa para sangrarme el pecho
> (*Richard* 39)

⤳

> [Poetry evolves from what I leave behind on my journey: flowers or the devil,
> poetry comes alone like a bird
> (I give it a red tree)
> and it perches savagely on my head, and it feeds on my sclera
> but now it is not only
> birdsong
> not merely the city
> Here, I say it's the coastal waves and the Revolution
> here poetry arrives with a beautiful lance to pierce my breast]
> (Tr. Linda Howe)

Anaphora, repetition, and transformation characterize these lines. The poet disregards earlier assertions, that poetry originates from the city, to claim that the revolution is the true source. In addition, the scheme of sensations has changed with two references to the color red, the tree and the bleeding chest, that might be associated with the symbolic red of communism. Rather than submit elements of the urban landscape to a surrealist hermetic gaze, the poet includes the metaphor of a beautiful lance that makes the poetic speaker's chest bleed. The pain the lovely lance occasions and the resultant flow of blood liken the process of creating poetry to that of the sacrifice needed for the revolutionary struggle and to a culminating moment of religiosity.

Morejón's angel of revolution that pierces the poetic speaker's breast recalls Bernini's altar in the Cornaro Chapel at Santa Maria della Vittoria, Rome (1645–52). There, in marble, Bernini has created the "Ecstasy of Saint Theresa," which includes an angel holding in its hand an arrow aimed directly at Saint Theresa de Avila's heart. Saint Theresa's gaping mouth and eyes looking upward reveal a combination of willing sacrifice and bliss. In her writings the saint claimed that she envisioned a smiling angel who repeatedly pierced her heart with a golden arrow, causing her to experience ecstasy: a seemingly contradictory mix of pain and infinite sweetness.

Morejón's verses are permeated with religious overtones of martyrdom; rapture comes about when the wounded body "bleeds" revolutionary images. She transforms the poet into a soldier of metaphors. By analogy, poets become commendable soldiers who willingly accept pain to fight for the eternal revolution and victorious glory.

The poet-soldier has returned to the city, this time giving priority to revolutionary and bellicose images that eclipse all other previous similes. To vindicate the guerrilla's labor is thus to pay tribute to revolutionary virtues. Has Morejón not corrected an earlier poem to bring it in line with official ideology? Her strategy is revealed in the poem's iconography. Morejón's revised sources of poetic inspiration are drawn from official accounts of Castro's guerrilla victory, and those images are based upon an iconography of heroism. This reformed version of "Amor, ciudad atribuída" supports the idea that Morejón modified content as well as form to close the gap between her poetics and the official aesthetic. It is in these poems of revolution and sacrifice that we also witness a shift in the poet's construction of the Cuban condition. There no longer exists an internalized spiritual torment. Rather, we see a militant spirit and a facsimile of a socialist future generated by revolution.

Throughout the 1970s and 1980s, Morejón reiterated the revolutionary spirit with undeniably politically committed poems in her collections. In *Parajes de una época*, Morejón's erstwhile assertiveness of form over content, subjective ambivalence, and enumeration of metaphors are displaced by an objective conversational style. We see this transfor-

mation through officially approved "purified" verse and more accessible language. Although Morejón includes other types of poems, the
political ones, such as "Una rosa," "Mitología," and "Meditación a med-
iodía por los caídos en Playa Girón," are nostalgic references to revolutionary icons and the military struggle against the Batista dictatorship.
They describe heroic battles at the Bay of Pigs and panegyric verse for
the fallen heroes Abel Santamaría and Camilo Cienfuegos. Her themes
also include Vietnam's nationalism, the indignities of U.S. racism, the
atrocities of Chilean concentration camps in the late 1960s, and support
for revolutionary struggle. By this time, Morejón had joined the ranks
of other poets of her generation (e.g., Barnet, Nogueras, Casaus) in establishing a tradition of government-sanctioned political poetry.

After a brief hiatus of three years, Morejón reaffirmed her commitment to the Cuban government with *Octubre imprescindible* (1982). The
text begins and ends with poems dedicated to Cuban nationalism.
Poems in the first and second sections refer to the Cuban missile crisis,
the Russian Revolution, and the Soviet presence in Cuba. The third
section comprises black themes: slavery and Afro-Cuban religion. The
fourth section consists of a variety of topics. Nicolás Guillén's influence
(*West Indies Ltd.*) is notable in such poems as "Hablando con una culebra" and "Güijes" (Luis, "Race" 94).

In *Cuaderno de Granada* Morejón gives equal attention to aesthetic
form and revolutionary content. Since for cultural authorities, too much
attention to form would be labeled "anti-revolutionary," it was perhaps
bold for Morejón to attempt to have it both ways.[5] Miriam DeCosta-
Willis states that in *Cuaderno* the verse is "too prosaic and the political
theses too heavy for the lyrical frame, as the poet subordinates image
and symbol to ideology ("The Caribbean" 240). Luis notes that "usually,
both form and content can complement each other, but within the context of the revolution, they are separate and mutually exclusive. In fact,
form is associated with an elitist and archaic past" ("Race" 98). He remarks that, in this volume, Morejón presents the revolution on her own
terms. She frames the leitmotif with two romances that begin and end
the text, gives much attention to formal characteristics, and applies a
highly polished style. During this period, Morejón maintained her status as a poet and a cultural representative and traveled abroad freely (98).

In *Piedra pulida* Morejón experiments with hermetic and aesthetic poetry and does not include revolutionary subject matter. Perhaps, since
Morejón had an international reputation and was a well-respected, established Cuban poet (in spite of fact that Cuban critics largely ignored

her works [Bianchi Ross, "Nanay Morejon" 33–34]), she ventured to alternate styles and topics. In *Piedra pulida* Morejón dedicates a poem to Pushkin, who was ostracized by the Russian regime after the revolution. Is she alluding to the political tightrope on which the artist balances cultural production in a country such as Cuba?

Morejón's mix of politically committed poems and hermeticism and cosmopolitanism confirms that her wavering aesthetic is a constant in her work. In 1988 Morejón published a collection of essays with the Lezamian title of *Fundación de la imagen;* the variety of themes corroborates Morejón's intent on aesthetic balance. Here, she gathers together the majority of her articles, brief essays, and studies previously published in journals such as *Revista de la Universidad de La Habana, La Gaceta de Cuba, Unión, Casa de las Américas, Bohemia,* and *Resumen Semanal de Granma.* This collection covers several diverse topics, including antislavery novels, the concept of transculturation, and the literary contributions of such figures as Mirta Aguirre, Jacques Roumain, and Edward Brathwaite. For the most part, Morejón presents these topics within the ideological framework of the revolution, with numerous explicit references to the ideas of Fidel Castro and Karl Marx.

However, Morejón's narrative strategies also illustrate fissures. She obviously wants to reiterate the importance of Lezama's poetic in Cuban letters. In the essay "A propósito de José Lezama Lima," she defends his hermeticism and his eminently asocial poetry, which Cuban cultural officials had castigated in the 1960s for its lack of revolutionary zeal and its impenetrable content. Morejón chose an unpopular position in 1977 when she published her essay supporting Lezama's work. Here, she disregards official opinion and favors Lezama's aesthetics and themes, insisting that his poetry is admirable even though it does not contain revolutionary ideas or conversational style. As noted, Cuban critics also criticized Morejón's lyrical style in *Mutismos,* comparing it to Lezama's hermeticism. In this case, Morejón's defense of Lezama's style in *Orígenes* may be understood as a device for her own self-defense. In an interview with Emilio Bejel, Morejón stated: "At first, many people said that the text [*Mutismos*] resembled Lezama's style, that it belonged to the hermeticism of *Orígenes;* but all the poetry of *Orígenes* cannot be classified as hermetic, and, furthermore, it is important to emphasize that these poems of mine weren't formally hermetic; when I wrote them, I was not familiar with Lezama's work" (*Escribir en Cuba* 229).[6]

When Morejón defends Lezama and her own poetic style of the 1960s, she may also be proposing that cultural critics should evaluate hermetics differently. Perhaps Morejón does not agree that hermeticism is a symbol of bourgeois decadence and individualism. Rather, she suggests that hermeticism has multiple meanings and does not necessarily imply an antirevolutionary aesthetic. She also protests literary criticism's tendency to pigeonhole literature into movements on the basis of common formal features.

Morejón also manifests a polemical relationship with aesthetics in her more recent poetry collection entitled *Paisaje célebre*. Her shifting perception of the Cuban condition over the years, from metaphysical anguish to revolutionary zeal, was never simple. With such poems as "Marina," she provides a new vision of the Cuban spirit by combining haunting images in the conversational style of the exteriorist poets.

In the 1990s Morejón adapted her own style of poetry to criticize contemporary circumstances. Her poems convey a degraded Cuban condition during the political and economic decline of the Special Period, when Castro invoked mandatory rationing and other severe economic measures, reflecting the rapid deterioration of the standard of living in socialist Cuba after the fall of the Soviet Union in 1991.

In "Marina," the third poem that refers to the Cuban spirit, Morejón epitomizes the plight of the Cuban condition with anchored ships that symbolize spiritual and moral descent:

> Frente a los barcos
> fondeados,
> hay una cartomántica
> que espera la opción cero
> y pone su pamela
> sobre el muro del malecón
> pasa un coche tirado
> por un caballo flaco
> frente a los barcos
> fondeados.
> La cartomántica vuelve la cabeza
> y ve los ojos del caballo flaco
> sin jinete y sin rumbo,
> frente a los barcos
> fondeados.
> Hay un caballo flaco
> y una mujer que aguarda
> la caída de la tarde,
> sin una dalia entre las manos
> frente a los barcos
> fondeados.

⌒≋⌒

[Facing the anchored
ships
is a fortune teller
who awaits nothingness
and places her wide-brimmed hat
on the sea wall of the Malecón
a carriage
hauled by a scrawny horse
passes opposite the anchored ships.
The fortune teller turns her head
to look into the eyes of the scrawny horse
without a rider and without a path,
facing the anchored ships.
There is a scrawny horse
and a woman who awaits
the twilight
without a dahlia in her hands
facing the anchored
ships.] (Tr. Linda Howe)

Morejón's poetic speaker anticipates "opción cero" and describes how "el caballo flaco" roams a metaphorical landscape of decay, lost hopes, and zombie-like figures. The first stanza meditates on Cuba's current problems, on the revolution's fate. We expect the poem to be about Cuba's reality, but it snatches back the reference to reality by repeating "sin" (without) before each descriptive word so that the result is an etching scribbled over broken dreams. This poem functions something like a phobia. As the actual signified (the Cuban revolutionary system in crisis) is repressed, displacement rears its head with variants (distressed, despondent figures walking aimlessly on the streets due to wrecked ideals, poverty, and shortages of goods), just as repressed symptoms break out elsewhere in the body.

The stanza on anchored ships that begins, intersects, and ends the poem lends it a dirge-like rhythmic solemnity. Unlike the quivering ship in the nineteenth-century Cuban romantic poet Avellaneda's famous poem "Al partir," which sadly abandons her "beloved Eden" (Cuba) and sets sail for exile, Morejón's ships cannot get out of the harbor. The Cuban spirit is a stagnated soul in a sea of bleakness. This desolate situation exists along the sea wall, as well. We see a fortuneteller who anticipates option zero, a scrawny horse with no rider and no objective, and a woman without a dahlia in her hand. There is absence everywhere.

Notable in "Marina" is this nonexistence of objects named. Their existence, asserted by the poetic speaker's description, is translated into mimesis of (spiritual) nothingness itself. The hierarchy of representations imposed from reference to reference pushes the meaning to a text not present in the linearity of the poem. Rather, one encounters a barren panorama that refers to a live spirit, a wasteland that represents the traveler rather than itself, a debased soul that is the memorial of a negated, nonexistent future. Thus, the poet's allusion to the absence of a dahlia (an archetypal funeral flower) is a deliberate play on its presence that disrupts our reading. We are told that the woman does not have a dahlia in her hands as she waits for the end. This play on the binary opposition absence/presence reinforces the dreary tone, bringing the flower into play not as a real object but as a poignant brush stroke of mourning. The Cuban condition is epitomized by souls trapped, held hostage by the island's sea of despondency, while their bodies roam aimlessly through a spectacle of misfortune.

While the absent dahlia exposes hardship and nothingness, the presence of "el caballo flaco" represents an absence of power and a deflated figure not mentioned. Since thin horses drawing carts can be seen on the streets in some parts of the city, the reference may be literal. "El caballo" may also make the well-known reference to Fidel Castro and, by synecdoche, the entire revolutionary government. Virgilio Piñera's poem "Paseo del caballo," although written in 1943, was censored in the early 1960s for the simple reason that Castro is disrespectfully known as "el caballo" (Dopico Black 120). John A. Crow informs us that Castro's enemies "refer to him as 'el caballo' (the horse) because his words come out kicking like a horse and because they believe he has no more ability to rule than a horse. Fidelistas say that he is 'strong as a horse'" (781–82). Since intellectuals have been careful not to refer to "el caballo" for fear of being accused of making a negative reference to Castro, perhaps Morejón is not consciously taking this risk. Nevertheless, the "caballo" is denied power three times in the poem, and one cannot help suggesting an interpretation that connects the present Cuban condition with the government's deflated image after the fall of the Soviet Union.

Likewise, in the poem "Paisaje célebre," Morejón reiterates states of despair, disillusionment, and physical decay. She conjures a sense of entrapment and isolation on an imaginary island. As I mentioned at the beginning of the chapter, the poem begins with the vision of Icarus falling into a bay off Alamar (literally "to the sea"), a coastal town near Havana where Morejón often writes. In her poetic sketch of introspection,

Morejón describes a lonely old misanthrope, inspired by Brueghel's work, who paints the spiritual vacuum and solitude of magnificent laborers.

In this poem, Morejón engages in intertextual plasticity with references to classical mythology and Renaissance painting. We also see a thematic link between Morejón's poem and the often-anthologized poems "Musée des Beaux Arts" (1938), by W. H. Auden, and "II: Landscape with the Fall of Icarus," by William Carlos Williams, from his collection *Pictures from Brueghel and Other Poems* (1962). However, in her poem Morejón stretches the myth across her canvas to create her own intimate examination of the Cuban condition.

According to the Greek myth, Icarus flies too high and too close to the sun while attempting to flee the prison-island Crete. The wax of his wings melts because of his exuberant carelessness, causing him to plunge into the sea. Both Auden and Williams allude to Brueghel's detailed landscape of busy peasantry on a high cliff (the painter foregrounds a farmer plowing behind his horse and a shepherd tending to his sheep). The backdrop consists of the blues and greens of the sea below, with a galleon sailing along the shore. The poignancy of human suffering, and nature's indifference to it are evident only moments later, when one discovers that Brueghel also depicts Icarus's fall; at the moment of impact, only two diminutive legs are sticking out of the sea in the right-hand corner of the painting. The boy's fatal plunge appears to be the painter's mere afterthought or a cruel joke about the paltriness of endurance and human life.

Auden's poem explores the metaphysical aspects of Brueghel's apathetic scene: "About suffering they were never wrong / The old masters: how well they understood / Its human position; how it takes place / while someone else is eating or opening a window or just walking / dully along" (179).

Auden's brazen tone with the term "dully" undermines the implications of such a disaster. Williams reiterates Auden's sarcasm as he studies Brueghel's scene and probes the sting of the matter. He describes inconsequential tragedy with sparse detail and stunning understatement:

> According to Brueghel
> when Icarus fell
> it was Spring
>
> a farmer was ploughing
> his field
> the whole pageantry

of the year was
awake tingling
near

the edge of the sea
concerned
with itself

Sweating in the sun
that melted
the wings' wax

Unsignificantly
off the coast
there was

a splash quite unnoticed
this was
Icarus drowning (4)

Williams's personification of the sea's edge, concerned only with itself, echoes Auden's prosopopoeia of the "expensive ship" that coolly glides along with its own purpose, inattentive to human catastrophe. Auden's adverbs "leisurely" and "calmly" doggedly portray life as viewed by a misanthrope who overlooks spiritual blows and flippantly ignores the duped youth's disaster:

> In Brueghel's *Icarus*, for instance: how everything turns away
> Quite leisurely from the disaster; the ploughman may
> Have heard the splash, the forsaken cry,
> But for him it was not an important failure; the sun shone
> As it had to on the white legs disappearing into the green
> Water; and the expensive delicate ship must have seen
> Something amazing, a boy falling out of the sky,
> Had somewhere to get to and sailed calmly on (179)

We hear the splash and the cry, and we grasp that the body, covered with scalding wax and doomed by rambunctious ambition, has dive-bombed into the chilly green sea. We fear that nothing will ever compensate for the unfathomable shiver of ruination.

Our knowledge of the landscape's indifference and the unnoticed sacrifice makes any attempt at repetition of such an act a tragicomic misstep. Surprisingly, Morejón does just that. She completes her intertextual study of the "Old Masters" by pasting her poetic "I" onto the tragedy. Unlike Brueghel, Auden, and Williams, Morejón does not invoke distance to advise her readers of the folly of human nature. Rather, she insists on intimate transference in the desire to possess the imperfect wings. Her collage is a patchwork of historical and artistic textures and coatings depicting a visceral undertaking. The allegorical poem announces sundown on the island, and the poet dreams monsters. We are drawn into a secret wish to make the quixotic journey of dubious heroics and flights of fancy. But we know this will have us gasping for air, if our cognizance of eternal blows does not kill us first:

> Ver la caída de Ícaro desde la bahía de
> azules y verdes de Alamar
>
> Un valle al que se asoma
> un misántropo encapuchado.
> . . . .
>
> Ese hombrecillo
> es pariente de Brueghel, el viejo, hermano mío,
> que pinta la soledad del alma
> cercada por espléndidos labradores
>
> Es el atardecer y necesito las alas de Ícaro (*Paisáje* 54)

⤳

> [To witness the fall of Icarus near the bay
> the blues and greens of Alamar Bay
>
> a hooded misanthrope
> approaches a valley.
> . . . .
>
> That little man
> is one of Brueghel's relatives, the old man, my brother,
> who paints the solitude of the soul
> encircled by magnificent laborers
>
> The daylight hours are coming to an end and I yearn
> to have Icarus's wings] (Tr. Linda Howe)

An ostensibly simple poem, it portrays the complexity of the Cuban condition and provides an antidote to the clichéd prose of mainstream revolutionary rhetoric like the slogan "Socialism or Death." In contrast, aphoristic enunciation and a prophetic voice accept the burden, a priori, of failure. More than the mere desire of a self-sacrificing hero, the plunge symbolizes a poet's contemplation of a demoralizing process of national meditation and self-mocking revolutionary dynamism. The poet mocks the bland and enervated victorious typography of revolutionary posters and billboards and newspapers with rhetoric boasting of "a better future." Morejón reveals the profound superficiality of tattered sloganeering about utopian sacrifice and heroism.

On another note, Morejón's reference to Brueghel's indifferent Nature, concerned with itself, contrasts with traditional organicist myths found in Latin American literature that posit Nature as a metaphorical landscape through which nations encounter their originality and uniqueness. Here, Nature pays no heed to the Cuban hero, the poet who would have wings.[7] With her projection of the imminent splash, Morejón distinguishes her myth from those of a nascent independence movement borrowed from José Martí's "Nuestra América." Whereas Martí establishes theories in support of "Cubanness" and nationhood based on Nature's magnificence, Morejón's poem is permeated with history's little ironies that posit Nature's indifference to Cuba's identity crisis in the Special Period.

If we juxtapose the poet's portrayal of the Cuban spirit in the two versions of "Amor, ciudad atribuída" and, later, in "Marina" and "Paisaje," we discover the absurdity and contradictions of the human condition generally and in particular the decline of revolutionary dreams. Do the poems' metaphors illustrate Morejón's ability to manipulate aesthetics, styles, and themes to criticize the government? Is she using literary strategies to polemicize her relation with authorities? She may be cultivating mechanisms and manners of speaking that simultaneously appear to be within but that go beyond the boundaries of official cultural expression. Her ambiguous metaphors leave her intentionality opaque—perhaps deliberately so.

Since the 1960s Morejón has sought to publish her works and has conformed to the highly politicized climate of official literary production. At the same time, she has attempted to call into question the objective representation of symbolic systems promoted by cultural institutions. Perhaps Morejón's fluctuating illustrations of the Cuban spirit also symbolize a gap between imposed aesthetic norms about revolutionary consciousness and some semblance of lived reality.

Is there a link between the most recent iconography of Morejón's anchored souls and contemporary rifts in the hierarchy of cultural institutions? Although in the 1980s a number of young poets who had demonstrated their indifference and irreverence toward revolutionary policy had already emerged on the cultural scene, it was rare for well-established intellectuals like Morejón to adopt this critical style in their works. However, by the early 1990s, as old cultural institutions adapted to the ongoing economic crunch, intellectuals took advantage of the government's lack of revenue to create illegal semiprivate foundations. Both the advent of the new institutions and the economic and political difficulties that faced the Castro government have contributed to a re-distribution of material resources for artists and writers.

Morejón's evolving metaphors, her fluctuating aesthetics, reflect her adept analysis of her position in the highly politicized context of the Cuban revolution. At the same time, she questions the mechanisms of cultural production to push beyond the limits of official policies. Her flexibility as a Cuban revolutionary intellectual is enigmatic and prob-lematic.

Another significant aspect of Morejón work is her artistic approach to Afro-Cuban themes. Her work on these questions has been a result of her individual experiences, both before and after Castro's revolution. In some cases, she has complicated her position by highlighting con-troversial issues within the Cuban revolutionary context, thereby test-ing the limits of official rhetoric and policy. At the same time, she has been extremely careful, as an officially sanctioned writer, never to openly controvert official policies and dogma. Cuban officials judged en-deavors to address racial issues in contemporary Cuba as "microfac-tional" and divisive in the overall scheme of a newly developing social-ist state.[8] Morejón, as a writer and a black woman living in Cuba during this historical period, was aware of these limits. And when she suffered serious political setbacks—such as El Puente's demise or the official suppression of the Cuban Black Power movement in the 1960s—she labored to distance herself from the controversy surrounding the groups under attack. She has often denied any affiliation with allegedly "sepa-ratist" pro–Afro-Cuban or women's movements and emphasizes her commitment to nationalist revolutionary activities.

Although Morejón may have avoided direct political confrontation with cultural officials, her insistence on themes of black heritage has been consistent since the late 1960s. In *Richard trajo su flauta* she pays homage to the black community by eulogizing her family members. In this collection there are also references to the Afro-Cuban journalist and politician Juan Gualberto Gómez (1854–1933) and an explicit recogni-tion of Afro-Cuban musical traditions (Luis, "Race" 82). In "Presente Brígida Noyola," "Presente Ángela Domínguez," and "La cena," she em-phasizes the importance of the family network and acknowledges Afro-Cuban women's role in society. She personalizes the Cuban black fam-ily's experience, venerating those who came before her.

In "Presente Brígida," the poetic voice recapitulates her grand-mother's affection and spirit: "Tú eres grano y volcán / cuarzo divino ancho" and "menuda en el espíritu / voraz morena / eres cañón carbón

descuartizada carne / hulla lastimosa de la noche / como la tierra creces tú" (*Richard* 11). [You are a grain of sand, a volcano / quartz divide
wide / . . . Diminutive in spirit / voracious black woman / you are a
cannon pulverized charcoal meat / pitiful soft coal of night / you grow
like the earth (tr. David Frye).]

With the simile "como la tierra creces" and the metaphor "cañon carbón descuartizada carne," the poet fuses blackness with the idea of for-
titude and describes Brígida as a woman of conflictive intrepidity. In
"Present Ángela," the poet paints a cheerful portrait of her other grand-
mother Ángela Domínguez's vitality: "Tú eres un poco más ligera / can-
tas con trovadores y guitarras / en la noche clarísima / clara como tus
ojos (*Richard* 14). [You weigh a little less / sing with balladeers and gui-
tars / in the night so clear / as clear as your eyes (tr. David Frye).]

Ángela, with her clear eyes, brightens the world and is also a queen
of laughter; her lighthearted nature bestows a contagious effervescence.
In both poems the tender description of the grandmothers' combined
strength and vigor radiates intimacy.

Likewise, in "La cena," the poet asserts that her mother is "como el
agua de todos los días" (*Richard* 12) [like our daily water (tr. David
Frye)]. Gabriel Abudu states that the simile comparing the mother to
water suggests woman as a biological, as well as a psychic, source of life
(81). By association, the aquatic metaphor, a recurring theme in Morejón's poetry, is linked to Yoruba cosmology. Water represents the powerful female "orisha," Yemayá. According to Migene González-Wippler,
Yemayá is the sea goddess and mother ocean who carries the weight of
humanity on her shoulders (111). Yemayá, like water, is a life-sustaining
element that enables the symbiotic relationship between mother and
child, as well as promotes the pilgrimage and the continuity of Afro-
Cuban society. Hence, the black community's endurance partially re-
sides in the mother's metaphorical, psychic, and biological bond with
her offspring. The poet's symbols foreground Afro-Cuban women's lives
and legacy.

In the same poem, Morejón emphasizes the father figure. The father's
backbreaking work and determination afford his child a better life and
allow her to transcend the father's difficulties (Abudu 81). William Luis
says that Morejón's inclusion of the black family and Afro-Cuban themes
indicates that she was attempting to embrace a larger audience and to
make her poetry more appealing to the masses ("Race" 92).

By the 1970s Morejón delved into themes linking historical and
contemporary black issues in her poetry, emphasizing the plight of the

Afro-Cuban woman throughout history. Her effort to formulate the Afro-Cuban woman's complex realities led the poet to question feminism. In an interview with Elaine Savory Fido, Morejón explains her hesitations: "I guess there are sometimes words which are a trap. . . . In our Western world there are certain feminist movements that I respect very much as a woman, but sometimes they don't go to the real point of our time and our societies" (266).

Morejón's preference for the term "womanism" reveals how she wants to connect Afro-Cuban women's endeavors with their socio-historical context: "I think the task of a womanist (let's talk with Alice Walker's term, which I love very much) in our region should be something related to our society and to our history" (266). Morejón's works complement Alice Walker's womanist approach with a pro–Afro-Cuban stance in ways that question how Western culture constitutes race and gender. She addresses the debates surrounding race and gender indirectly in her poetry and essays and directly in her interviews.

Morejón's application of the ideas about black women's strength and the importance of the black community's survival, articulated in Walker's *In Search of Our Mothers' Gardens,* permits her theoretically to cross over from North American society to Cuban society. In Walker's context, womanism implies establishing a legacy of "foremothers" by exploring the works of African American female writers. She emphasizes African American cultural contributions and considers sociohistorical racial specificity an essential element in gender analysis. Walker explains that the term "womanist" derives "from womanish. . . . A black feminist or feminist of color. . . . Usually referring to outrageous, audacious, courageous or willful behavior." She also emphasizes that womanism is about commitment to survival and the wholeness of people, male and female. Walker describes a daring black woman who supports the black community's well-being. She stresses an identification with African American history and culture and redefines black women's artistic heritage to embody narrative strategies that enable them "to have their voices heard and their histories read" (Butler-Evans 13). Walker's womanism qualifies feminism with a critical look not only at the variable sex/gender but also at race. Her concept of racialized gender underscores how Western/Euro-American feminist theories often exclude race issues. Walker criticizes the universalizing power of the sex/gender system, the allegedly ethnocentric and imperializing tendencies of European and Euro-American feminisms.

Because Morejón explores racial and gender issues within Cuban revolutionary politics, we need to consider briefly how post-1970 Afro-American feminist debates surrounding the womanist perspective broadened critical notions of race and gender. Morejón was probably aware of these polemics because she has visited universities in the United States since at least 1983 and has read several black female writers and critics' works (and, of course, the initial quotation shows her familiarity with those works, if not her investment in them). Her interest in the Afro-Cuban woman's social position corresponds to some extent with womanism, as well as with other theories of "women of color," inasmuch as those theories are a critique of gender and racial politics. For example, Barbara Smith, Hazel Carby, and bell hooks criticize the universalizing power of the sex/gender system set up by Euro-American feminisms as blurring distinctions relevant to African American women and/or Third World women. In 1977 Barbara Smith's "Toward a Black Feminist Criticism" addressed both racial and sexual politics. She reassessed Western white feminist scholarship and black, primarily male-oriented, scholarship concerning race and gender. According to Smith, this scholarship distorts or excludes the black female experience and specifically the works of African American female writers. Smith's work and that of other critics resulted in the development of new theories with specific methodologies applied to the interrelatedness of class, race, and gender. The successful marketing of Afro-American female writers such as Alice Walker, Gloria Naylor, and Toni Morrison and the subsequent advent of revisionary literary historiographies also contributed to the appraisal of black cultural production. By the 1980s several African American female critics had established a body of critical writings about black female artists and writers.

Smith and others propose the reconstruction of gender and race to include alternative views about literary and artistic traditions with specific consideration of Afro-American women's cultural contributions. In their distinct interpretations of black feminism, they explore ways of analyzing the literature and the images of Afro-American women. In most instances, they combine racial and gender theories to create hybrid approaches that question hegemonic notions of identity. Furthermore, they posit black and female as legitimate categories for historical and political discussion. Since essential elements of womanism include dialogue and discursive diversity, these narrative sites posit a rereading of gender and ethnicity. Critics of African American literature, with a

wide range of theoretical approaches, have utilized womanism's symbolic power to give voice to the heretofore underrepresented female
perspective.

In Morejón's appropriation of Walker's term, many questions remain
unanswered. For example, how does Morejón incorporate the womanist perspective into her writings within the parameters of postrevolutionary politics in Cuba? Why does she simultaneously question Western ideas, talking about "consumer-society imports" (Savory Fido 266)
even as she adopts the paradigm of an Afro-American writer like Alice
Walker? Does not a Western-based womanist theory maintain a "Third
World"–"First World" demarcation and focus primarily on the problems of black feminists in a capitalist country? Indeed, Morejón does not
use Walker's term without questioning it. However, the obvious strength
of the theory is its challenge to "white" feminisms to deal with the complex spectrum of women. Morejón enlarges the context and, at the same
time, reshapes the tradition of Caribbean protest discourse to embrace
the Afro-Cuban woman's perspective. In this sense, we might say that a
womanist approach for Morejón constitutes black women controlling
their own history and culture.

Caribbean literary critics have debated the application of an exogenous womanist theory to Caribbean literature. For example, the Caribbean writer and critic Sylvia Wynter considers the feminist/womanist
discussion a transitional step for Caribbean feminist scholars. She rejects
the use of Eurocentric discourses of any feminist stance, since these discourses ally formally with "patriarchal" discourses that historically vic-
timize the Caribbean female subject. Kathleen M. Balutansky points out
how Wynter's model of a "new Caribbean epistemology" resists "the in-
trinsic character of feminist criticism" and calls for a space "outside all
current discourse(s)" (542). Although Wynter must also utilize Eurocentric discourse to emphasize her argument, Balutansky perceives the
polemic on the womanist theory to be essential to the development of a
Caribbean feminist tradition. According to Balutansky, debates and
dialogues about this theory and others are inevitable for Caribbean
critics, as they have been for black feminists in the United States. These
critics are linked by the dilemma of "whether or not to give precedent
to the 'race variable' and racial oppression over sexism" (543).

Perhaps a womanist theory that reflects the concerns facing a black
female intelligentsia in the United States has little to do with Afro-
Cuban women in the revolutionary period. Morejón's rationale for
using the womanist position is that it disputes more widespread, naive

feminist notions that do not address Caribbean women's reality. In her interview with Savory Fido, Morejón points out the urgent need to differentiate between the Western world's feminist projects and womanist theory in a Caribbean setting. Although Morejón prefers womanism because it underscores black women's experience, she detects serious problems with this approach for Cubans. She says that Caribbean peoples "cannot import certain patterns of these movements from Western Europe or developed countries because we are underdeveloped countries" (Savory Fido 266). It is unclear, however, which aspects of feminism or womanism Morejón does not wish to import. She does not explain which components simply fail to correspond to Cuban reality; she insists on claiming, yet editing, aspects of Walker's theories, saying that her country is "too underdeveloped" for any of them to take root (Savory Fido 266–67). The idea of a black literary environment in which female writers flourish is a complex one that perhaps exists in consumer societies, like the United States. On the surface, Morejón appears to bridge particular points of contact she shares with Walker's theory: the black communities' plights and the need for black solidarity among men and women. Without a doubt, Morejón realizes the complexities of applying Walker's questioning of gender and race policies to Cuban revolutionary politics.

Morejón appeals to Walker's womanism to hint at the black female intellectual's lack of power in Cuban cultural affairs. By referring to Walker and womanism, she calls attention to Afro-Cuban women's invisibility in the national literary canon. She originates a cross-cultural theoretical position and superimposes it on Cuba's entirely unique political climate. Morejón's ideas beg the question as to whether past official policies on racial and gender politics have had an adverse effect on black female intellectuals' concrete expression in the field of cultural production. If Morejón's ambiguous reference to the womanist theory alludes to the paucity of contemporary Afro-Cuban female writers, she mitigates and mediates a womanist demand for more representation in Cuban cultural production.

In her interview with Savory Fido, Morejón justifies her appropriation of an exogenous theory when she states that she views the Caribbean region as cross-cultural and enriched by racially mixed populations. She finds a parallel to this racial amalgamation in Caribbean people's ability to synthesize cultural ideas by borrowing freely from diverse cultures. When Morejón adopts Walker's concept, she cites traditional Caribbean cross-cultural exchange to justify her appropriation of an Afro-American writer's theoretical position. What may be most interesting about her revised womanist perspective is that it highlights the Afro-Cuban female's position in Cuban society. She reinforces her own critical womanist view by focusing on the Afro-Cuban woman's specific situation and by breaking the perimeters of Cuba's literary racial and gender representations, emphasizing the significance of black issues, not as divisive but rather as promoting a necessary dialogue with previous literary traditions and race and gender representations.

Morejón deals with real problems that Afro-Cubans have confronted throughout history in several of her poems and essays.[9] She highlights specific historical, literary, and political traditions to explore her own dialogue within these traditions. As William Luis concludes, Morejón "has been careful and systematic in developing poems about blacks and the issue of race in her books"; he adds that perhaps her "greatest poetic contribution has been her attempt to keep the history and voice of blacks alive in contemporary Cuba" ("Race" 101).

Morejón's dedication to history and to Afro-Cuban issues is a continuation of the work of the early Guillén and other Afro-Caribbean poets, but Morejón highlights gender in addition to race (see Rosegreen-Williams and DeCosta-Willis). For example, in her poetry she manifests continuity and rupture with regard to the Negritude and Negrismo movements of the Caribbean. Protest poetry is a significant aspect of this Afro-Cuban poetic movement of the 1920s, 1930s, and 1940s. In the worst cases, poets depicted blacks as representative of erotic animalism. However, the Negrismo movement also included poems that criticized the dehumanizing effects of racist representations and called attention to Afro-Latin Americans' degrading and impoverished lives. These themes can be found in such poems as "Actitud" by Emilio Ballagas, "Evohé" by Marcelino Arozarena, "Hermano negro" by Regino Pedroso, and Nicolás Guillén's "Pequeña oda a un negro boxeador cubano."[10] These poets reacted to the ideology of European colonialism and racism by describing experiences of and struggles against discrimination. They also highlighted problems of black identity and consciousness and rejected artistic submission to Eurocentric aesthetics, which severely limit Afro-Latin American images. Their Afro-Cuban consciousness consists, in part, of a return to slave rebellion. These poets utilize the past to criticize the present and to empower a new black voice to challenge racism.

While the protest poetry of Negrismo demands social change for the Afro-Cuban male, its notions of the female subject are quite narrow. Negrismo poets, for the most part, have perpetuated stereotypical images of the Afro-Cuban woman and have dehumanized her with simple erotic descriptions. Even Nicolás Guillén's attempt to displace the erotic metaphorization of Afro-Cuban woman in "Mujer nueva" resulted in an idealized future goddess. The difference between Morejón's concept of an Afro-Cuban woman in her poem "Mujer negra" and Guillén's concept in "Mujer nueva" is that Morejón's version does not limit the construction of the female merely to a future ideal.[11] Rather, her poem implies that women's strength, defiance, and active participation already existed in Afro-Cuban history. While Morejón does not speak specifically to the often-discussed metaphorization of the Afro-Latin American woman as embodiment of sexuality, fertility, or sensual nature, her poems deal with real problems Afro-Cuban women have confronted. I suggest that she manifests these ideas in "Mujer negra" and "Amo a mi amo."

In "Mujer negra" and "Amo a mi amo," Morejón appropriates themes of slavery and racial discrimination from nineteenth-century antislavery narratives and from the twentieth-century Cuban Negrismo movement, rewriting them to include gender. In "Mujer negra," Morejón grafts the Afro-Cuban female slave's voice onto the historically rebellious black voice and amplifies the black woman's role in the revolutionary era. The poetic speaker and her descendants come down from the "Sierra" (an obvious reference to the Sierra Maestra mountains from which Castro's guerrillas waged battles against Batista's army) to put an end to capitalist exploitation. "Amo a mi amo" is an Afro-Cuban female slave's response to sexual servitude; she rebels against her white master in a dream. The slave's rebellion against her master-lover reminds us that a mixture of collusion, compromise, and insurrection are constants in Afro-Cuban history.

I discuss both "Mujer negra" and "Amo a mi amo" within the context of Morejón's concepts of transculturation and its relation to racial mixing. In the 1977 essay "Mito y realidad en Cecilia Valdés," Morejón argues that the mulatta Cecilia, the main character of Cirilo Villaverde's nineteenth-century antislavery novel, reflects the agonies of transculturation. Morejón's definition of transculturation is adapted from the ethnologist Fernando Ortiz's original conception. For Ortiz, transculturation challenges the Eurocentric notion of acculturation—the complete assimilation of an "inferior" civilization by a "superior" civilization on the basis of a priori cultural and historical value judgments. Ortiz's term signifies constant interaction among cultural components, which creates a two-way transformation and, as a result, a provisional third cultural grouping. Morejón, like Nicolás Guillén, the outstanding Afro-Cuban poet of the Negrismo movement, before her, goes beyond Ortiz to insist on a nation-building concept of transculturation. She believes that the mestizo population represents the "new race," as well as Cuba's national character ("Mito y realidad" in *Fundación* 14).

Transculturation has different meanings and uses depending on the sociohistorical moment of the thinkers who have analyzed the concept in relation to the effects of cultural mixing. Moreover, the changing political and socioeconomic status of blacks and mulattos also influences the application of the word. (The fact that these racial categories are scientifically baseless further complicates the issue.) While Ortiz's definition responded to a European concept of acculturation, Morejón's interpretation corresponds to Cuban society's progress toward a nonracist society and to Cuba's Soviet-funded interventions in Africa in the 1970s.[12] Morejón points out that, in the case of Cuba, "la Revolución socialista ha determinado de modo diáfano y tenaz una vocación decidida a encontrar y proclamar las más legítimas raíces de nuestra identidad" (*Fundación* 15). In its attempt to rescue the African in Cuban culture, the government officials have rhetorically created a new people, the Afro-Latin Americans. Linked to this notion of national identity is Afro-Cubans' changed status since the revolution. Indeed, the Castro government's efforts to eliminate institutional discrimination benefited many poor blacks. As Frank F. Taylor confirms, "It is indisputable that the Revolution did indeed advance the material welfare of the Afro-Cuban population, having from the outset attacked the manifest inequities of class and race that it encountered in the social system" (23).

Morejón recognizes these positive changes for Afro-Cubans and sees, by extension, that the Cecilias of Cuba have been somewhat vindicated. Cecilia, as a mulatta, is the incarnation of transculturation and *mestizaje* (the cross-breeding of "races"), and—like Cuba—she is a product of this process. However, as an Afro-Cuban female, she is a victim of the slave system's legacy, subject to both racism and sexism.[13] In "Mito y realidad," Morejón conjures up the illusion of a revolutionary space in which Cuba can achieve racial harmony and in which all the contradictions Cecilia suffers—racial injustice, sexism, and marginality—are resolved.[14] Since racial equality is not a reality, Morejón resorts to a literary device and invokes the nineteenth-century figure Cecilia Valdés in order to illuminate Cuba's contemporary race relations. Written eighteen years after the revolution, the essay suggests that much remains to be done.

The polemical use of Cecilia reveals Morejón's attempt to interrelate Afro-Cubans' current social and political concerns with those of their predecessors. She persuasively engages with official rhetoric about gender and race by juxtaposing the image of the new nation—the Afro-Americans living in a racist-free Cuban society—with a disturbing message that, since prejudice prevails, the black struggle in Cuba must continue. This is not to say that she is discouraged that government measures have not eradicated racism. On the contrary, she believes these goals should be pursued with zeal.

We witness Morejón's reconstruction of the Afro-Cuban woman in "Mujer negra," as well. Published in the journal *Casa de las Américas* in 1975 (88: 119–20), the poem is a first-person narration that maps out the history of the Afro-Cuban female:[15]

> Todavía huelo la espuma del mar que me hicieron atravesar.
> La noche, no puedo recordarla.
> Ni el mismo océano podría recordarla.
> Pero no olvido el primer alcatraz que divisé.
> Altas, las nubes, como inocentes testigos presénciales.
> Acaso no he olvidado ni mi costa perdida, ni mi lengua ancestral.
> Me dejaron aquí y aquí he vivido.
> Y porque trabajé como una bestia,
> aquí volví a nacer.
> A cuánta epopeya mandinga intenté recurrir.
>
>   Me rebelé.
>
> Su Merced me compró en una plaza.
> Bordé la casaca de Su Merced y un hijo macho le partí.
> Mi hijo no tuvo nombre.
> Y Su Merced, murió a manos de un impecable *lord* inglés
>
>   Anduve.
>
> Ésta es la tierra donde padecí bocabajos y azotes.
> Bogué a lo largo de todos sus ríos.
> Bajo su sol sembré, recolecté y las cosechas no comí.
> Por casa tuve un barracón.
> Yo misma traje piedras para edificarlo,
> Pero canté al compás de los pájaros nacionales.
>
> Yo misma traje piedras para edificarlo,
> pero canté al natural compás de los pájaros nacionales.
>
>   Me sublevé.
>
> En esta misma tierra toqué la sangre húmeda
> y todos los huesos podridos de muchos otros,
> traídos a ella, o no, igual que yo.

Ya nunca más imaginé el camino a Guinea.
¿Era a Guinea? ¿A Benín? ¿Era a Madagascar?
  ¿O a Cabo Verde?

        Trabajé mucho más.

Fundé mejor mi canto milenario y mi esperanza.
Aquí construí mi mundo.

        Me fui al monte.

Mi real independencia fue el palenque
y cabalgué entre las tropas de Maceo.

Sólo un siglo más tarde,
junto a mis descendientes,
desde una azul montaña,

        bajé de la Sierra.

para acabar con capitales y usureros,
con generales y burgueses.
Ahora soy: Sólo hoy tenemos y creamos.
Nada nos es ajeno.
Nuestra la tierra.
Nuestros el mar y el cielo.
Nuestras la magia y la quimera.
Iguales míos, aquí los veo bailar
alrededor del árbol que plantamos para el comunismo.
Su pródiga madera ya resuena. (*Where the Island* 86–88)

                    ❧

[I still smell the foam of the sea they made me cross.
The night, I can't remember it.
The ocean itself could not remember that.
But I can't forget the first gull I made out in the distance.
High, the clouds, like innocent eye-witnesses.
Perhaps I haven't forgotten my lost coast, nor my ancestral language.
They left me here and here I've lived.
And, because I worked like an animal,
here I came to be born.
How many Mandinga epics did I look to for strength.

        I rebelled.

His Worship bought me in a public square.
I embroidered His Worship's coat and bore him a male child.
My son had no name.
And His Worship died at the hands of an impeccable English *lord*.

        I walked.

This is the land where I suffered mouth-in-the-dust and the lash.
I rode the length of all its rivers.
Under its sun I planted seeds, brought in the crops,
but never ate those harvests.
A slave barracks was my house,
built with stones that I hauled myself,
while I sang to the pure beat of native birds.

      I rose up.

In this same land I touched the fresh blood
and decayed bones of many others,
brought to this land or not, the same as I.
I no longer dreamt of the road to Guinea.
Was it to Guinea? Benin? To Madagascar?
  Or Cape Verde?

      I worked on and on.

I strengthened the foundations of my millenary song and of my hope.
Here I built my world.

      I left for the hills.

My real independence was the free slave fort
and I rode with the troops of Maceo.
Only a century later,
together with my descendants,
from a blue mountain,

      I came down from the Sierra

to put an end to capital and usurer,
to generals and to bourgeois.
Now I exist: only today do we own, do we create.
Nothing is foreign to us.
The land is ours.
Ours the sea and the sky,
the magic and the vision.
My equals, here I see you dance
around the tree we are planting for communism.
Its prodigal wood resounds.] (Tr. Kathleen Weaver)

We read of her plight as she crosses the Atlantic in a slave ship to the
New World, then, as a slave, becomes a maroon (a runaway slave) and,
still later, a fighter alongside Maceo in the war of independence and
finally a participant in the 1959 revolution. The poetic speaker claims:
"Me dejaron aquí y aquí he vivido. / Y porque trabajé como una bestia, /
aquí volví a nacer." It is through her hard labor in the slave system that

Cuba became a modern nation. Reciprocally, her presence in this new nation caused her rebirth: the creation of the Afro-Cuban people. We are reminded that African elements have had a profound impact on Cuba.

Morejón also foregrounds the Afro-Cuban woman's different historical and political moments as an active protagonist, not often written about in the social protest tradition. Her protest poetry links Afro-Cuban history with gender politics. It is through the repetition of verbs of action—"me rebelé," "anduve," "me sublevé," "me fui al monte," "bajé de la sierra"—that she creates an implicit paradigm of possible active positions for the Afro-Cuban woman.[16] These key words, which underscore explicit acts of independence and rebellion, also sustain the poem's general theme of resistance to racism.

Morejón's allusion to black separatism, "mi real independencia fue el palenque," refers to blacks' historical struggle with Cuban authorities over black consciousness. The allegorical "palenque" of Cuba—a metaphorical space where black consciousness survives in spite of official repression—finds its roots in the history of Afro-Cuban slaves' marooning activity. The runaway slaves formed communities in remote areas called palenques. The poet reenacts antislavery discourse and suggests that Afro-Cubans felt true freedom only when they had their own separate societies, untouched by white rule. "Mi real independencia" also addresses the fact that, although white Cuban liberals recruited and encouraged blacks to fight in the war of independence, they did not consider them equal by any means. In fact, most Cuban whites feared blacks and believed that their increasing numbers would enable them to revolt as had happened in Haiti (Luis, *Literary Bondage* 60–61). The fact that Morejón retells this story from an Afro-Cuban woman's first-person perspective underscores the serious gap with regard to her historical and literary representation.

Morejón uses understatement to reveal another dimension of the slave's experience. The victim speaks of the trauma of sexual servitude and of her child's subsequent illegitimacy: "Su Merced me compró en una plaza. / Bordé la casaca de Su Merced y un hijo macho le partí / Mi hijo no tuvo nombre." Rosegreen-Williams comments that Morejón's use of "subtlety, indirection and ellipsis" in this line "to convey protest" is "more powerful in its impact because the disconnection between the act of embroidering for her master and the result of bearing his child points starkly to the reality of sexual exploitation of the black woman" (9). Scholars have only recently begun to document that black female slaves suffered triple oppression: racism in general and sexism (economic and

sexual oppression) on the part of both black male slaves and white masters (Bush 8).[17] These lines particularize and historicize the black female
slave's complex plight. More important, they reveal a black woman's
strong will to survive and rebel in spite of her circumstances.

Morejón's insertion of the concept of *mestizaje* in the lines "pero canté
al natural compás de los pájaros nacionales" and "Nada nos es ajeno. /
nuestra la tierra" calls to mind the themes of national identity and hy-
bridization of which she speaks in her study on Guillén (*Nación* 23–37).
In that essay, she downplays the significance of the African component
of the term "Afro-Cuban" and foregrounds Cubans' homogeneous nationalistic identity. Morejón states that Guillén utilized racial issues only
as a stepping stone to rebellion and communism and not as a separatist
racial politics. Her disclaimers about Guillén's black politics are ironic
since, by the 1980s, it was evident that Guillén's ideological desire for
racial equality had not been achieved. Moreover, Morejón had witnessed several conflicts in the revolutionary period between blacks and
the government (Moore, *Castro* 310–11). Although she personally experienced disillusionment with authorities' severe measures against
blacks, Morejón converts her poetic speaker in "Mujer negra" into an
echo of official rhetoric proclaiming communism a solution for Afro-
Cubans' advancement:

> Nuestros el mar y el cielo.
> Nuestras la magia y la quimera.
> Iguales míos, aquí los veo bailar
> alrededor del árbol que plantamos para el comunismo.
> Su pródiga madera ya resuena. (88)

> ✑

> [The land is ours
> Ours the sea and the sky,
> the magic and the vision.
> My equals, here I see you dance
> around the tree we are planting for communism.
> Its prodigal wood resounds.] (Tr. Kathleen Weaver)

In light of this ending, one must ask whether Morejón's assertion that
communism is a panacea for black struggle is a strategy to include black
politics in the national agenda by encompassing them within revolutionary poetics. Certainly the poem's ending conveys clear-cut political
commitment to the revolution, or, at least, these verses offer a utopian
resolution to racism. Repetition of the possessive adjective "nuestros"
or "nuestras" attests to the communal sharing and equal distribution of

goods. Moreover, the jubilant dance-celebration around the tree of communism alludes to the black woman's satisfaction with the new order of
things. The metaphor of the tree's resounding wood proposes that
blacks can look forward to a bright future. However, the poet leaves us
with an open-ended interpretation. Even though the poetic "I" praises
communism, we are not told whether the planted tree bears fruit or blos-
soms. Is Morejón walking a political tightrope with her poetics?

One might note that Morejón wrote the poem in 1975, at the two-
thirds point of an officially imposed "silent" period between 1967 and
1979. During that time she could not get any poetry volumes published
in Cuba. She was suffering the consequences of her affiliations with the
literary group and publishing house El Puente and possibly of her role
as a black activist or her association with those who were.

Obviously, Morejón must have understood the correspondence between her change in poetic style and themes and the willingness on the
part of the editors of *Casa de las Américas* to publish "Mujer negra." Later,
she included the poem in *Parajes de una época*, the volume that signaled
the end of the ban on her publications of poetry volumes and gained her
much-deserved recognition as a Cuban poet (Luis, "Race" 92).

In "Mujer negra" Morejón grafts a revolutionary guerrilla voice onto
an enslaved Afro-Cuban female one, thereby incorporating the black
woman's role into an official one. The poet develops a black female body
politic to include black women within the definition of national identity.
Although Morejón emphasizes the black woman's significant position,
she is careful to balance politics and aesthetics. Indeed, in an interview
with Rafael Rodríguez, Morejón denies that she wrote "Mujer negra" to
consciously promote ethnic or gender politics: "Si por otra parte ese
poema le es útil a aquellos hombres y mujeres en el mundo que—no so-
lamente negros—tienen conflictos raciales o son oprimidos y les sirve de
estandarte y bandera, me parece mucho mejor. Pero tampoco lo escribí
tratando de reconstruir a través de un yo épico—no es Nancy Morejón—la historia de una parte del pueblo cubano, las mujeres de este
país" (25). [If, on the other hand, that poem is useful for the men and
women in the world—not only blacks—who have racial conflicts or
who are oppressed, if it serves as a standard and a nationalistic position,
all the better. But I did not write it to reconstruct through an epic self—
it is not Nancy Morejón—the history of some sector of Cuban society,
the women of this country (tr. Emma Claggett and Linda Howe).]

Morejón's determination to steer her writing clear of anything that
could be qualified as "microfactional politics" has prevented her work

from addressing black politics or feminism even when the situation seems to demand it. However, as Yvonne Captain-Hildalgo points out, Morejón's denial that she engages in Afro-Cuban politics does not necessarily mean they are nonexistent in her works. She states that, despite Morejón's claim to the contrary, her reiteration of black themes forces us to consider that Morejón's has convincing opinions about culture and ethnic identity (601).

Indeed, Morejón constantly invokes black issues under official scrutiny. Her themes do not always adhere to official discourse on racial equality, nor do they heed the government's prohibition of Afro-Cuban religions, which was officially enforced until the 1980s. We witness the poet's flirtation with such taboos in poems such as "Hablando con una culebra," "Güijes," "Richard trajo su flauta," and "Amo a mi amo."

As we saw in "Mujer negra," Morejón links the Afro-Cuban world not only to slavery and pain but also to sedition. In "Amo a mi amo," the female poetic speaker proposes violent rebellion, parallel to expressions of love and subjugation. The empowered and rebelling voice eventually defies domination through a vision of a fierce uprising against the master. The slave woman speaks of love for her master but simultaneously sees herself with a knife in hand, "desollándolo como a una res sin culpa" (*Where the Island* 75). Throughout "Amo a mi amo," the Afro-Cuban enslaved female develops a consciousness of the mediatory nature of language and the manipulative ramifications of her master's narrative. Her master controls and seduces her with a language she admits she never completely comprehends. Eventually, she realizes that there is a correspondence between the master's abuses of which the old black overseers speak and her own subjugated position:

> Oyendo hablar a los viejos guardieros, supe
> que mi amor
> da latigazos en las calderas del ingenio,
> como si fueran un infierno, el de aquel Señor Dios
> de quien me hablaba sin cesar. (74)

~≈~

> [Hearing the old field guards talking, I learned
> that my love
> gives lashings in the cauldrons of the sugar mill,
> steaming like some Hell, the Hell of that Lord God
> he used to talk about unendingly.] (Tr. David Frye)

She discerns that language is a tool of seduction and control that has a real and negative effect on her life and on other Afro-Cubans' lives. In anger, she questions her own denigrated situation and mediative role, loving and serving the master in ways that mitigate his harshness and abuse.

At first, the voice of the enslaved woman, in her apparently submissive and loving devotion, echoes and complements the master's discourse (the dominant discourse). However, the master's ability to overpower the slave with his own language and culture, which are not similar to hers, is undermined by her apparently neutral description of his warlike feats:

> Amo a mi amo
> recojo leño para encender su fuego cotidiano.
> Amo sus ojos claros.
> Mansa cual un cordero
> esparzo gotas de miel por sus orejas.
> Amo sus manos
> que me depositaron sobre un lecho de hierbas:
> Mi amo muerde y subyuga.
> Me cuenta historias sigilosas mientras
> abanico todo su cuerpo cundido de llagas y balazos,
> de días de sol y guerra de rapiña.
> Amo sus pies que piratearon y rodaron
> por tierras ajenas.
> Los froto con los polvos más finos
> que encontré, una mañana,
> saliendo de la vega.
> Taño la vihuela y de su garganta salían
> coplas sonoras, como nacidas de la garganta de Manrique.
> Yo quería haber oído una marímbula sonar. (74)

～

> [I love my master
> I gather firewood to light his daily fire.
> I love his clear eyes.
> Meek as any lamb,
> I scatter drops of honey on his ears.
> I love his hands
> that laid me down on a bed of grass:
> My master bites and subjugates.
> He tells me silent stories while
> I fan his whole body, full of sores and bullet wounds,
> of days in the sun and plunderous war.
> I love his feet that buccaneered and wandered round
> those foreign lands.
> I massage them with the finest powders,
> which I found one morning

while leaving the tobacco field.
He strummed his guitar and from his throat emerged
sonorous verses, as if born from the throat of Manrique.
I felt I had heard a *marímbula* humming.](Tr. David Frye)

In these verses Morejón uses images that refer to the enslaved
woman's subservient activities: gathering brushwood, pouring drops of
honey in his ears, fanning his body, and rubbing powder on his feet.
These images contrast sharply with the master's brutal force. Furthermore, her manifest admiration for the master's culture, symbolized by
the mention of melodious *coplas* of the fifteenth-century Spanish poet
Jorge Manrique, is overshadowed by the memory of familiar, African-
based marimbula sounds she longs to hear.

We sense that the master's seduction of the slave is mimicked by the
slave's seductive language. Her words imply that she loves everything
about her master. However, she admits that language is also the medium
through which misreading and confusion occur:

Amo su boca roja, fina,
desde donde van saliendo palabras
que no alcanzo a descifrar
todavía. Mi lengua para él ya no es la suya. (74)

∾

[I love his delicate red mouth,
from which spill words
that I cannot quite decipher
yet. My tongue for him is not now his own.](Tr. David Frye)

For the poetic speaker, the master's language is less a form of communication than a vehicle for mutual incomprehension. Yet, it is interesting here that Morejón proposes a relation between the power of sensual language and the seductive power of language. Her use of the
female slave's conflicting images and sentiments makes it difficult to
establish an absolute binary opposition between master/slave—and, by
extension, abuse/resistance. Rather, Morejón describes a relationship
that cannot be clearly defined as an unproblematic dichotomy. The poetic speaker employs a language the master simultaneously can and
cannot understand. Ultimately, the enslaved female is able to compre-
hend the manipulative process of language when she overhears the old
black overseers confirm her already irresolute position in relation to
the master's discourse: she finds out the master whips the other slaves.
These images of whippings and other aspects of the slaves' hellish

conditions at the sugar mill shock the enslaved woman to anger. Her evolving awareness of the master's abuses causes the slave to question her collusion with him: "¿Qué me dirá? / ¿Por qué vivo en la morada ideal para un murciélago? / ¿Por qué le sirvo? / ¿Adónde va su espléndido coche? / tirado por caballos más felices que yo?" (76–77). [What will he tell me? / Why am I living in a lair built for a bat? / Why must I serve him? / Where could he go in his splendid carriage, / drawn by horses happier than I? (tr. David Frye).]

Clearly, the master is skilled in the art of seductive language. Yet, the female slave can no longer tolerate the false relationship that upholds her love: "Mi amor es como la maleza que cubre la dotación / única posesión inexpugnable mía." [My love is like the weeds that cover my garden plot / the only possession I can call my own (tr. David Frye).] She curses the veils that conceal her enslaved body: "Maldigo / esta bata de muselina que me ha impuesto / estos encajes vanos que despiadado me endilgó / estos quehaceres para mi en el atardecer sin girasoles" (76). [I curse / this muslin robe he has imposed on me; / these vain lace dresses he forced on me without pity; / these chores of mine in the sunflowerless afternoon (tr. David Frye).]

She recognizes language as an obstacle that disguises her abuse. She rejects the language of entrapment that has left her scarred, bitter, and resentful:

> esta lengua abigarradamente hostil que no mastico;
> estos senos de piedra que no pueden siquiera amamantarlo;
> este vientre rajado por su látigo inmemorial;
> este maldito corazón. (76)
>
> ⤳
>
> [this baroquely hostile tongue that I can't get between my teeth;
> these stone breasts that can't even suckle him;
> this womb, raked beyond memory by lashings;
> this accursed heart.] (Tr. David Frye)

Here, Morejón distinguishes between the figurative speech of devotion and the history of sexual degradation and slave labor. In the end, the enslaved woman's latent rebellion manifests itself in her "condemned heart" when she vows love and murder in the canefield:

> Amo a mi amo, pero todas las noches,
> cuando atravieso la vereda florida hacia el cañaveral
> donde a hurtadillas hemos hecho el amor,
> me veo cuchillo en mano, desollándolo como a una res
> sin culpa.

Ensordeceres toques de tambor ya no me dejan
oír ni sus quebrantos, ni sus quejas.
Las campanas me llaman . . . (76)

[I love my master but every night,
when I cross the flowery pathway to the cane fields
where we have surreptitiously made love,
I can see myself with knife in hand, butchering him like
an innocent cattle
Deafening drumbeats no longer let me
hear his sorrows, his complaints.
The tolling bells call me . . .] (Tr. David Frye)

The canefield is a bittersweet territory of seduction, a metaphor of economic and sexual servitude. This colonial and postcolonial space of production and reproduction is where the master subjugates the slave on several levels. It is, as the narrator states, the place "donde a hurtadillas hemos hecho el amor" [where we have surreptitiously made love]. In reality, love in the canefield is an activity that dupes the slaves.

The canefield is also the symbolic ground for the sacrifice of the master. The very same discursive space in which slaves suffer abuse is transformed into a space for resistance and violent rebellion. In her vision—within which African drumbeats accompany her act of murder in the canefield—is another space where the woman's language and identity, different from those she displays in her discourse with the master, sustain a distinctive and irreducible beat.

Seen in this light, Morejón's writings reveal her pro Afro-Cuban politics and womanist consciousness. Womanist politics emphasizes the African community in Cuba and recognizes racial, historical, and political differences in feminism.[18] She makes a collaborative effort to engage gender and race with poetic strategies that defy the aesthetic universalization of Afro-Cuban identity. Her poetic "voicing" in "Mujer negra" and in "Amo a mi amo" constitutes a critical rereading of official gender and racial concepts. On the one hand, several exogenous discursive fields— among them Eurocentric aesthetics and western feminism—have played key roles in creating negative or misleading characteristics of "Afro" and "female." On the other hand, internal discursive fields—including Negrismo poetry and Cuban revolutionary politics—have contributed to adverse constructions of Afro-Cuban female subjectivity. Morejón reassesses aesthetic and political interests by rewriting the notions "black" and "female." Her poetry voices Afro-Cuban concerns by means of a black female consciousness in the absence of an officially recognized political or cultural movement. More important, Morejón underscores the Afro-Cuban woman as a significant element in Cuban culture, history, and politics.

Morejón was among the elite young intellectuals who took part in projects to reformulate Cuban literary aesthetics, national identity, and Afro-Cuban images. In the 1960s and 1970s she participated in the political and cultural debates and battles about what kind of aesthetics best corresponded to Cuba and revolutionary socialist society. She discovered early on with the El Puente scandal (1965) that the rules of cultural production consisted of both official constraints and self-censorship. Cultural officials imposed restrictions on literary expression and rewarded those intellectuals who adopted styles and genres congruent with revolutionary thinking. Morejón's response to the politicization of Cuban literary output reveals divergent discourses in her writings, not only with regard to aesthetics but also in reference to the significance of Afro-Cuban society.

Morejón encountered problems in her development as an intellectual in the revolutionary period. Both she and Barnet experienced a professional setback with the El Puente scandal and, as a consequence, made an effort to remove their stigma of "decadent" aesthetics (with cautious disclaimers and a new scholarly focus on officially accepted themes and genres). The fact that Morejón posits an Afro-Cuban womanist consciousness underscores how she reassesses revolutionary aesthetics within the symbolic realm of black and feminist politics. Morejón's constructions of the black female and Yoruba-based mythology in Afro-Cuban society flirt with subversion insofar as they promote the status and significance of black women and the repressed practices of Afro-Cuban society. Her Afro-Cuban imagery foregrounds the manipulation of languages, the mechanisms of censorship, and the intellectual's ability to call into question the power of official discourse without actually upsetting the hierarchy of the dominant language. She presents the fissures and fragments that are contrary to a colorblind society and the erasure of differences in an ideally constructed homogeneous society that has not sufficiently dealt with discrimination, racism, and other legacies of slavery. In spite of her efforts, it is clear that Morejón, like Barnet, experienced the pressure of the government's censorship. The institutionalization of cultural policy bound her to a particular literary aesthetic and taught her skills in subtle verbal bravado.

Morejón's writings are inscribed in the socialist and nationalist polit-

ical system of the Cuban government. Her apparently innocuous promotion of Afro-Cuban society is in keeping with the limits most intellectuals accepted after the 1971 Padilla affair, which symbolized the end
of the era of experimentation and freedom of expression in the realm of
cultural production. Yet, she demonstrates an ability to say and mean
things without saying and meaning them too explicitly. Ostensibly, she
gets the game of political control and discursive conventions and, in all
probability, responds to particular demands with self-censorship when
she deems it necessary. At other times, her themes of love, woman, spiritual angst, Afro-Cuban elements, and societal decay have lacked
reverence with regard to officially sanctioned literature. Nonetheless,
Morejón manages to promote the triumphalism of the Cuban revolution while she conveys her preference for hermetic style and certain
racial and gender issues and remains true to her core concerns with
modest dignity.

Her wavering aesthetic and the variety of themes in her works cor-
roborate Morejón's participation in battles of cultural politics in Cuban
letters after 1960. Morejón investigates black consciousness and alternative voices with regard to race and gender problems in order to raise
seriously the questions of constructive change for blacks and women.
Morejón does not uphold nationalistic discourse about racial harmony
and national unity. Rather, her aesthetic changes reveal a political compromise, a kind of corralling of imagery and creativity. It also is possible
to view her work as a demonstration of what cultural production, like
the tormented souls of her poetry, is always up against in Cuba.

In the end, Morejón's writing is also characterized by avoidance of
explicit themes of separatist black politics and gender politics, a factor
that undermines historical and political analysis. It presents the image
of blacks encoded with the ideals of the new socialist society. Morejón
had the difficult task of maintaining her professional positions as an
intellectual and a writer in the unpredictable climate of revolutionary
cultural politics. Throughout her career, she tried to balance stylistic
changes, themes, and images of black society that both upheld and
pushed beyond officially limited discursive sites and symbolic spaces
of the Cuban revolution.

Morejón continues to write in the 2000s and to reshape her views on
aesthetics and Afro-Cuban society. As I have suggested, during that
period, Cuba's difficult economic situation affected the role of Cuban
cultural politics. It remains to be seen how scholars will assess the
Castro government's treatment of intellectuals and the heterogeneous

components of Cuban society under different historical and political phases. Morejón remains active in literary life, and, as a result, she constantly grapples with historical, social, and economic changes in her country. Seen in historical and political context, her work exemplifies how official constraints have affected the production of poetry in revolutionary Cuba. Her works also reveal the way she conjures what is Cuban under the most challenging political and spiritual circumstances.

4

Miguel Barnet's Creative Oeuvres

Religious Iconography, Revolutionary Hagiography, and Erotic *Jineteros*

Since the early 1960s there has been more than one identifiable Miguel Barnet. I do not mean to suggest that Barnet the writer has a split personality. My point here is that he is a chameleon-like littérateur whose astute adaptations to changing cultural policies have enabled him to produce his artistic creations. *Biografía de un cimarrón* (1966) and *La canción de Rachel* (1970) are among his most significant contributions to Latin American literature and to the testimonial genre. A sample of Barnet's poems and prose pieces reveals a repertoire that draws on a variety of literary forms and styles; his oeuvre of layered genres—whether under the guise of "scientific" ethnology laced with testimony, pure fiction, or poetry—displays a plethora of voices, historical sketches, and challenging images that allude to the political, social, and cultural milieu of his times.

We should never assume that a given work has a univocal meaning or that literary language is transparent. Literary effects often obscure an indisputable interpretation of both text and author. Nevertheless, it is notable how Cuba's politics and economics have shaped cultural production and permeated the contexts of Barnet's writings since the 1960s. For example, at times he has favored political positions and aesthetics that dovetailed with officially sanctioned policies. In the 1960s, when authorities wanted to eradicate Afro-Cuban religions, he aestheticized

religious practices while downplaying their religious and political import. In the late 1980s, when the Castro government demonstrated a
new-found tolerance for religions and lifted restrictions on them and
authorities even allowed Communist Party members to declare themselves religious (Oppenheimer 343), Barnet and other intellectuals began to revise their earlier opinions about African-based religions; Barnet declared that previously outlawed Afro-Cuban religious ceremonies
were significant lived practices of society. In *Nganga Kiyangala* (1991), a
documentary on Afro-Cuban religious practice, he explains divina-
tions and trance experience (e.g., how "orishas," or Afro-Cuban gods,
"mount" their mediators to speak through them) and says that he does
not adopt "orthodox" religious or political positions.

Although it is difficult to assess exactly how politics get in the way of
cultural production, Barnet's contributions are intriguing because his
work cannot be easily defined. To what purpose does Barnet blend and
blur incongruent thematics and traditional literary boundaries? Do his
literary works reveal anarchical tendencies within the constraints of
officially sanctioned literature? Is he a product of Cuban cultural production's institutionalized stinginess or an exception to some of the
stodgy socialist realism that was produced in the 1960s and 1970s?
Officials used Che Guevara's ideal of the self-sacrificing "new man" to
encourage artists and intellectuals to join the masses and to mortgage
the present for a distant utopian future.

Some critics suggest that Barnet's curious literary fusion is an affir-
mation of his independence, a strategy to defy categorization and, in-
dispensably, a survival tactic that has worked during periods of revolutionary puritanism (Sklodowska; Luis "Politics of Memory"). Indeed,
Barnet maneuvers his hybrid discourses, miscellaneous in character and
quality, to many ends. He often affirms his independence through his
literary production. And, yet, the more he establishes his autonomy
through belletristic eclecticism, the more he constitutes himself as the
ex-bourgeois bohemian and talented dandy (à la Wilde) with socialist
overtones. He has scavenged voraciously through Cuba's underground
(e.g., the testimonial writings and the Afro-Cuban poetry) to create brilliant alternative versions of "real" historical events and fictitious versions
of life. Yet, he has shrewdly veiled other issues within the cultural clut-
ter of his texts; rather than take any absolute position, he has chosen to
jumble obscurity and verisimilitude and to weave literary subterfuge
into the fabric of his protean creativity.

Biografía de un cimarrón is a vivid tale of the audacious and independent Montejo, a former Afro-Cuban slave who was a maroon in the midnineteenth century and whose solitary life consisted of harrowing experiences and survival tactics. Like a pseudodocumentary, the work features Barnet's chronologically framed epic account of Montejo's monologues, descriptions of his life as a worker in the sugar factories, a runaway slave hiding in caves, and a soldier fighting in the independence wars. It is a narrative purportedly composed of an informant's pure memory, along with the ethnologist's historical and sociological interventions on the scene. Unlike Flaubert's intimate one-on-one literary relationship with Emma Bovary, characterized by Flaubert as "Madame Bovary c'est moi," Barnet transforms his narrative hero into a collective voice, a sort of "Montejo c'est nous." The author gives birth to accounts of the "other"; personal "rescued" histories represent the marginalized lives of the masses.

There is a slightly different focus and a female voice in *Canción de Rachel*. Here, Barnet eavesdrops on a devilish and ferociously beautiful cabaret entertainer at Havana's best music halls through first-person narrative, interspersed with newspaper clippings and comments by other characters. A composite of the stories of several women who sang and danced in cabaret-style theaters and dance halls, the tale is a pretext for historical retrospection, especially regarding the early decades of twentieth-century Cuba, a period of heightened social turmoil and political corruption during which Cubans struggled for economic independence and democracy. With vibrant dry wit and a certain voyeurism, the author pursues Rachel's tumultuous adventures with love affairs, fame, and money while she performs at the celebrated Alhambra theater.

Barnet has created various personalities that radiate human strength and suffer weakness in distinct social settings and historical periods. His poetic voices of the early 1960s demonstrate intimate knowledge of Afro-Cuban religious ritual and portray slave resistance to the unconscionable cruelties of the system. His first two collections, *La piedra fina y el pavorreal* (1963) and *Isla de güijes* (1964), reflect the early phase of the Cuban revolution, before the complete bureaucratization of culture. Subtle and lean representations of Afro-Cuban religious iconography are practically devoid of political rhetoric and impervious to restrictive cultural expression. In contrast, by the late 1960s, Barnet's personalized, guilt-ridden, antibourgeois voice proposes his earnest integration into Cuba's nascent revolutionary society. In the poetry of the late 1970s and the 1980s, he describes Afro-Cuban religious fables, acknowledges

Cuban cultural personalities (e.g, the writer José Lezama Lima and the
singer Bola de Nieve), depicts travel in foreign countries, and pays homage to Latin American leftists such as Che Guevara, Fidel Castro, Roque
Dalton, and Víctor Jara. In the early 1990s Barnet concentrates on romantic and erotic poems, philosophical musings, and haiku poetry.

In some of his writings of the 1990s, during the Special Period (the
economic crisis that began in Cuba after the disappearance of the Soviet
Union), he manifests an ironic perspective on contemporary political
and social problems, such as the government's contradictory policies
toward prostitutes, marginals, and homosexuals. In the poem "Hijo de
obrero," Barnet borrows from the Alexandrian Greek poet Constantine
Cavafy to illustrate the grievous life of a disconsolate young man who
"wastes away" under working-class circumstances and sexual hustling.
Loaded with caustic social criticism, the poem is equally charged with
what T. S. Eliot calls the symbolic weight of dead poets and literary tradition. Barnet conjures up Cavafy's poetics and homoerotic themes to sit-
uate historically gay expression in Cuba. While Cavafy merely laments
the fading beauty of a young man, Barnet rewrites Cavafy's poem to suc-
cinctly describe how a young man's "temptation" to possess material
things leads to prostitution, AIDS, and death.

Similarly, the prose of his short story "Miosvatis" is intercut with disquieting undercurrents of economic dislocation and spiritual vacuous-
ness. A somewhat cynical narrator returns to his native Cuba in the
1990s, bearing gifts (from Wolfgang, a German friend) for a Cuban
woman named Miosvatis. She is physically absent from the story, which
symbolically accentuates her employment; she is constantly "out there
turning tricks" on Havana's streets. A metaphor for pragmatic and illegal business skills on an island with austere resources, Miosvatis is a *jinetera* who caters to foreign tourism and purportedly prostitutes herself
out of economic necessity.[1] Barnet has a penchant for characters and settings charged with symbolic sexual overtones with underlying and
scathing social commentary.

Barnet's writings attest to his erratic professional development, but
also to his political resiliency. Immediately after the revolution, the government founded new cultural institutions that displaced the existing
independent writers and publishing houses. By 1968 several institutions
were promoting a literature of revolutionary idealism that echoed official versions of social reality. Barnet's own background was eclectic. He
studied ethnography and entered the Seminario de Etnología y Folclor;
later, he taught folklore studies in the Escuela de Instructores de Arte

(1961–1966). He and the writer Lydia Cabrera are considered literary disciples of the prominent Cuban anthropologist Fernando Ortiz. Barnet was also a researcher for the Instituto de Etnología y Folclor de la Academia de Ciencias and in the José Martí National Library. At the Institute, he studied under María Teresa Linares, Isaac Barreal, and Argeliers León. His formal preparation influenced the development of his writing into a sort of amalgamation that incorporated both popular icons and official rhetoric. The mix was socialist ethnology, prorevolutionary iconography, highly stylized Afro-Cuban religious imagery, erotic poetry, angry realist prose, and conversational poetry.

However, Barnet's literary savvy and political skills were not sufficiently honed to allow him to dodge bureaucratic bullets during different phases in Cuba's highly charged cultural politics. He has experienced professional and personal highs and lows since the early 1960s and was affected by such ominous realities as the closing of Ediciones El Puente (1965), the Padilla affair (especially 1968–70), and his friend Reinaldo Arenas's complex problems with officialdom.

I Saw the Best Minds of My Generation . . .

Barnet was close to the inner circle of El Puente members; his relationship with the group brought him publishing opportunities and political discord. In 1964 Ediciones El Puente published his second collection of poetry, *Isla de güijes*. The publishing house also selected Barnet's poem "¿Dónde están?" for the collection *Novísima poesía cubana* (1964), edited by José Mario and with a prologue by Reinaldo Felipe and Ana María Simo, who were all key members of the group. The prologue served as a literary manifesto in response to accusations by young rival "revolutionary" intellectuals that El Puente produced merely "pure" poetry. In addition to official scrutiny because of its antirevolutionary aesthetics, the El Puente group was damaged by an irreparable blemish—the memorable (to say the least) visit by Allen Ginsberg to Havana in 1965. As described in chapter 1, the subsequent arrests of José Mario and Manuel Ballagas, two young El Puente members who spent much time with Ginsberg in Havana, caused a sensation of another kind. Ballagas had translated fragments of Ginsberg's "Kaddish" and other poems into Spanish and was working on "Howl."

Ostensibly, Ginsberg's openness about his homosexuality and his boisterous protest against the conservative mores of the Cuban revolution offended and threatened the government bureaucrats.

Inadvertently, Ginsberg's forthrightness contributed to the stigma of homosexuality that attached itself to El Puente, to the group's infamy, and, ultimately, to its demise.

Barnet was implicated in the scandal of El Puente but distanced himself from several members after they officially fell from grace (officials also detained and interrogated Ana María Simo). Perhaps Barnet's response to the scandal was to withdraw his works published by El Puente from circulation, or perhaps Cuban editors chose to delete his El Puente publications in the lists of publications included in Barnet's later works. In any case, *Isla de güijes* was absent both from Barnet's lists of credits in later publications and from anthologies of his subsequent works, as if El Puente had never published the text. The airbrushing of the El Puente episode and the publications from his professional dossier creates a sort of literary erasure effect that always leaves some trace; that which disappears is emphasized by its absence. Evidently, after its demise, El Puente was an undesirable association for any young writer in revolutionary Cuba.

Despite the negative ramifications El Puente caused for Barnet, several powerful cultural bureaucrats supported him. Roberto Fernández Retamar and Lisandro Otero wrote favorable critical reviews of his works, especially of his poetry. *Biografía de un cimarrón* is a popular text that has been translated into several languages. However, Elzbieta Sklodowska says that Barnet's internationally acclaimed *Biografía* did not gain him official recognition. William Luis joins in speculation with Sklodowska that it was not until 1967, when Barnet clarified his ideological position in the poetry of *La sagrada familia* (The Holy Family), that he was accepted by the Cuban literary establishment. Enrobing this poetry collection with the title of Marx and Engels's seminal text *The Holy Family* may have helped to convince some officials of Barnet's political solidarity. The text was of great interest to Communist Party officials for its condemnation of bourgeois values in a corrupt capitalist world.[2]

However, Barnet's publication of *Biografía* and *La sagrada* did not ameliorate the tension between him and officialdom. Even though Casa de las Américas awarded Barnet literary mention for *La sagrada* in 1968, he was not able to publish poetry again until 1978. Apparently, he had not been able to shed the label of nonconformist intellectual because of other factors.

Barnet had close ties with the enfant terrible of Cuban letters, Reinaldo Arenas, an iconoclast intellectual who clashed with cultural officials. Barnet's friendship with Arenas was no secret to anyone in Havana's cultural milieu. Arenas was the "bad boy" from the countryside who was considered unrefined but almost brilliant, and scandalously gay at a time when everyone—that is, everyone who wanted a place in Cuban culture—had to appear straight. Even Arenas had gone so far as to marry a friend in response to the official repression of gays. Some authorities harassed Arenas for his defiant behavior and "antirevolutionary" works. Officials apprehended Arenas and confiscated his manuscripts because they found his work "controversial" and irreverent. For a time, he became a fugitive on his own island and finally fled Cuba during the 1980 Mariel exodus.[3] Although officials put an end to the UMAP forced labor camps in 1968, harassment of nonconformists was looming on the horizon (this is confirmed by the purges in the universities and the theater during the so-called gray years, 1970–1975).

The events of 1967 and 1968 marked a period without publications for Arenas, Barnet, and others (Nancy Morejón, also an El Puente contributor, experienced her "silence" during this time). In 1967 Arenas submitted *El mundo alucinante* to the UNEAC literary competition, and, in 1968, Barnet submitted *La sagrada familia* to the Casa de las Américas literary competition. Officials gave literary mention to *El mundo alucinante;* it was published in Argentina in 1968, but not in Cuba. Barnet received literary mention for his work. Barnet's close relationship with the "unconventional" and unruly Arenas, coupled with El Puente's demise, may have caused strained relations for him.

Another barrier that may have impeded Barnet's complete integration into the mainstream cultural milieu was that he wrote about "Afro-Cuban" issues. Cuba's racism did not simply vanish when officials outlawed racial discrimination, despite the contention of many whites that the state's new racial policies were sufficient to do away with racial inequities. It was also argued by some that there was no need for Afro-Cubans to promote a separate black agenda that went beyond official measures: some authorities decided that Afro-Cubans' radical action would result in "microfactional" political divisions for the nation. Elzbieta Sklodowska says that, in spite of racial tensions, officials may have considered Barnet's writings acceptable: "Although the new dominant ideology favored a materialistic interpretation of Cuba's past and present, in the early 1960s the constraints of Marxist doctrine were still not so inflexible as to ban the exploration of what was Barnet's main interest: Afro-Cuban folklore, with all its magic, 'irrational' cults, beliefs, and myths" (3).

This statement is partially true, since the predominantly white cultural establishment continued to harbor racism. Barnet's writings, both ethnological and poetic, went beyond systematic scientific and historical research to reveal deep sympathy and transference with regard to religious practices. Moreover, his writing was unlike that of Manuel Moreno Fraginals and Pedro DesChamps Chapeaux, whose undertakings were viewed as "legitimate" historical rewritings of Cuba's sugar economy and slavery. Conceivably, Barnet's ethnology and Afro-Cuban religious writings were a harder sell; they represented undefined boundaries and were nonscientific works that highlight "atavistic" cults and "primitive" religious ceremony. Since officials sought to obliterate religious practices in order to forge Cuban society into a modern socialist nation, Barnet's obsessions may have seemed frivolous and even suspect.

In fact, it was often the case that different officials unpredictably, unevenly, and randomly dealt with artists' and writers' works. For example, while some authorities praised Barnet's use of "popular" culture, several white cultural bureaucrats chided him for promoting Afro-Cuban issues. Barnet says that Alfredo Guevara, Carlos Franqui, and others insinuated pejoratively that he was an ideologue for blacks. Some officials displayed racism and materialist antireligious rhetoric, showing an aversion to Afro-Cuban religions.

It may have been both a literary and political challenge for Barnet to write about and for Afro-Cubans during the politically charged 1960s. Barnet was a "white" Cuban working within a predominantly white cultural establishment. Some Afro-Cubans writers and artists mistrusted him for meddling in "black" affairs. (Barnet's dilemma echoes Fernando Ortiz's paradoxical situation as a white researcher who studied secret black religious sects.) This was not surprising, since the government restricted separate black expression and arrested or harassed several Afro-Cuban intellectuals for their gatherings and writings.

If Barnet's writing inadvertently tested white officials' "tolerance," or created suspicion among Afro-Cubans, this did not appear to deter him from pursuing research on Afro-Cuban culture and religions. Similarly, Afro-Cuban iconography in his poetry attests to his persistent use of Afro-Cuban culture in his literature. In the early collections *La piedra fina y el pavorreal* and *Isla de güijes* he produced lyric sequences that emphasize components of Afro-Cuban belief systems. The titles of the collections allude to objects of spiritual and cosmic import in Afro-Cuban religions; the poems depict significant religious pantheons and are both a personal examination and a lyrical exposé of sacred ceremonies and song.

For example, in "Mito" the poetic speaker foregrounds a chant for Yemayá (the Afro-Cuban goddess of the sea and fertility) that gives rise to a mystical atmosphere:

> Oigo el canto de Yemayá sobre las algas:
> Iyalé, yalé, yaluma O
> Yalé, o mi yalé
> allabwa mío
> Todo la tierra resuena.
> El aire de la espuma alisa las piedras. (*La piedra fina* 49)
>
> ∽
>
> [Listen to Yemaya's chant over the seaweed
> Iyalé, yalé, yaluma O
> Yalé, o mi yalé
> allabwa mío
> The earth resounds
> The foam breeze burnishes the stones.] (Tr. Linda Howe)

The Afro-Cuban chant depicts Yemayá's powers over nature. Intimate and lyric, the consonance and vocalic rhythms of the chorus provoke a spiritual state of mental delirium in the believer: "No pienso demasiado/ Abro y cierro los ojos/ Reposo / Todo vive en mí" (50). [I don't think too much / I open and close my eyes / Rest / Everything lives within me (tr. Linda Howe).] The speaker succumbs to the enchantment of song and to the goddess Yemayá's "presence," which dominate the ethereal realm. The suggestive lyrics portray the complexities of rites, as well as the poetics and the rhythms of sacred chants. We hear voices singing to the gods, a chorus that calls upon the supernatural world to provide a path to inner peace.

Barnet provides a glossary of terms for his hybrid text of ethnology and poetry. He includes colloquial words for animals, objects, and instruments that connote communication with sacred beings (e.g., "la ceiba" "el güije," "la lechuza," "el pavo real," "la piedra fina," "los caracoles," "la siguapa," "el caldero," and "el tablero"). He emphasizes—as Fernando Ortiz, Lydia Cabrera, Nicolás Guillén, and Alejo Carpentier had done before him—that the foundation of the cosmos is in nature and in common objects. Both Guillén's Afro-Cuban poetry and Carpentier's narrative illustrate aesthetic innovation of African-based culture and language. Their work to retrieve and collect "folkloric" components and "afronegrismos" reflected a commitment to vernacular art. For example, in the novel *Ecue-Yamba-O!* (1933), Carpentier incorporates religious song and ritual, vernacular language, and ethnographic references. Barnet's use of the musical chorus, colloquial language, and black oral expression also recalls Guillén's poetry of *Motivos de son* (1930) and *Sóngoro Cosongo* (1931). Guillén's use of the Cuban *son* to create poetic versions and multiple voicings of popular music precedes Barnet's incorporation of Afro-Cuban musical chorus.

While "Mito" appears to be ethnology-in-verse and depicts innocuous formal traditions, other poems stand for the demonic and destructive nature of some religions. For example, in "La ciudad," Roque's burial and the arrival of Ikú Arayé suggest that evil ways and witchcraft are ominous warnings of imminent death among members of Lucumí religion (60). Mystery and violence allude to murder with disquieting effects. The poem begins with a deceivingly conventional list of multiple urban scenarios. However, the poet's progressive exploration of Havana's unexplored secrets takes on brutal overtones, and we end up in the tentative horror of the city's dark underbelly.

Impressionistic sketches of the African-based religions narrow the gap between "high" culture and "low" folklore. Is Barnet a literary raconteur and an anthropologist rummaging through the religious underworld of secret ceremony and "atavistic" belief systems to enhance a poetic medium? Or is he merely establishing a personal encounter with the gods and a significant ethnic experience? His writings resemble both the work of a religious informant, scribbling down knowledge in sacred notebooks, and that of an ethnologist whose curiosity and creativeness have led to the aestheticization of the divine. In the end, the interlocutors, who in this case could be the Cuban literary critics, judge the value of these texts.

Some critics favor Barnet's use of national "folklore" that displaces "high art" to break the chains of foreign cultural dominance and bourgeois literary traditions. Poetry that constituted national cultural elements challenged the foreign cultures that dominated Cuba for centuries. To some degree, Barnet also models his poetry after the "anti-poems" of the Chilean Nicanor Parra and the "conversational poetry" of the Nicaraguan Ernesto Cardenal. However, he latches on to Afro-Cuban religious ceremonies and iconography to express his notion of "Cubanness." Critics also viewed his work as a model for the "nationalization" of culture. For example, Lisandro Otero, Victor Casaus, and Roberto Fernández Retamar praise Barnet's poetry of Afro-Cuban folklore and the revolution. Otero says that Barnet's unique poetry is "exteriorista" because it avoids "excessive glitter" and is rooted in Cuban identity (Bernard and Pola 67–68). Otero contrasts exotic and foreign elements of hermetic poetry with Barnet's expression of "real" Cuban things. Casaus likens Barnet's style to that of the Cuban Eliseo Diego in his *En la calzada de Jesús del monte*, but he clarifies that Barnet differs because he takes into account the effects of the revolution ("Inventario" 144). Casaus's weakly veiled criticism slights Diego's poetry and implies a lack of substantive thematics and political conviction. Casaus resorted to political rhetoric to prescribe literary styles and themes.

Similarly, Fernández Retamar singled out Barnet as one of the first young writers to produce a conversationalist poetry with "proper" thematics. Barnet is the archetype of a young intellectual who creates "new" writing for the revolution:

> De los poetas surgidos con posterioridad a la Revolución, con la cual se halla desde luego estrechamente identificado, Barnet es uno de los primeros en encontrar voz propia. En sus poemas, las preocupaciones concretas animan también sus estudios sobre el país, unidas a un penetrante lirismo directo, le permiten una mirada cubana, según su voluntad, dentro de una línea que puede ya considerarse característica de la expresión nacional. El surgimiento de esta poesía joven, desaliñada, vuelta con cariño sobre las cosas reales del país, es una de las alegrías de la literatura cubana más reciente. ("Prologue" *La piedra fina* 3–4)

> [Of the poets who emerged after the Revolution (with which they closely identified) Barnet is one of the first to find his own voice. In his poems, concrete concerns stimulate his research about the country. They are linked to a direct and penetrating lyricism that affords him a deliberately Cuban perspective, according to his will, within a trend already considered characteristic of national expression. The emergence of this young, untidy poetry, affectionately focused on the country's reality, is one of the joys of the most recent Cuban literature.](Tr. Emma Claggett and Linda Howe)

Otero, Casaus, and Fernández Retamar turned themselves into the main subjects of their writing and highlighted their own transformations into communist "new men."[4] Often, and to varying degrees, they measured works against formal and universal revolutionary standards of socialist realism. Both Fernández Retamar and Otero, powerful influences on the Cuban literary journals *Casa de las Américas* and *Gaceta de Cuba*, were heavy-handed in shaping Cuban literature after the revolution.

They extolled the principles of their own perception of official literature to generate politically committed work in the cultural realm.

Official constraints shaped representations of "otherness" through the reformed self of the artist and writer. Many intellectuals felt or professed to feel indebted to the guerrilla revolutionaries who had won the military and political victories of Castro's revolution. Intellectuals were to become the literary spokespersons and intellectual soldiers of the new government. In "El otro," Fernández Retamar writes exemplary guilt-ridden verse to project these ideological sentiments:

> Nosotros los sobrevivientes,
> ¿a quiénes debemos la sobrevivida?
> ¿Quién se murió por mí en la ergástula,
> quién recibió la bala mía,
> la para mí en su corazón?
> ¿Sobre qué muerto estoy yo vivo,
> sus huesos quedando en los míos,
> los ojos que le arrancaron, viendo
> por la mirada de mi cara,
> y la mano que no es su mano,
> que no es ya tampoco la mía,
> escribiendo palabras rotas
> donde él no está, en la sobrevida? (Vitier 188)

~

> [We, the survivors,
> to whom do we owe our continued existence?
> Who died for me at the gallows,
> who took the bullet
> meant for my heart?
> At whose expense am I alive
> the dead bones within mine,
> the eyes they tore from him, seeing
> the look on my face,
> and the hand that is neither his,
> nor is mine,
> writing broken words
> where he is absent, among the survivors?] (Tr. Linda Howe)

Feelings of culpability, remorse, and duty overwhelm the poetic speaker. Fernández Retamar postulates a counterpoint to the egotistical bourgeois artist. Idealized heroes overshadow the dwarfed and ineffectual intellectual, who plays no serious role in the revolution unless he is able to dedicate his pen to the cause. Fernández Retamar rejects the aestheticism of yesteryear and calls for a direct social language to reflect Cuba's new, putatively independent culture. He urges artists and writers to create didactic literature and to relinquish the cosmopolitan ideas and influences afforded them by their privileged backgrounds. Likewise, in his lengthy essay *Calibán*, he prophetically envisions intellectuals who endorse rupture with Western modes of symbolic domination to produce a national literature, unfettered by exogenous artistic movements with "imperialistic" tendencies: "Those intellectuals who consider themselves to be revolutionary must break the ties with their own class (the petty bourgeoisie in many cases); they must also break their ties of dependency with the metropolitan culture that gave them its culture, its language, its conceptual and technical apparatus" (83). Cuban writers and artists were encouraged to become public servants to express the nation's collective experience; poetry was to be developed into a vehicle for raising patriotic consciousness and revolutionary sentiments.

The Cuban critic José Prats Sariol asserts that Barnet possesses revolutionary qualities because he has knowledge of Cuba's "ethnic and social roots, customs and rites, and struggles and dreams" (158). In "Che, tú lo sabes todo," we witness how the poetic speaker resorts to the official mythology of Che as Cuba's representative guerrilla hero to discuss the diminutive role of the intellectual:

> Che, tú lo sabes todo,
> los recovecos de la Sierra
> el asma sobre la yerba fría,
> la tribuna
> el oleaje en la noche
> y hasta de que se hacen
> los frutos y las yuntas
>
> No es que no quiera darte
> pluma por pistola
> pero el poeta eres tú (*Carta* 90)
>
> ⤛
>
> [Che, you know everything,
> the nooks and crannies of the Sierra Maestra,
> asthma over cold grass,
> the speaker's platform,
> the swell of the sea at night
> and even what makes plants grow
> how oxen are yoked

It's not that I want to give you
a pen instead of a pistol
but the real poet is you] (*When Night Is Darkest* 59)

Apostrophe and the informal "tú" in the line "Che, you know everything" create an intimate experience for the reader; we address Guevara
using the familiar, rather than the more formal, construction. Che's dedication spreads out across geographical and spacial metaphors. Barnet
emphasizes Che's relationship with Cuban flora and fauna to show how
Che was intimate with Cuba, from the Sierra Maestra to Santa Clara,
where he had fought and won major battles for Castro's movement. The
lines "It's not that I want to give you / a pen instead of a pistol / but the
real poet is you" recall the classic debate about whether the pen is might-
ier than the sword. Here, Barnet affirms that the fighting has been the
single most important factor in the emergence of Cuba's new society.
The poem's submissive tone also attests to the intellectual's vision of the
need for exemplary individual sacrifice. Che's revolutionary spirit permeates the island, and the poetic speaker sings praises to the guerrilla
in an acquiescent tone. Che is linked to sacrifice, nature, and wisdom.
Like José Martí, the national hero of the nineteenth-century independence wars, Che died in battle. Each man was an intellectual force, as well
as a fighter for Cuban independence. Reverent verses describe Che's
omnipotence and omnipresence. We imagine the Cuban photographer
Korda's optimistic and famously romanticized photographs of Che wear-
ing his beret and wisely gazing off to a distant utopian future, or the
poster art of the 1960s that idealized Che as universal guerrilla fighter.

Barnet embraces the organic role of the intellectual as zealous advo-
cate of the revolution's martyrology. His disdain for the allegedly decadent culture of prerevolutionary Cuba can also understood within the
context of his own North American–influenced bourgeois background.
He says that his commitment to writing came about because he felt like
a stranger in an unknown land in his own country: "Entonces, cuando
llegó la Revolución, empecé a salir, y en esa salida encontré muchas
cosas, me encontré con el mundo, con Cuba, y me fasciné a tal punto que
me dio por estudiar toda la historia de Cuba, toda la geografía, la
economía, el folclor, la etnografía. . . . Decidí que ese era mi camino, es
decir, estudiar la cultura nacional" (*La fuente viva* 21–22). [So, when the
Revolution came, I started to explore, and I discovered many things, I
discovered the world, Cuba, and I was fascinated to such a point that I
devoted myself to studying the entire history of Cuba, all the geography,

economy, folklore, ethnography. . . . I decided that was my path: to study the national culture (tr. Emma Claggett and Linda Howe).]

Officials encouraged Barnet's generation to produce literature to differentiate itself from previous ones, but with the added political encumbrance that it reflect the radically changing circumstances after 1959. In the United States or Western Europe, the decision whether to embrace what Tom Wolfe called "radical chic" was a personal one. For writers and artists in Castro's Cuba, radicalism was not merely chic— it was obligatory if you wanted to position yourself well in cultural politics.

Barnet demonstrates this commitment in *La sagrada familia,* in which he offers up political poems replete with "tender anger." He reveals a poetic multiple-personality complex that combines nostalgia, painful transitions, and rebellion against the pillars of bourgeois society and family values (Forgues 57). This collection is a milestone because the ideal poetic voice of self-effacement not only rejects cosmopolitanism but also emphasizes authentic components of "Cubanness."

Both Afro-Cuban themes and the disintegration of traditional bourgeois family values fill the pages of this collection. In "Revolución," Barnet's poetic alter ego depicts the revolution's impact on society:

> Cuando llegó la Revolución
> la multitud entró en mi casa
> Parecía revolver las gavetas, el armario,
> cambiar el cesto de la costura
>
> Aquel silencio viejo cesó
> y mi abuela dejó de tejer memorias,
> dejó de hablar,
> dejó de cantar
>
> Esperanzado vi, había que ver,
> cómo entraba la luz en aquella sala
> cuando mi madre abrió las ventanas
> por primera vez (109)

⟨≋⟩

> [When the Revolution arrived
> the multitudes came in to my house
> They seemed to shake up the drawers, the cupboards,
> and even change the sewing basket
>
> That old silence ceased
> and my grandmother stopped spinning tales,

> stopped speaking,
> and stopped singing
>
> Filled with hope I saw, I had to see,
> how the light entered that room
> when my mother opened the windows
> for the first time] (*When Night Is Darkest* 29)

Movement, sound, and light signal inevitable change. In a rebellious tone, the poetic speaker confronts old-world views. Repetition of the verb "stopped" signals the momentous ceasing of the grandmother's speech, song, and her memories. Revolutionary upheaval brings her power over the family to an abrupt end. Light penetrates the house and forces open doors and windows, which symbolizes victory, change, and hope. Things fall apart as a "former silence" vanishes and insular bourgeois steadfastness and tradition disappear through the exposed spaces. Mirta Yáñez emphasizes the poem's "shameless iconoclasm," because Barnet fuses personal catharsis with political indoctrination in a conversational tone (15).

Overall, the poetry is replete with "realistic" representations and social commentary in favor of the revolution. There is more emotional intensity than intellectual intricacy. Although Cuban bureaucrats found redeeming political value in *La sagrada familia,* there is nothing particularly innovative or distinguished about this poetry. Rather, it derives its "value" from its blend of politics, officially sanctioned literary style, and cultural matter.

Barnet also includes laudatory verse for Cuban revolutionary heroes and martyrs and denunciation of slavery, and he includes a plethora of descriptive Afro-Cuban ceremony and vocabulary. His black protest, antislavery themes, and African-based mythology echo Ballagas, Arozarena, and Guillén's poetry of the Negrista movement.

In "En el monte" and "Ceremonia para un gallo y un pez," the poetic speaker alludes to animal sacrifice as offerings to the gods. Barnet aestheticizes syncretic religious ceremony; practitioners drain blood from a goat's head or from a black rooster during Abakuá ceremonies. The esoteric iconography conveys private meditation with the gods. The critic Eugenio Matibag suggests that these poems belong to an insider's language, "a language that can only seem opaque to the uninitiated reader" (120). In "En Santiago" and other similar poems, Barnet depicts carnivalesque celebrations, religious ritual, sacred music, and dance with ambiguous and obscure references to religious practices.

At first glance, these poems seem superficially exotic and "primi-
tivist," as do some Negrista poems of the 1920s and 1930s. The icons
suggest, but do not reveal, a veritable world of lived-religious practices
and a cultural underworld. Barnet argues that his poetry exemplifies
Cuba's vox populi and is part of a new literary tradition confirming
Cuban nationalism. He employs a conversational style in other poems
of *La sagrada* that expose details of slave exploitation. For example,
"Peregrinos del alba" and "Negroes" are retrospective critiques of slavery. They describe the Middle Passage and the slaves' unbearable conditions:

> Ahora pienso en la travesía, aquellas cabezas
> negras, aquellos brazos pulidos, comidos por la
> malaria y el tifus
> Pienso en la fiereza del mar batiente
> Y los cráneos amarillos abajo
> ("Peregrinos" in *La sagrada* 215)

> [Now try to think about the long journey back, those black
> heads, the glistening arms eaten away by
> malaria and typhus
> Think about the ferocity of the churning sea
> and the skulls all yellow at the bottom of the hull]
> (*When Night Is Darkest* 35)

> Levantaron la proa de los galeones
> y toda la dotación
> se bautizó de orín
> en brazos y pupilas

> Fue la razón del alboroto
> el espectáculo
> la noche del primer suicidio
> Luego los cantos y las oraciones
> el peso
> del oráculo en el horizonte

> Y sin mirar atrás
> por una vez
> la sombra
> la ausencia de la arena que cubrió sus pechos
> el miedo de estar juntos sin los dioses
> ("Negroes" in *La sagrada* 211)

[They lifted the bow of the galleons
and all the crew
was baptized by the sweat and urine
of arms and pupils

It was the cause of the uproar
the spectacle
the night of the first suicide
Later, songs and prayers
the immensity
of the oracle on the horizon.

And, for once,
without looking back
the gloom
the absence of sand on their chests
the fear of being together torn from their gods]
(Tr. Linda Howe)

Dispersed among slave enclaves, Afro-Cubans faced the obliteration of their languages, collective belief systems, and religious practices. Survival and active forgetting were indispensable features of the slaves' psyche. Barnet describes the horror of uprootedness and the distress and abhorrent conditions of the Middle Passage, represented by the slaves' disease-wracked bodies, consumed by typhus and malaria. Overlapping allusions to urine and the holy water for Christian baptism produce scatological commentary and sacrilegious imagery. We discover that, in some cases, captured slaves responded to the humiliating and abhorred conditions with the ultimate act of resistance: mass suicide.

Barnet dedicated "Negroes" to Malcolm X in an obvious gesture of solidarity with American black radicalism of the 1960s. He intersects antislavery themes with Cuba's problack internationalism and "anti-imperialist" policies. However, since Cuban officials perceived a localized Black Power movement in Cuba as a microfactional threat to national politics, Barnet's homage to Malcolm X inadvertently exposes the contradictions in Cuba's racial policies. Cuban officialdom promoted "black" politics internationally and created an "Afro-Cuban" image for the island. Nevertheless, the government actually displaced politicized local Afro-Cuban expression with "folkloric" studies and historical research on slave societies.

Officials warned that to write about Afro-Cuban concerns did not mean to write against the national political grain. From the beginning of the revolution, Castro had implemented institutional policies of racial equality but advocated José Martí's whitewashed nationalistic rhetoric about racial harmony: "To be Cuban is more than being White, more than being Black. A Cuban is someone who belongs to no race in particular!" ("Cuba es más" 1–3).

Castro restates Martí's words to propose a racism-free contemporary Cuban society without political "separatism." Martí, who wanted to prevent racial bloodbaths, was attempting to appease whites in the nineteenth century who feared black rebellion. Castro's speech carries the historical weight of Martí's discourse but contends with the context of the revolution, the U.S. civil rights movement, and radical black activism. Castro's rhetoric prioritizes national unity and promotes "color-blindness" in a unique sociohistorical context.

Within that context, Barnet fuses his ideas about black culture with official rhetoric to eradicate the "cults." In *La fuente viva*, he creates his own "black" writing, making use of historical and would-be scientific (Marxist) theories to incorporate black issues into the officially sanctioned national agenda. One of his discursive strategies has been to invent a representative "black" voice: "Yo creo que políticamente yo soy un negro también, en la medida que tengo que tomar conciencia de la cultura nacional, y la cultura de mi país ha sido muy enriquecida por la cultura africana. Identificarme con los problemas de los negros es natural, no lo hago por exotismo sino por asumir una cultura que tanto tiene que ver conmigo, con la cultura cubana. . . . Los problemas de los negros son mis problemas" (28). [I think that politically I am also black, insofar as I have to be conscious of the national culture of my country, which has been enormously enriched by African culture. To identify myself with the problems of the black people is natural; I do it not out of exoticism but because I absorb a culture that has so much to do with me, with Cuban culture. . . . The problems of black people are mine also (tr. Emma Claggett and Linda Howe).]

Barnet qualifies the value of Afro-Cuban religion and constructs cultural components within a pseudo-Marxist framework. He advocates the eventual disappearance of Afro-Cuban religious practices while emphasizing their stylistic richness:

> En Cuba se ha hecho evidente que cultos como la santería han ido perdiendo su preeminencia desde los primeros años del triunfo de la Revolución. La nueva sociedad, que resuelve y garantiza la estabilidad económica, la salud, y crea incentivos de vida que permiten ampliar las perspectivas humanas, irá prescindiendo cada vez más de estas estructuras religiosas.

De la santería, de la riqueza de sus cantos y bailes, de su mitología, irán quedando aquellos valores permanentes en el orden
puramente estético. La alegoría a sus patrones filosóficos y cos-
mogónicos también será válida en la creación artística y literaria." (*La fuente viva* 196–97)

⤚⤙

[In Cuba, it has become evident that cults like Santeria have been
losing their preeminence since the first years of the Revolution.
The new society, which resolves and guarantees economic sta-
bility, health, and creates incentives that broaden human perspectives, will gradually eliminate these religious structures.
  Of Santeria, its wealth of songs and dances and its mythology—those permanent values in the purely aesthetic order will
remain. The allegory of its philosophy and cosmological patterns will also be valid in artistic and literary creation.] (Tr. Emma
Claggett and Linda Howe)

Gleaned artistic palimpsests of "former" lived-practices, Barnet's
texts are filtered through historical and social-scientific methodology.
Was it possible to limit Afro-Cuban religious practices to aesthetic expression while harnessing such expression politically? Is Barnet's cultural patchwork of religious iconography suitable for a revolutionary
framework?

Barnet does attempt just that. In *La fuente viva,* he refers to the events
that occurred on 1 January 1959, when a dove landed on Castro's shoulder during his speech in Havana. According to popular belief, the Afro-
Cuban high priests determined that this was a sign that Oddúa had con-
doned and abetted Castro in his revolutionary victories (doves are
associated with Oddúa). Here, religious iconography dovetails with
political discourse and design. Oddúa blesses Castro's victory and
endorses the 26 of July Movement (Castro's guerrilla organization):

> En Cuba, los patrones de la mitología africana, especialmente la
> de origen yoruba o lucumí, como la llamamos popularmente,
> han servido para interpretar y determinar hechos políticos de
> gran trascendencia. . . . Oddúa representa en Cuba la vida y la
> muerte: es una divinidad dual: simboliza la fuerza organizada,
> el gobierno, la ejecución. Su fecha onomástica es el 1^0 de Enero,
> día en que triunfó nuestra Revolución. Sus colores pueden ser el
> rojo y el negro; colores con que también se identifica la bandera
> de nuestro Movimiento 26 de julio; su animal es la paloma,
> clásico símbolo de la paz. . . .Todos estos elementos con-
> tribuyeron para que nuestro pueblo asociara a Oddúa con la Rev-
> olución, con el 1^0 de Enero, fecha clave, con los colores de la ban-

dera del Movimiento 26 de Julio; y a la paloma de Oddúa con la paloma que se le posó en el hombro a nuestro líder Fidel Castro el día que pronunció su primer discurso ante el pueblo. . . . Los adeptos decían sin titubeos que el líder de nuestra Revolución era un hijo de Oddúa. (158)

꧁

[In Cuba, the conventions of African mythology, especially of Yoruban and, as we commonly say, Lucumí origin, have served to interpret and to determine political acts of great significance. . . . In Cuba, Oddúa represents life and death: he is a dual deity; he symbolizes organizing power, the government, and achievement. His saint's day is January 1, the day our Revolution triumphed. His colors can be red and black, colors associated with the flag of our 26 of July Movement. His animal is the dove, the classical symbol of peace. . . . All these elements contributed to our people associating Oddúa with the Revolution, with January 1, and Oddúa's dove, with the dove that landed on the shoulder of our leader, Fidel Castro, the day he made his first speech before the public. . . . Without hesitation, the [religious] leaders said that the leader of our Revolution was a child of Oddúa.] (Tr. Emma Claggett and Linda Howe)

Black and red colors symbolize Oddúa's power and represent Castro's 26 of July Movement, founded immediately after his failed attempt to take over the Moncada military barracks in Santiago de Cuba in 1953. Although Castro's and his rebels' first military action to oust Batista from power was a failure, it marked the beginning of the dictator's end.

Barnet's final observation that the high priests declared Castro to be Oddúa's son reinforces the leader's affiliation with the Yoruba pantheon. It is unclear to what degree Barnet links politics to religious iconography; does he suggest here that Castro might have a connection with the divine powers of the orishas?

Barnet's Afro-Cuban voices are inextricably bound to his own ideological, social, and political position in cultural production. I find Russell Berman's theory of the mask useful in explaining how intellectuals and writers project different identities to represent "the very thing that is being repressed." Intellectuals' position-taking is a "form that identity must assume in order to appear in a repressive society, and it bears the marks of repression while denouncing them mutely." Berman explains that the mask is simultaneously the antithesis and the product of the mechanism of subjugation: "Appearance as a mask corresponds to identity as the tension between empirical facticity and social

representation, and the mask is consequently the interface where antithetical processes cross; as the denial of the merely given, it overcomes
nature by repressing it; as visible appearance, it names the particular
and salvages the same mimetic substance that had just undergone
repression" (18).

If we apply Berman's concept to Barnet's mimetic act of "blackness,"
we see him attempting to reconcile "blackness" in contemporary Cuban society. He wants to "rescue" authentic Cuban culture by media-
tion of "blackness" and religion through official rhetoric (e.g., Oddúa's
blessing).

His poetry also reflects Barnet's endeavor to aesthetically mediate
and shape Afro-Cuban heterogeneous voices into "palatable" cultural
representations. In *Akeké y la jutía* (1978) and *Orikis y otros poemas* (1980),
he rewrites traditional Afro-Cuban tales and invents variations on *orikis*
(laudatory Yoruba songs directed toward Afro-Cuban gods or "re-
markable" people). He blends traditional apostrophe to the Afro-Cuban
gods with anonymous medieval poetry and popular contemporary
song, dedicating them to poets and performers such as the poet Nicolás
Guillén and the entertainer Bola de Nieve. The outcome is a hybrid form,
like "Oriki para Bola de Nieve." Barnet's creation of the poem parallels
Guillén's use of traditional Spanish and Italian Renaissance madrigals
to produce twentieth-century "mulatto madrigals." Guillén combined
the musical rhythms of the *son* with the loose formal qualities of the
Renaissance madrigal.[5] Barnet reworks the *oriki,* intercut with medieval
verse. Likewise, he imitates both Bola de Nieve and Guillén, who studied popular medieval lyric and traditions of Spanish verse and incorporated them in their works.

Bola de Nieve, also known as Ignacio Villa Fernández, was a well-
known Afro-Cuban composer, pianist, and singer. He played piano for
the famous Cuban singer Rita Montaner and was associated with the
music of the Cuban composers Ernesto Lecuona and Alejandro García
Caturla. Later, he became a celebrated *chanteur.* When he died, Guillén
wrote "Oración fúnebre a Bola de Nieve" and read the poem at Bola de
Nieve's burial. Solano's tune "El Caballero de Olmeda" was played at
Bola de Nieve's funeral procession in Guanabacoa, Cuba.

Barnet's use of contemporary popular culture to further enrich poetic
tradition characterizes Bola de Nieve as musical personality and Afro-
Cuban *juglar* (minstrel):

> Caballero de Olmedo,
> juglar herido por la flecha de Ochosí, el cazador,

> ven en tu trineo de yaguas
> y enciende las calabazas
> Dueño de la fragua y del colmilo de jabalí,
> Sumérgete en la espuma de las cinco palanganas de Ochún
>
> . . . .
>
> Vamos, despréndete de los cascos,
> salta estremecido del Puente a la Alameda
> y déjanos tu capa de lagarto raída
> tu ronquera ancestral
> tu canto antiguo . . . (*Orikis* 7)

> [Lord of Olmedo
> minstrel wounded by the hunter Ochosí's arrow
> come in your sleigh of palm fronds
> and light the gourds
> Lord of the furnace and fang of the wild boar
> submerge yourself in the foam of Ochún's five wash basins
>
> . . . .
>
> Shed your hooves
> leap from the Bridge into the Alameda
> and leave us with your frayed lizard's skin
> your ancestral hoarseness
> your ancestral song . . .] (Tr. Linda Howe)

Aesthetic beauty and homage to the Cuban pianist, singer, and popular cult figure characterize the poem. Barnet also alludes to the fact that
Juan Solano's modern version of the anonymous song "El Caballero
de Olmedo" and the popular Peruvian *vals* "La flor de la canela," by
Chabuca Granda, were part of Bola's successful repertoire. Solano's mel-
ody echoes the well-known verses from "Sobre el llanto del caballero,"
by the sixteenth-century musician Antonio de Cabezón. Lope de Vega
popularized the verse in his play *El Caballero de Olmedo*. In the play, men
from Medina murder Don Alonso (el caballero de Olmedo) while he
travels to see his love, Inés. Don Alonso dies after hearing a field worker
sing the witch Fabia's omen:

> Que de noche le mataron
> al caballero,
> la gala de Medina,
> la flor de Olmedo
> Sombras le avisaron
> que no saliese,
> que no fuese
> el caballero,

la gala de Medina,
la flor de Olmedo. (de Vega 77)

⤝

[They killed him in the night
the lord from Medina,
the flower of Olmedo
The shadows warned him
not to leave,
not to venture out
the lord,
the gala from Medina,
the flower from Olmedo.] (Tr. Linda Howe)

Lope de Vega establishes an interplay between popular theater and medieval verse (the song was based on a real incident) to invent dramatic effect. Ultimately, Barnet transforms Solano's song to create even more intricate layers. The song represents several generations of deviations from the original medieval version, and Solano adds Lorca-influenced images (the ominous moon and enigmatic gypsies) to the medieval verses that Lope de Vega had popularized in the sixteenth century.

Onto this palimpsest Barnet affixes new layers to emphasize the intertexuality common to literary genres and poetic tradition. He invokes the already symbolically weighty Caballero de Olmedo to create a syncretic, melancholic elegy for Bola de Nieve. Phrases and words like "minstrel," "wounded by Ochosi's arrow," "ancestral song," and "ancestral voice" attest to the presence of medieval *juglares* and African ancient voices that sing *orikis*. Apostrophe to Ochosí and the descriptive elements that characterize religious ceremony and the gods (Ochún's five wash basins, the gourds, the Lord's lizard skin) underscore Bola's religious affiliations. It was rumored in some artistic circles that Bola practiced Afro-Cuban religions and that he was possibly even a *palero* (a practitioner of Palo Monte religion), although others who knew him claim that this rumor is unfounded.

The juxtaposition of *oriki,* anonymous medieval verse, and popular song places the reader in the sacred landscape of Ochosí within the poetic framework of traditional Spanish lyric. Barnet's genre bending, if you will, also underscores the cultural significance of Bola de Nieve and his success with songs like "Caballero de Olmedo" as a worldly *chanteur.*

Barnet published *Carta de noche* (1982), *Viendo mi vida pasar* (1987), *Mapa del tiempo* (1989), and other testimonial writings during that period. Poems in *Carta de noche* display Barnet's devotion to the revolution, impressions of foreign travels, dedications to writers, and interests in love compositions and Afro-Cuban religious themes. *Viendo mi vida pasar* is a compilation of poems, including previously unpublished ones. Themes comprise meditations on death, politics, and travels from China to Mexico's Chiapas region—in the willfully idiosyncratic voice of Barnet's previous poems. We sense the familiar downtrodden narrative lyricism that he initiated in *La sagrada familia,* but his standard political commitment is balanced by philosophical reflection and aesthetic drive. In *Mapa,* Barnet recapitulates topics from *Carta* and includes metapoetics and erotic motifs. Although he has written about love and erotica in the past, he beefs up the poetic style and formal features in "Con pies de gato." In an artificial realm of mad desire, Barnet conceives metaphors of fire and a hunter/lover stalking his prey:

> El viento ha quemado mi pelo
> el viento frío, arrasador
> Con pies de gato camino en lo oscuro
> Cautelosamente, como una fiera prevenida,
> me acerco a tu corazón
> El olfato y la noche son mi brújula (226)

> [My hair aflame in the wind
> the cold, devastating wind
> I walk in darkness on cat's feet
> cautiously, like a stalking wild animal
> I go for your heart
> Instinct and the night are my compass.]
> (Tr. Linda Howe)

Antithesis, simile, and symbols of seduction and passion characterize the verses. Hot wind, like fiery breath against the skin, burns the lover's hair. Cold wind that burns like icy fire produces an oxymoronic effect reflecting mixed sentiments. Longing heats up the body, while the possibility of rejection cools it off. Hot and cold also allude to lovers "on fire," who experience waves of sexual yearning. Lust expressed on the pages arouses the reader's expectations as the lover approaches the object of desire. On cat's feet, he tracks his prey, like a stalker or a wild animal snatching victims in the night.

References to rain and nature intermingle with libidinous thirst:

> Entre tú y yo se cierne sólo la lluvia
> que espejea tus brazos
> No puedes verme porque voy cubierto de árboles

Feroz, bebo de tu desnudez hasta que mis labios
se sequen o se olviden. (226)

[Between you and me, only a drizzle of rain
like a sheen on your arms
You cannot see me because I am covered by trees
Ravenous, I drink of your nakedness until my lips
become parched or forget.] (Tr. Linda Howe)

We expect a sensual climax as the hunter/lover, camouflaged by trees like an Afro-Cuban god, "drinks" the nakedness of his prey. This is Diana, Cupid, Zeus-the-swan, the sirens, and the Afro-Cuban pantheon all rolled into one syncretic sexual metaphor.

Likewise, in *Con pies de gato* (1993), "Fax" and "Memorandum XI" reflect the poet's indulgence in erotica. In *Bocetas de Haiku* (1991), Barnet experiments with haiku poetry, imitating the famous poet Basho to create facsimiles of the seventeen-syllable Japanese poems with antithetical themes. Like the avant-garde Mexican modernista Juan José Tablada's radical experimentation with Japanese haiku poetry and Apollinaire's ideogrammatic poetry (which he borrowed to infuse Latin American poetry with innovative forms), Barnet's creation of haiku is a purely formal exercise with variations on nontraditional poems of strict rhyme and syllable count.

The haikus signal Barnet's departure from conversational poetry. By the 1990s, Barnet was experimenting with a variety of topics and styles. His concern for political issues gave way to more diverse themes and styles. In Cuba, poets discovered that conversational poetry proved insufficient in form and content to fill the gap produced by the loss of Cuba's rich poetic traditions. As the Cuban critic Víctor Fowler Calzada suggests, the prerevolutionary hype for conversational and antipoetry from the 1950s, which dominated aesthetics of the 1960s, had waned by the early 1970s and 1980s ("La tercera orilla" 70–71). By the late 1980s, after the production of much mediocre literature, official policies were relaxed and restraints on cultural production were lifted. Consequently, many artists and writers began to explore an array of themes and styles.

For more than thirty years, Barnet as writer, poet, and ethnologist prudently carved out a space for his oeuvre in the conflictive and controversial history of Cuban cultural production. It is no surprise that his writings of the 1990s, such as the short story "Miosvatis" (1998) and the poem "Hijo de obrero" (1994), are critical of Cuba's socioeconomic and political problems. In the last decade of the twentieth century, Cuban cultural production was multifaceted, self-critical, and critical too of the government's treatment of disparate sectors of society (e.g., Cuban exiles, gays, blacks, religious practitioners, and independent intellectuals). Both Barnet and his contemporary Nancy Morejón are well-established writers who have no particular need to take literary pot shots at the system merely to gain literary notoriety (unlike younger and relatively unknown writers such as Zoè Valdés, who came into the international literary limelight with her first novel *La nada cotidiana;* published in France, Spain, and Germany, this text is a personal account and a brutal critique of Cuba's ramshackle state of affairs). Barnet and Morejón are seasoned writers who have overcome setbacks and scandal; they are attuned to Cuban literary trends and to the political quirks of the system.

While many young people have produced exceptional works during the Special Period, a seasoned writer like Barnet finds his own way of tweaking the prevailing styles of cultural production. His short story "Miosvatis" and his poem "Hijo de obrero" appear to be intentionally deceptive in their simplicity, but they are full of parody and irony.

The "New" Whore and the Old Sea Wall

The final lines of "Miosvatis" summarize Barnet's stinging gaze at sex tourism and other contradictory realities of contemporary Cuban society: "At that hour the Malecón [Havana's sea wall] was almost deserted. Only a tourist couple in Bermuda shorts and a sad and sickly dog, like Giacometti's, were silhouetted against the landscape" (74). Giacometti's skeletal dog and the billboard-like tourists are all that the narrator encounters in his search for the lovely and mysterious Miosvatis, whore par excellence. Barnet mockingly links prostitution and tourism to economic necessity and hunger. He portrays prevalent and "unofficial" prurient activities instigated by the government's courting of foreign tourists in search of cheap "goods."

The Italian Futurists claimed that Venice was a tawdry whore of yesteryear. Barnet's fresh prostitute (*jinetera*) lives in Old Havana, where prostitution was prevalent before the revolution—the Old Havana of Cecilia Valdés, the exploited nineteenth-century mulatto female protagonist of Cirilo Villaverde's novel *Cecilia Valdés*. Cecilia may be Miosvatis's predecessor. The modern, beautiful, and erotic Afro-Cuban female seductress could represent a remake of Cecilia, except that, after we are a few pages into the text, the author reveals that Miosvatis has

inherited the legacy of slavery and recycled historical racism and sexism. She is a victim of economic subjugation sustained by a revolution that
promised her something better. The predicament that slavery imposed
on Cecilia has worsened for Miosvatis, who, in her Cuban brothel, is a
symbol of the impoverished conditions in 1990s Havana. A synecdoche
for the physical and spiritual wasteland of contemporary Cuba, Miosvatis operates from her rundown neighborhood.

Both women are denied legitimacy, but, unlike Cecilia (whose loyalty
was divided between Spain and Cuba), Miosvatis is loyal to no one. Is
this, perhaps, a bad political in-joke; Cubans plunge into financial debt
and low moral depths? Foreign tourists seek out national "resources"
purely for carnal pleasure.

Irregular economic circumstances and the concomitant corruption
lead to rampant degradation of the poor. Barnet returns to the most
striking feature: Giacometti's sculpture of a mangy dog. We see it as a
postcard and then as a recurrent image flashing off and on in the narrative. The stick-figure dog exudes hunger and recalls Cervantes's bony
metaphors in his seventeenth-century novel about Spain's decadent fall
from political power and idealism. Is this the eternal return of Don Qui-
jote and his horse, Rocinante? What can we make of this convergence?

By design, Barnet insinuates picaresque scenes as Cuba is transformed from an archetypal socialist state into a state overwhelmed by
economic deprivation and political exhaustion in the years following
the disappearance of the Soviet Union. The narrator gives a personal account of events surrounding Miosvatis's life with ironic distance, which
recalls the pervasive irony of the picaresque tradition—emaciated but
experienced *pícaros,* like Guzmán de Alfarache, symbolic of Spain's corruption and farcical state of affairs, make a mockery of quixotic visions
and utopian settings as they swindle the guileless, the helpless, and, of
course, one another.

The female *pícaro* Miosvatis can be viewed as a hybrid form, a mestizo version of Dulcinea. Perhaps Miosvatis is just a contemporary
grifter, a female incarnation of Guzmán de Alfarache with retooled skills
and a "new" product "Made in Cuba." While she appears to be Wolfgang's dream-like princess from a distance, up close we see her in an
impoverished and haggardly world of prostitution (*jinterismo*). She is a
businesswoman who survives the economic woes of 1990s Cuba by dup-
ing foreigners, as she is "duped" by them.

The narrator's journey to bring gifts (fine perfume and an elegant
watch) for Miosvatis takes him to her residence, which is surrounded

by decomposing garbage and feces; the stench of the piled-up debris and the deteriorating environment nauseate the reader. We want to leave the poverty and filth behind to imagine the object of Wolfgang's affection, but the squalor permeates the pages of the text. You have to see, smell, and appreciate Barnet's reality. The description carries with its words an unexpungeable odor of exploitation.

There are also misunderstandings and irksome incidents. We witness lives inured to misery and one or another of the routines that are socially recognized in a marginalized and alienated world. Miosvatis's world of poverty and sex-for-sale forecloses the possibility of any ideally designated role. Skepticism abounds as her sister confuses the gift from Wolfgang with that of another man. Clearly, it is difficult to distinguish among the various suitors, since, conspicuously, there is a steady stream of men and presents.

To add to the squalid atmosphere, there is an old woman who lives downstairs. A counterpoint to the sisters, who are the "new" capitalists, she is a decrepit harpy, a gossip, and an envious bag of bones who spies on Miosvatis and her sister. As the narrator learns, she never passes up an opportunity to criticize their behavior to anyone who will listen. The neighbor's resemblance to members of the neighborhood Committees for the Defense of the Revolution, who were responsible for ferreting out antirevolutionary activities, is uncanny. In the 1990s, some of these official organizations decayed into centers of gossip, bribery, and revenge, since making illegal deals was part of daily life in every neighborhood. As in the case of the old woman, during the Special Period, many committee members preferred to look for possible bribes or lucrative business transactions than to spy for the revolution.

The old woman's presence and the narrator's visit to Miosvatis's apartment are pretexts for throwing the reader into the seedy and equivocal world of social and political decline. We view the current state of affairs within a surreal world encircled by the ominous Malecón (often facetiously referred to as the "Wall of Berlin" on the streets of Havana). Although there is nothing apparently surrealistic about the narrative in "Miosvatis," Barnet's anecdote refers to the surreal framework of a repugnant and bizarre yet real world "out there" beyond the pages. Barnet barely scratches the surface of Havana's 1990s underworld parade of disease-wracked entrepreneurs and clients of the sex trade.

The closest the reader actually comes to a surreal moment in the text is the eternal return of the dog. Barnet has the tattered dog leap from a postcard to the Malecón at the narrative's end. Such an image recalls

Buñuel and Dalí's famous short film *The Andalusian Dog*. In both the surrealist film and the modern short story, the suggestive canine facsimile
disconcerts the reader; we are unable to fathom the philosophical and
intellectual predicaments of both works. We are haunted by the de-
nominator of the common dog, which remains hidden on the surface and
leaves tooth marks on our subconscious.

For Buñuel and Dalí, religious angst illustrated by the disorder of
things and by sacrilegious imagery manifested themselves in chaotic
subconscious barking and sexual desires. Barnet's fleshless carcass of the
wiry dog circles the narrative relentlessly like a greyhound at the dog
track. The quirky recurring image of the dog connotes both the act of
writing and the Cuban condition. Writing is always an act of repetition
and a willful go-around with a persistent debt to tradition. It implies a
circular act insofar as it ultimately refers to itself and to the process of
creating literature.

Likewise, the persistent go-around and the chase of the decoy to the
point of exhaustion are literary leitmotifs and symbols of Cuban society's contradictions. With regard to writing, the story and the metaphors
repeat themselves like a literary tradition. As for society, the canine's
hunger and Miosvatis's prostitution repeat themselves as revolutionary
Cuba suffers a reversal in terms of rules and principles. Socialist discipline and virtues are abandoned, except for regard for money, which,
once again, makes the hustler and the prostitute the privileged sector of
society.

Both the casual references to Giacometti's dog and Miosvatis's haunting destitution intimate a sort of national stream of consciousness, a collective madness. The narrative hints at what actually goes on between
the lines of the text, behind official battle lines, and on the back streets
in Cuba. With regard to writing, representation has that intermittent
erasure-like effect and never gets at the thing it purports to represent.
With regard to politics, the Cuban people, who "support" the continued revolution, fight a clandestine economic cold war with the government. Cuban people receive low wages, but the economy demands
a high cost of living, forcing Cubans to resort to the black market.
As the value of incomes falls and government subsidies diminish, the
flourishing black market stands for widespread economic rebellion.
However, this story is about not just economic crisis and social decay but
also the messy nexus of living and surviving, surrounded by tempting
commodities for sale. We surmise that, as night falls, Havana is a constant circus parade of hustlers, pimps, whores, and tourists.

Fantasies and extravagant and risky behavior reign and turn into chaos. We suspect a hardening of the souls like Miosvatis, who collide, and turn numerous tricks, with countless tourists. The machinations they must go through to earn dollars replace the possibility of altruistic relationships and romantic love. Everything is permissible. Such behavior would be unthinkable in an ascetic revolutionary society of sacrifice and utopian dreams.

"Hijo de obrero": The Diseased Body Politic

Whereas the poetic voice in the early poems of *La sagrada familia* passionately condemns bourgeois family values and alludes to significant revolutionary changes, in both "Miosvatis" and "Hijo de obrero" Barnet's voice is subtle and detached. These are not conspicuously emotive pieces but carefully crafted portrayals of downtrodden souls and bodies for sale.

In "Hijo de obrero," Barnet's irony and subterfuge stand for metacriticism of the official restrictions on cultural production that limit any emotional response to the adverse consequences of prostitution and AIDS. The poetic speaker describes a young man who, with lugubrious sensuality, prostitutes himself in exchange for commercial goods, inadvertently contracts AIDS, and dies. We enter a young hustler's world and realize that his utilitarian state of mind is divorced from any notion of revolutionary ideals. His actions represent the plunge of the Cuban spirit into the depths of national despondency:[6]

> Hijo de obrero,
> trabajaba en ocasiones como auxiliar de cocina
> en hoteles de lujo.
>
> Usaba para su trabajo ropa corriente,
> Sus manos gruesas y jóvenes mostraban
> algunos signos delatores
> y sus ojos no sostenían la mirada hacía ningún punto.
> Caída la noche del sábado,
> le entraban deseos de una extraña voluptuosidad
> mezcladas a un sentimiento que él sabía mezquino.
> Todo lo que durante la semana había visto
> en las tiendas de moneda convertible
> se volvía una obsesión: un blue jeans de etiqueta tejana,
> unas gafitas redondas,
> una camisa de seda
> que jamás se exhibía en vitrinas.

Para lograrlo vendía su cuerpo al primer postor,
sin distinción de sexo, desde luego,
Lo importante era la pieza, la quimera soñada,
el blue jean
Como Kavafis, me pregunto si en los tiempos antiguos
poseyó Alejandría un joven más bello,
más perfecto que él.
Arrojado al olvido acabó penosamente
devorado por una enfermedad
que fue el azote del siglo.
Lo recuerdo en una calle de La Habana
preguntando la hora
a un reloj asesino (*When Night Is Darkest* 118)

⤚

[He was the son of a laborer
and worked now and then as kitchen help
in luxury hotels.

He wore ordinary clothes to work,
his thick young hands showed
telling signs
and his eyes could not stay focused on one thing for long.
When night fell on Saturdays,
he would be overcome by strangely voluptuous desires
mixed with a feeling he knew was sorry.
The things he'd seen all week
in the stores where only tourists could shop
became an obsession: blue jeans made with Texas labels,
small round sunglasses, a silk shirt,
the kind you never see on the streets.
To get these items he would sell his body to the highest bidder,
and soon he didn't care which sex,
because all that mattered was the hotel room, his dreams,
the new clothes.
Like Cavafy I ask my self if there was ever
a boy so beautiful or perfect
in Alexandria in ancient times.
There were no statues of him, no oil paintings, not even
a tacky photograph,
and he was cast into oblivion, devoured
slowly by a disease
that was the scourge of the century.
I remember him on a street in Havana
checking the time
on a killer watch. (*When Night Is Darkest* 119)

The nameless boy's erotic adventures turn into mock pleasure, but the verses lead to disease and death. Barnet's wit and acerbic comments on prostitution and AIDS in the Special Period are especially poignant since he makes intertextual reference to C. P. Cavafy's poetry. A particularly transparent mirroring of Cavafy's "Days of 1909, '10, and '11," the poem is coded in hedonism and homoeroticism. However, Barnet focuses not only on personal indulgence and economic exploitation but also on the politics of gay expression. His use of Cavafy's thematic as a source for his poem can be viewed as a ploy to criticize official limits on aesthetics or, at the very least, to emphasize "prohibited" themes. Cavafy's and Barnet's poems share themes and metaphors, but Barnet departs from homoerotic musings to depict the problematic consequences of the selling of young beautiful bodies to tourists in the Cuba of the 1990s. Barnet ameliorates the explicit contemplation of male beauty and portrayal of homoerotic desires because he has chosen one of Cavafy's somber poems about exploitation:

> He was the son of a harassed, poverty-stricken sailor
> (from an island in the Aegean Sea).
> He worked for a blacksmith: his clothes shabby,
> his workshoes miserably torn,
> his hands filthy with rust and oil.
>
> In the evenings, after the shop closed,
> if there was something he longed for especially,
> a fairly expensive tie,
> a tie for Sunday,
> or if he saw and coveted
> a beautiful blue shirt in some store window,
> he'd sell his body for a dollar or two.
>
> I asked myself if the glorious Alexandria
> of ancient times could boast of a boy
> more exquisite, more perfect—lost though he was:
> that is, we don't have a statue or a painting of him;
> thrust into that awful blacksmith's shop,
> overworked, tormented, given to cheap debauchery,
> he was soon used up. (161)

Cavafy laments that a good-looking working-class boy and a son of a sailor is "wasting away" at hard labor in a blacksmith's shop and at cheap peddling of his body on the streets. While Cavafy presents an individual response to working-class conditions, Barnet's antihero represents a younger generation of Cubans whose parents and grand-parents, like Che, dedicated their lives to the revolution and, later, to the Castro government. The alienated children of the Special Period experience quite a different Cuba. Although their responses vary, some take a sinister crash course in economic survival and get lost in a world of black marketeering and prostitution.

In the beginning lines of his poem, Barnet juxtaposes incongruous images of the proletarian son with words like "luxury hotel" and "kitchen help." The young man's sumptuous workplace overshadows his coarse appearance. His "telling signs" and blank stare betray a dead-end job, indifference to the revolution's ideal work ethic, and a disbelief in a better future. The pathetic condition of some Cubans who become impoverished and are treated like second-class citizens in their own society offers a stark contrast with the luxurious and privileged world of tourism. The young man window-shops for superficial things he cannot afford. The evocation of vulgar ambition against a background of official rhetoric about the "pioneers" who unconditionally sacrifice (without material gain) to make a better society is probably meant to shock. Pimping for material goods and practicing idolatry of mass consumption generates pathological pride.

Barnet's allusion to male beauty going to waste on hard labor and pimping also recalls Cavafy's "In the Street." Here, we sense the anxiety of influence as Barnet layers his own poem with various characteristics of Cavafy's. Barnet's unfocused boy recalls Cavafy's young man with chestnut eyes who looks "dazed" as he wanders to solicit sex: "he drifts aimlessly down the street, / as though still hypnotized by the illicit pleasure, / the very illicit pleasure that has just been his" (67).

Likewise, in "Passing Through," Cavafy combines innocence and sexual desire to depict a young man who "stays out all night" to have sexual encounters:

> The things he timidly imagined as a schoolboy
> Are openly revealed now. And he wanders around,
> Stays out all night, gets involved. And as is right (for our kind of art)
> his blood—fresh and hot—
> is relished by sensual pleasure. His body is overcome
> by forbidden erotic ecstasy; and his limbs
> give in to completely. . . . (70)

Barnet converts Cavafy's figures into an original composite of a young man whose lost innocence and forbidden fantasies lead him to prostitute himself to "clients of either sex." The young man's strange voluptuousness and penurious sentiment bring to mind kinky sex for trade. The worker's son "resolves" his parsimonious conditions by responding to the clients' sumptuous sexual appetite. In a sacrilegious gesture of sacrifice, the man gives of his flesh (libidinous favors) in exchange for commodities.

Sinister craving for goods leads to avarice, and debasement triggers erotic and willfully obscene behavior. In the early 1990s, coveted commercial goods (e.g., blue jeans, silk shirts, and sunglasses) were not available in state stores. However, they were displayed in hotels and in diplomats' stores for foreigners. In Barnet's world, the double monetary system of dollars and pesos reduces the worker's real worth; his "son" degenerates into a sexual parody of his father's revolution. The older generation of Che's self-sacrificing "new man" fades into the background. Rather, we are presented with an antihero, who thinks only of self-satisfaction and who uses his fine-looking body to attain it. Understatement, euphemistic language, and a poised gaze at the youth's body suggest the sexual act: "Like Cavafy I ask my self if there was ever / a boy so beautiful or perfect / in Alexandria in ancient times."

In the end, neglect and deprivation transform the boy's statuesque beauty into a disease-wracked apparition. Sadly, unlike the statues of the ancient world that project beauty in the most pristine form, the young man leaves no trace of his former beauty. Both Cavafy and Barnet's poetic speakers lament that no statue, no painting, nor even a vulgar photograph of their beautiful young men remains. We sense a contrast to the negligence of the forgotten working sons in Cavafy's "Tomb of Evrion," which describes an ornately designed tomb, symbol and monument to a handsome and noble youth's attractiveness:

> In this tomb—ornately designed,
> The whole of syenite stone,
> Covered by so many violets, so many lilies—
> Lies handsome Evrion,
> . . . .
> But we've lost what was really precious: his form—
> like a vision of Apollo (50)

Also, in "Orophernis" a four-drachma coin serves as a frivolous tribute to a handsome boy's "young charm" and as a "sensuous commemoration" of his loveliness:

> his body perfumed with oil of jasmine,
> he was the most handsome, the most perfect
> of Ionia's handsome young men

. . . .
His end must have been recorded somewhere only to be lost:
Or maybe history passed over it
And rightly didn't bother to notice
A thing so trivial. (60)

In his poetry Cavafy also emphasizes the classical Greek contemplation of the perfect male body. In "Pictured" the male gaze on a young
boy's splendor epitomizes the homoerotic spirit of ancient Greece:

In this picture, I'm gazing at a handsome boy
Who is lying down close to a spring,
Exhausted from running.
What a handsome boy: what a heavenly noon. (59)

Although the reference to Cavafy's musings emphasizes sexual
yearnings, Barnet redefines the seductive gaze. His focus resembles that
of a documentary. Barnet pans the youth's hustling on a street corner to
make social commentary and to link deadly sexual disease to sexual
peddling. The stark reference to the devastation of AIDS is in contrast
to Cavafy's sensual evocation of open pleasure. In "Hijo," the perfect
male body is "tossed away and erased." The man is "devoured" by a disease that was "the scourge of the century." The contemplative pause
and suspended gaze are devoid of self-indulgent sexual connotations.
Rather, the emphasis is on the "wasting away." Barnet distorts the elegy
for those who made an ultimate "sacrifice" for the Cuban revolution. The
poem ends with meditation on a discarded and forgotten pariah who
peddled sex: "I remember him on a street in Havana / checking the
time / on a killer watch."

With synecdoche and metonymy, Barnet cleverly gives us the part for
the whole. He places the blame for youth's death on the watch. The reference to the assassin-watch can be read in various manners, none of
which is an exclusive interpretation: the watch (1) reveals the method
that Cuban hustlers use to make contact with foreigners, asking them
the time of day; (2) stands for the presence of the client (tourist) and, by
extension, for capitalist encroachment of Cuba; (3) emphasizes the
transmission of AIDS from the client to the exploited "pure" Cuban
body; (4) superimposes the metaphor of death and illness on the Cuban condition. It can also be read as a fairly traditional memento mori;
that is, as a reminder that even youth is subject to time, which kills us all.
Youth and beauty are frighteningly mortal. The complex series of synec-
doches and metaphors produces a multilayered paradoxical effect.

Perhaps Barnet also poignantly foregrounds AIDS as a killer virus. For years, Cuban officials proudly issued statistics that suggested a low number of AIDS cases on the island. At some point, people become aware of that which official propaganda had tried to obscure. Officials did not provide systematic protection from socially transmitted diseases to prostitutes and to the general population during the apogee of prostitution in the early to mid-1990s. By the mid-1990s, there was rampant prostitution in Cuba, yet condoms were not readily available. On the street, Cuban prostitutes were known to provide unprotected sex for little money, or for a few extra dollars. Officials required HIV-positive patients to remain quarantined in hospitals (for example, at Los Cocos) as a preventive measure to avoid contamination of the general population. "Hijo del obrero" accentuates a contradiction: thousands of foreign tourists who had sexual contact with Cubans were never tested for AIDS upon entry into Cuba. Perhaps the reference to illness and crisis unveils the catastrophic consequences for the Cuban economy and society after the collapse of idealism and the moral downturn. Barnet's portrayal of the young man's predicament discloses the Cuban condition as "afflicted." Since AIDS eventually reduces one's immune system to nil, and the patient eventually dies of AIDS-related complications, Barnet has set the stage for incessant national suffering and, perhaps, for the death of a system. And, if the young man is the embodiment of younger generations of Cubans who are prostituting themselves at risk, there are "ailing" bodies everywhere, like a multivehicle pileup on the postrevolutionary turnpike.

Despondently, in "VIII" (1993), Barnet alludes to the metaphor of illness to describe his attachment to Cuba in spite of the nation's plight:

> No me cures de la tristeza Señor,
> déjame disfrutar este paisaje
> como un convaleciente disfruta
> los restos de su enfermedad
> (*Con pies de gato* 334)

> [Don't cure my sorrow Lord,
> allow me to take pleasure in this landscape
> like a convalescent enjoys
> the remnants of his affliction]
> (Tr. Linda Howe)

The poetic speaker prefers to wallow in sadness and to savor his malady. Poetic disconsolation used to express a nation's sentiment recalls

José María Heredia's neoclassical "Niágara" and Martí's romantic "Dos patrias." In both poems, idealistic views of nationhood are expressed through metaphors of pain and suffering. Martí's insistence on sorrow as patriotic sense of duty is an essential element of the Cuban condition.

Is Barnet's disheveled and derelict "Hijo de obrero" the powerful and mocking antithesis of Korda's photographic martyrology of Che as iconic revolutionary hero? As the protégé of diaphanous sexual fantasy adorned with Tommy Hilfiger-like "rags" and Ray Ban sunglasses, the boy is a sadly diminished figure in a buyer's sex market. With a sense of alienation and the motif of a deadly disease, Barnet ponders collective behavior that reflects cultural alienation and economic strife.

The poignant anecdote attests to his outspokenness in response to the social dilemmas posed by the Special Period. Many intellectuals have taken advantage of the crisis to delineate the negative social ramifications of the collapse of the Soviet Union. They have settled accounts with the Cuban government over its imposition of aesthetic limits and censorship. Perhaps Barnet resorted to exogenous poetry (Cavafy's aesthetics and poetic images reflect a voluntarily prosaic poetry explicitly depicting homosexual desire) to comment on the restrictions on culture and to insert outlawed controversial themes into his repertoire.

As a final note, Barnet's implicit use of Cavafy's homoerotica would have been considered antirevolutionary or decadent aesthetics in the Cuban literature of the 1960s and 1970s. Cuban writers had already witnessed how Lezama Lima's infamous "gay" chapter 8 in *Paradiso* (1966) caused a scandal after officials finally discovered that the text contained homoerotic themes and condemned it to oblivion. Apparently, the censors had been baffled by Lezama's neobaroque style and obscure metaphors a la Góngora and were unable to detect the homosexual allusions. The official banning of Lezama's work confirmed the institutionalized repression of "gay" and "decadent" themes.

Within the range of multiple meanings, Barnet's writing can be viewed as his manner of positioning himself within the parameters of a precarious and competitive Cuban cultural milieu. As the revolution became more institutionalized and officials clarified the guidelines for cultural production, Barnet adjusted his aesthetics through distinct historical periods, but he also was innovative in style and pushed the envelope with regard to controversial thematics. He produced his works during sometime hostile phases of Cuban cultural production.

He aestheticizes Afro-Cuban religious components that, in reality,

are incompatible with communist thought and official political policies. His essays and testimonial writing reveal his attempt to justify his
role as a writer. He gives voice to the heretofore underrepresented
masses, particularly the "black voice." His attempt to represent Afro-
Cuban religious ceremonies in order to preserve them recalls the filmmaker Sara Gómez's effort to emphasize the "Afro" in Cuban culture.
In her documentaries and her full-length feature film, she takes inventory of Afro-Cuban religious experiences that the Castro government claims have "disappeared." Both Barnet's and Gómez's works
underscore how "esoteric subcultures" get in the way of "official" history. The "popular" components of culture prove to be lasting in the face
of authorities' attempt to obliterate them; the stubborn heterogeneous
elements of the culture persistently impose themselves and challenge
"nation-building" projects.

Barnet may have felt the strain of microfactional "black" politics and
responded by conforming to a more palatable version of black expression. He echoes the writings of the Afro-Cuban writers Alberto Pedro
and Rogelio Martínez Furé, who moderated their political "separatism"
after falling out with officials; their writings focus on "folkloric" aspects
of Afro-Cuban culture or on rhetoric that favors Afro-Cuban integration
into revolutionary politics. Barnet limited his research on Afro-Cubans
to "discovering" the roots of Cuban culture in Afro-Cuban iconography.
While black writers sought to fold Afro-Cuban studies into national
rhetoric, Barnet attempted to integrate Afro-Cuban imagery into "materialist" ethnology. On the other hand, he contends with otherness and
disputes official efforts to achieve "sameness" by insisting on the existence of an Afro-Cuban culture. Whether he accomplishes this is beside
the point. Underlying tension always exists between "real" Afro-Cuban
society and official control and representation of it. Officialdom has
always been wary of various aspects of Afro-Cuban society.

On another level, Barnet's creation of "Afro-Cuban" voices to connect with the roots of Cuban culture forms a counterpoint to his bourgeois upbringing and prior lack of interest in Cuba's national culture
and peoples. His testimonial work on Montejo and his generally self-
dramatizing "black" and revolutionary poetry may have alleviated his
common bourgeois sense of guilt, shared by many Cuban writers and
artists after the revolution. Often, Barnet has commented on this transformation. At any rate, his persistent attention to Afro-Cuban issues
and his aestheticization of Afro-Cuban culture in his literary works
are unquestionable. Moreover, as the founder and director of the

Fernando Ortiz Foundation for more than a decade, he has persistently promoted scholarly studies and published works on Cuba's multicultural and racial components.

Barnet's literature reflects a personal vision of the social, political, and cultural changes that took place after the 1959 revolution. He has not only differentiated himself from the previous generation of poets and writers but also searched for ways to express Cuba's radically changing circumstances. He has discovered new meaning for "subcultures" and created unique imagery. An overview of his writings verifies that he offers no resolutions to racial or religious issues or to sexual politics. In fact, his representations of cultural otherness muddle racial questions and sexual/textual theories, and he fails to wrap anything up neatly.

Nevertheless, his talent lies in the ability to tap into several genres and literary traditions to aesthetically "harmonize" ostensibly incongruent elements. His cross between ethnology and fiction may oblige the reader to analyze the degree of fictionalization in the works, but this does not detract from the works' artistic proficiency. The writer reveals partial pseudoworlds, and his characters respond to sociohistorical circumstances and imaginary representations of parts of Cuban society. He positions himself inside and outside his characters' subconscious; he exposes problems in situ with a combination of ethnography, sociology, and fantasy.

Barnet's hesitancy or inability to publish other "gay" works may suggest the precarious nature of independent expression in a highly politicized cultural milieu. Despite the hype over Cuba's new-found freedom of expression, resulting from economic crisis and the influx of tourism, and the production of works like the movie *Fresa y chocolate*, a combination of "gay stigma," self-censorship, and official limits in the face of multifarious and incendiary expression continue to set the boundaries for artists' and writers' cultural production.

Barnet's intertextual reference to Cavafy's work does not so much push the envelope for "gay" writing in Cuba as much as it underscores the relationship between foreign tourism and the AIDS epidemic in Cuba. At any rate, "Hijo de obrero" and "Miosvatis" are representative of Cuban cultural production of the 1990s Special Period. Foreboding, sarcastic, and satirical, they are unique precisely because they convey abrupt change and spare no hideous detail. Like historical and cultural artifacts, they encode the marginal societies and circumstances that surface and proliferate in the urban scene of post-Soviet Cuba.

Likewise, representing "lo cubano" is a volatile and unrealizable goal. Barnet's attempt to do so locates his writing in the Latin American literary tradition. Traditionally, Latin American writers have attempted to resolve political and historical conflicts and problems of representation through the myth of writing (González Echevarría, *Myth and Archive*). For example, the controversy in political and intellectual circles over the veracity of Rigoberta Menchu's testimonial (as fictitious as it is real) is actually not a recent debate on testimonial writing or on the literary representation of the autochthonous. The literary critics Roberto González Echevarría, Seymour Menton, William Luis, Elzbieta Sklodowska, and Miriam DeCosta-Willis have questioned the goal of Barnet's literary representation and manipulation of materials to create voices "without history." His multiple voices are constructs within political, historical, and ideological confines that he has maneuvered and constructed for his own ends. His poetic representations suffer a similar fate insofar as they both fictionalize and distort composites of real people and actual lived practices. In the end, Barnet has remained afloat in a highly incendiary cultural sea of aesthetic debates and politicized expression. His assembled writings may have been sufficiently complex for him to avoid the official demands to produce exclusively politically committed literature and, paradoxically, sufficiently political for him to intersect with "new" literary trends produced after the revolution of 1959.

Conclusion

After the tumultuous 1959 revolution Cuba was transformed into a socialist state and a liberating force, paying a high price for its economic independence from the United States. It became the model for self-determination in the developing world; the revolution paved the way for a rush of leftist uprisings and for political strife between autocratic regimes and guerrillas all over Latin America and Africa.

The year 1990 marked another historical moment of extraordinary change on the island. The dissolution of the Soviet Union brought on Cuba's so-called Special Period of economic hardship; the government implemented severe domestic restrictions and sought out joint business ventures and foreign tourism to stave off the system's collapse. Revolutionary rhetoric was on the back burner for most Cubans, who waited in long lines for increasingly fewer rationed products. Surrounded by billboards that attested to the ordinary citizen's revolutionary zeal to overcome hard times, Cubans prevailed, albeit haphazardly.

Both the 1959 milestone and the 1990 maelstrom brought to the fore political leaders, artists, and writers who expressed exhilaration over the former and shock and dismay over the latter. Official efforts to sustain socialism's supremacy through cultural media vacillated between the initial promotion of myriad forms and aesthetics and purges and censorship that stifled dissent of many kinds to the distracted and tempered response to the explosive artistic output of the 1990s. Most writers and artists went beyond worn-out revolutionary themes to reflect on past mistakes and to criticize the Cuban government's contradictory economic and political policies during the Special Period.

Understanding Cuban art and writing since the 1990s is impossible without a retrospective view of how officials, writers, and artists have shaped culture since the revolution. Officials implemented measures to unify intellectuals, to raise their level of political consciousness, and to encourage work that reflected the everyday life and struggles of the people. Revolutionary iconography and socialist realism became part of Cuba's cultural lexicon; art ought to reflect the reality of change, the mythification of revolutionary heroes and guerrilla victories, and the magnificence of socialism. If the 1960s are remembered essentially for the marriage between art and politics, in fact the institutionalized romance calcified aesthetic standards. That fact that officials placed restrictions on much artistic output was ignored in Cuba until recently.

In the widespread revolutionary climate that lasted from the late 1960s into the late 1980s, professional advancement in the cultural realm was based more on adherence to the official aesthetic than on the quality of the work. Some cultural officials, suspicious of and hostile toward foreign (especially U.S.-influenced) cultures and bourgeois art, espoused revolutionary art that was "authentically" Cuban. They rejected art influenced by European modernism and by capitalist notions of commercialization and marketing as self-indulgent and thoroughly antirevolutionary.

The official institutionalization of culture was stifling to independent cultural production. One can only imagine an alternative history of Cuban culture without this autonomous artistic impulse. Cultural bureaucrats offered unprecedented support for literature, the visual and performance arts, and the theater, while stigmatizing independent publishers, noncommunist intellectual cliques, gays, and "militant" blacks. Gradually, after the initial deluge of creative forces unleashed by the revolution subsided, an atmosphere of censorship, intrigue, paranoia, and purges prevailed. The overriding message was that intellectuals had a moral obligation to the revolutionary cause and therefore should neither engage in divisive politics nor create works without significant political content within the revolution. In some cases, opportunistic individuals took note of the political shifts and set about eliminating rivals. Several mediocre writers and artists thrived by spouting revolutionary rhetoric. Likewise, cultural officials gained power through the promotion of prorevolutionary themes and iconography. Clashes broke out between those who supported the cultural policies and those who did not or were simply too radical and independent to conform.

Iconoclastic intellectuals responded, with varying consequences. Some writers and artists remained outside the inner circle of the politically committed intelligentsia. They eventually either conformed, disappeared from the scene of production, or left the country. The creation of the infamous UMAP camps for "antirevolutionary misfits" and institutional purges tainted the image of an open and utopian revolutionary society. Official suppression of Afro-Cuban gatherings and black expression also called into question the revolution's righteous path. The Cuban government did not tolerate what it perceived to be the "divisive" politics of a group of Afro-Cuban intellectuals and activists who it feared would promote ideas critical of the Cuban government's treatment of blacks. Several Afro-Cubans adjusted their politics to comply with the revolution. Officially, the rhetoric of the Black Power movement was valuable for its criticism of U.S. capitalism, racism, and imperialism, but such criticism was not to be directed toward internal racial politics in Cuba.

Similarly, young or otherwise uninitiated writers and artists found it difficult to avoid adhering to the imposed cultural policies if they hoped to produce work and have it acknowledged by revolutionary officials and presented to the public. The poet Nancy Morejón and the ethnographer/writer Miguel Barnet, like so many budding artists of the 1960s, were caught in the ideological crossfire at the beginning of their careers, but, later, they became adept players of cultural politics. By the time they were seasoned intellectuals, in their fifties, both had received Cuba's National Prize for Literature: Barnet in 1994, Morejón in 2001. I have analyzed the works of Barnet and Morejón within the context of the Cuban revolution in an attempt to understand the somewhat radical changes that occurred in their aesthetics. In the case of writings about Afro-Cubans, Morejón and Barnet danced around the more controversial racial politics, while emphasizing previously neglected aspects of Afro-Cuban culture and society.

In hindsight, perhaps, Barnet, Morejón, several Afro-Cuban intellectuals, and other iconoclastic individuals in the arts scene were apt to believe that their initial inexperience had prevented them from understanding the significance of appropriate intellectual output on the revolution. Eventually, those who wanted to produce within the system would have to resign themselves to the necessity of politics rather than self-determination and creativity. What choice did many young people have if they were to remain in Cuba and wished to become an integral part of the culture? They succumbed to the prevalent aesthetic and carved a niche for their own personalized articulations of Cuban culture.

The debates about aesthetics, cultural politics, and Afro-Cuban expression came to a head around the closing of El Puente, the private publishing house, and the cultural isolation of the loosely knit group of young intellectuals whose works had been published by that press. This period, from the mid- to late 1960s, not only signaled an end to semi-independent publications but also ignited controversies between some officials and Afro-Cuban intellectuals, which led to the stifling of black political and cultural expression. Out of fear that the Black Power movement might incite national and political divisiveness, some officials prevented Afro-Cubans from practicing radical black politics in Cuba. Barnet's and Morejón's works are intrinsically linked to the controversies over Afro-Cuban politics and artistic expression. The government reacted negatively and stifled local Afro-Cuban gatherings and works by and about Afro-Cubans. Influenced by the writings of Malcolm X, the influx of Black Panther Party members into Cuba, and the internationalism of the Black Power movement, Afro-Cubans were inspired to participate and to analyze race relations in Cuba. If and when they did produce works, they were subdued versions of black political consciousness that deferred to prorevolutionary or Marxist-oriented ideology. A good example is Pedro Serviat's *El problema negro en Cuba y su solución definitiva* (The definitive solution to the black problem in Cuba), published in the 1960s. According to Serviat, communism and not radical black politics would purge Cuban society of the capitalist-induced ills that had produced racism in the first place.

Given that Morejón and Barnet personally experienced the government's encroachment on independent publishing, I have scrutinized events surrounding the 1965 closing of El Puente. The demise of El Puente confirmed what the closing of the literary supplement *Lunes de Revolución* had already implied: a definitive end to semi-independent presses and aesthetic freedom. The purging of El Puente alerted a whole generation of young Cuban intellectuals to the need to heed the imposed standards of revolutionary aesthetics and politics.

Ostensibly, Morejón and Barnet understood the message and made aesthetic adjustments; yet both insisted on writing about black themes in spite of the tensions between Afro-Cuban intellectuals and officials. Although the Cuban government appropriated the anti-"Yanquism" of the radicalized U.S. blacks, it discouraged individual manifestations of Black Power. As a black woman, Morejón also downplayed politics that would incite censorship. Although her initial work was in a purely symbolist style, later she used her talents to rewrite the role of black women in Cuban history. In her works, Morejón examines culture and identity in Cuba and emphasizes the significance of the Afro-Cuban community throughout Cuban history. Her later works demonstrate a return to pure aesthetics and a dedication to social commitment, with a minor alteration: they focus criticism on Cuba's current situation.

Barnet's discursive sites for blacks in his ethnology and poetry reveal his desire to rewrite Cuban historiography. Since he became an entrenched cultural and political figure in Castro's Cuba, his notions of Afro-Cuban identity, while shedding new light on black issues, also may have inadvertently neutralized the radical politics of the black intellectual voice of the 1960s.

Barnet's and Morejón's artistic and political skills are undeniable. As they became well-known intellectuals, they offered palatable forms of official politics and aesthetics but also promoted their own modest agendas to promote black Afro-Cuban culture. Thus, they were able to express some critical notions about the social, political, and cultural milieu of the revolution. Throughout their careers, their contradictory positioning with regard to politics and writing attests to how they brought their own idealism to terms with the hard realities of Cuban cultural politics. They produced poems, stories, and essays that take into account the heterogeneity of Cuban culture and society during exceptionally tumultuous and impassioned times. Some of their fiction and poetry of the 1990s critically reflects on the "decadence" of the revolution and the social and moral decay of postrevolutionary Cuban society.

Perhaps, through an impressionistic lens of literature, theater, painting, dance, and the diverse manifestations of Afro-Cuban culture, one can begin to understand the complex and paradoxical interrelations among heterogeneous expression, prolific production, and official control. Official institutionalization of cultural production caused ideological struggles and factionalism among party members, officials, and independent writers and artists. Intellectuals and officials battled over what should be the appropriate aesthetic and ethical standards for cultural production. Myriad social, historical, political, and artistic threads created a loosely defined Cuban cultural fabric that endures. This culture is shaped by conflictive phases of contemporary Cuban history and policies and by the differing responses of artists and writers to the official requirements of aesthetics and politics.

The conflictive denouement for Cuba's ideal notions of autochthonous national expression, stripped of exogenous influences, reached its culmination in the post-Soviet phase of Cuban history. From the late 1980s into the 2000s, artistic production provides a tableau of disillusionment with heroics, stoicism in the face of hardship, and scrutiny of the revolution's wane. Artists' and writers' willingness to maneuver under such difficult circumstances ought to make us aware of the political content of their works. Differing approaches include backward glances and decade-long flashbacks tinged with revolutionary fervor. Appalled by Cuba's noblesse oblige to embrace world markets and to receive venture capitalism—which created joint business ventures, corrupted Cuban bureaucrats, and fostered rampant black marketeering, prostitution, and hustling—artists also were fascinated by the paradoxes inherent in Cuba's dilemma. With humor and poignant reflection, they depicted the social and moral decline spawned by economic hardship and uneven distribution of new wealth in a socialist society.

The works of the 1990s and the early 2000s show both continuity with past intellectual output and innovation. As the "Che" poems of the 1960s and 1970s converted the guerrilla into a symbol of revolutionary vision and myth, so the caustic vision of self-deprecating but determined characters in such works as Raúl Martín's staging of Virgilio Piñera's play *Los Siervos* and Marianela Boan's dance piece *Blanche* set the tone and ingredients of art after the collapse of the Soviet Union. The 1990s brought on the "bad" writing of Zoé Valdés; the more "poetic" works of Abilio Estévez and Ena Lucía Portola; Olympya's paintings that depict the paradoxical underworlds of socialist Havana seething with the previously banned religious practices of Santería and concealed sexuality; and Cuban art's playful mockery of former utopian dreams and dollar-driven morality. Psychological despair, the bitterness of disillusionment, and the deluge of painful reflections heralded new cultural production in an atmosphere of Special-Period angst. All Cuban reality confirmed it: a relentless depression and economic woes, in spite of great efforts and sacrifice on the part of the Cubans.

This wobbly revolution could not sustain the status quo; nor could its artists and writers soldier on, propping up the system with standard revolutionary zeal. The former creators of the socialist utopia combined energies and scarce resources to transform culture and to keep their own subsistent lives afloat. Their image of antihero emerged and projected incongruous images on the revolutionary mind's eye: the emblematic new organic entrepreneurs were procapitalist taxi drivers, hotel personnel, black-market hustlers, prostitutes, and globe-trotting artists and writers who sold their wares abroad.

The fate of Cuban culture and the feat of Cuban culture are to produce work that expresses the Cuban condition in all its glory, defeat, and contradictions. Cuban writers and artists faithful to their trade continue to do just that.

Notes

Bibliography

Index

Notes

Introduction

1. I elaborate on Santamaría's contributions to the development of Cuban culture in "Haydee Santamaría."

Chapter 1. Art in Revolutionary Cuba

1. González explains that Cuban critics now call these years of official repression, particularly from 1970 to 1976, "the gray years," a period that also coincided with the formation of the Ministry of Culture (18). The closing of El Puente and the opening of the UMAP camps presaged the purges of the 1970s. They mark the beginning of the official marginalization of gays, hippies, and other nonconformists.

2. Both Seymour Menton and Hugh Thomas have documented three decades of Cuban cultural and social history after the 1959 revolution.

3. The 26 of July Movement began when Castro met with friends and fellow conspirators in Havana on 19 July 1963, just before the planned attack on Moncada that occurred on 26 July (Thomas, *Cuba* 867). The group consisted of Haydée Santamaría, Pedro Miret, Lester Rodríguez, Vilma Espín, Frank País, Armando Hart, and Carlos Franquí, among others (867–68).

4. According to Blight and Welch, the Kennedy administration flaunted the Alliance for Progress as "a plan for the reconstruction of Latin America," while Cuban officials perceived it to be "nothing more than bribery money with which to keep poor Latin American countries anti-communist and [thus] anti-Cuban" (147). Likewise, Cubans viewed the OAS as an aggressive organization that attempted to isolate Cuba from the rest of the world.

5. Julian Schnabel tacks some scenes from *P.M.* onto his film *Before Night Falls* (2001), which depicts the life of Cuban writer Reinaldo Arenas and is based on Arenas's autobiography.

6. In August 1961 the state created the Union of Cuban Writers and Artists (UNEAC, Union de escritores y artistas Cubanos), which created new journals.

7. The Cuban critic Victor Fowler's *La maldición: una historia del placer como conquista* is the most comprehensive study of gay literature by a Cuban scholar in Cuba.

8. In *Dharma Lion,* Ginsberg reveals his intimacy with the young men and his protective behavior toward them. José Mario also provides some details of Ginsberg's visit in "Allen Ginsberg en La Habana."

9. Cuban musical tradition called *filin. Filin* is a Spanish transliteration of "feeling," a musical style influenced by crooners such as Nat "King" Cole.

10. Roger Reed writes that Mario accepted that El Puente become a part of UNEAC in 1964 (264).

11. Casal says that members of the group were accused of a "number of aesthetic (transcendental), moral (homosexualism), and, primarily, political (being unreliable as revolutionaries) sins" ("Literature and Society" 450).

12. Elzbieta Sklodowska provides important details and astute speculation about the aesthetic direction Barnet takes during that period.

13. Cuban theater critic and playwright Raquel Carrió states that the trajectory of Díaz's Teatro Público "is a recodification of the vernacular and the strictly literary" (37). Carrió suggests that casting a historical text in an ironic, postmodern context displaces audiences' predictable emotional responses. Thus, Díaz parodies Cuban directors' past attempts at traditional representations of classic plays and expands the audience to lump together the elite with the street.

14. These photographers show continuity and rupture with the intellectual framework and ritualistic connotations of the exiled Cuban performance artist Ana Mendieta (1948–1985). Jane Blocker emphasizes that Mendieta's body art represents "the dichotomy of nature and culture" that is tied to birth and death and the perpetual return to origin. According to Blocker, Mendieta's body-in-touch-with-nature-and-ritual images reflect the desire to reestablish identity and to produce an ephemeral effect that alludes to the womb as the initial sanctuary. The body-as-art symbolizes "a fragile and fleeting existence" and "a transcendent substitute for Mendieta's lost nation" (56–57).

15. Some of Olympya's recent paintings appeared in the Cuban film *Honey for Oshun* (2001), by the renowned Cuban director Humberto Solas.

16. Both James M. Saslow and Robert Eisler make reference to antique sources for the story of Pan and Olympus (the mortal boy whom Pan seduced) that were well known in the Renaissance period.

17. In the same year, the painter Carlos Guzmán created an alternative and capacious space, which he called "La Kahlo," within an official space, "La casa cultural," in Central Havana. A diverse group of artists performed in the space, drank homemade grapefruit wine, exhibited art, read poetry, and listened to music. Among the artists who showed or performed in the Space were "Angelito" (Ángel Delgado), Manuel Videl, Dagoberto Pedraja, Los Hermanos Saínz, and the group Extraño Corazón.

18. Boán's dance company is internationally recognized for its innovative and experimental mixture of dance, song, and theater. See articles by the Cuban critics Vivian Martínez Tabares and Noel Bonilla Chongo for a comprehensive analysis of Boán's works.

19. In *The Agüero Sisters* (1997), Cuban American writer Cristina García af-

fixes a hard-edged price to unrationed sex. In the novel, Dulce, a young woman managing a life in Havana, describes Cuban youths' pragmatic solution for survival in the 1990s: "Sex is the only thing they can't ration in Havana. It's the next-best currency after dollars. . Almost everyone I know my age, male or female, turns a trick once in a while" (51).

20. This study does not represent an exhaustive list of writers and artists from this period. However, excellent works by Cuban writers—Antonio Jose Ponte's *In the Cold of the Malecón*, Alejandro Aguilar's *Figuras tendidas*, and Jorge Ferrer's *Minimal bildung* — are worthy of mention for their uncompromising and unsentimental depiction of Cuba's decadent predicament and the pathos in the midst of physical and spiritual squalor. In *Brevísimas demencias: Narrativa joven cubana de los 90*, Amir Valle provides a comprehensive view of narrative writing in the 1990s.

21. There is a plethora of Cuban, French, Italian, American, Latin American, and Spanish writers, critics, and journalists who have provided opinions and analysis on this period in Cuba. For example, the Spaniard Vázquez Montalbán narrates converging events surrounding the historical visit of Pope John Paul II to Havana to discuss Cuba in the 1990s in *Y Dios entró en La Habana*. Another noteworthy example is Alma Guillermoprieto, an authoritative figure on Cuban and Latin American culture and politics. Her articles on Cuba are perceptive and informative; they often appear in the *New York Times, The New York Review of Books*, and *The New Yorker*, as well as in several major Latin American newspapers and journals.

Chapter 2. Revolutionary Politics, Cultural Production, and Afro-Cuban Intellectuals

1. In 2000 Stubbs and Sarduy published a book of interviews with Afro-Cuban intellectuals titled *Afro-Cuban Voices: On Race and Identity in Contemporary Cuba*. In their introduction, Sarduy and Stubbs provide a more critical, albeit brief and schematic, approach to race issues and racism.

2. Gerardo Mosquera points out that often the term "popular" does not have the connotation of "mass" or "consumer" culture "Rather its closest equivalent might be 'grass roots' or 'community-based.' . . In precapitalist cultures, the popular can be pointed to as a set of lived practices, possibly a whole way of life" ("Africa" 38). He proposes that Cuban anthropology's approach to Afro-Cuban culture makes use of this particular definition of the popular.

3. Alejandro de la Fuente's *A Nation for All: Race, Inequality, and Politics in Twentieth-Century Cuba* is a significant contribution to the study of shifting racial politics in Cuban society and history.

4. The Black Panther William Lee Brent says that Cleaver enjoyed the privileged status of a high-ranking Black Panther Party official in Cuba until he began organizing a Panther chapter in Havana. Under pressure, Cleaver left Cuba and went to Algeria (*Long Time Gone* 174).

5. Torrents, Bethell (118–19), Bunck, and Stubbs provide information about Cuban women writers, women's organizations, and current gender debates.

6. Kutzinski's study on Cuban nationalism and the influence of the economics

of sugar production on the literary erotization of blacks and mulattos exposes historically negative racial and gender constructions. Kutzinski links the erotics of sugar with new problems black women in Cuba face and asks why there are so few contemporary Afro-Cuban women writers.

7. Nancy Morejón elucidates how the mulatta Cecilia, the main character of Cirilo Villaverde's nineteenth-century antislavery novel, becomes a victim of racism when she attempts to move up the social and economic ladder by marrying into the elite white society of the Cuban Creoles ("Mito y realidad en Cecilia Valdés" in _Fundación_ 14).

8. A 1997 issue of _Temas_ is one of the first published critical discussions on contemporary racial issues after 1959.

Chapter 3. Nancy Morejón's Precarious Wings

1. I analyze this poem, and Morejón's portrayal of the Cuban condition, more elaborately later in the chapter.

2. In addition to _Lengua,_ Morejón also published _Recopilación de textos sobre Nicolás Guillén_ (1974), a compilation of essays on Guillén's works.

3. Ángel Díaz says that his greatest influence was his father's music, which was the traditional Cuban _trova. Filin_ was a hybrid form of American music and traditional Cuban rhythms (Contrera 22).

4. Abudu makes reference to several untitled poems (_Amor_ 35–41) that exemplify Morejón's formal experimentation, deliberate confusion of images, and lack of punctuation (72–74).

5. Both Casaus ("La más joven poesía" 10) and Casal ("Literature and Society" 541) emphasize the extremism of young revolutionary authorities like Jesús Díaz who vehemently condemned the emphasis on aesthetics over politics.

6. Emilio Bejel's interview with Cintio Vitier (_Escribir en Cuba,_ especially 379–87) elucidates Lezama's problems with the Castro government and the rehabilitation process in favor of Lezama's works that began officially in 1980 (i.e., after his death).

7. Roberto González Echevarría explains that these ideas are founded on classical and romantic notions of nature and nationalism, as is evident in the works of the Cuban poets José María Heredia and José Martí (_The Voice of the Masters_ 4–5). These poets linked strong sentiments about political exile and nation building with Nature's magnificence and expressed their spirituality and emotions through elaborate descriptions of the elements of nature. Vicky Unruh argues that, during the vanguard period of the 1920s and 1930s, Latin American writers upheld some myths but were intensely critical and ironical of organicism in the rhetoric of their manifestoes (126).

8. In chapter 2 I have discussed the fate of several Afro-Cuban political activists and their works.

9. In "Nancy Morejón's 'Negrismo' in the Revolutionary Era: The Question of Gender and Race in Cuba," I analyze Morejón's critical essay on the mulatto woman as a sexual and racial category. I also explore her representation of the Afro-Cuban woman in the poems "Amo a mi amo" y "Mujer negra."

10. Jackson thoroughly discusses these poems by Guillén, Pedroso, and

Arozarena in *The Black Image in Latin American Literature* (121–30). G. R. Coulthard provides a thematic study of blacks in Antillean literature.

11. The critics Pérez-Firmat and Kutzinski have commented on the issue of machismo and the sensuality of Afro-Cuban woman in Guillén's poetry. Pérez-Firmat argues that Guillén's "mulatto madrigals" project the image of Afro-Cuban woman as poetic muse. He states that the poems are important "because the woman they portray—the woman they invent—is Guillén's vernacular muse, the source and sometimes the subject of his mullatto verses" (85). In response to Pérez-Firmat's attempt to limit Guillén's characterization of the mulatto woman to "pure literariness," Kutzinski comments: "I take this to mean that poetics and/or aesthetics are not gendered, which, especially in light of Pérez-Firmat's own unbounded male enthusiasm for 'uterine utterance,' 'thinking with your thighs,' and 'the tropical fruits of [the Black woman's] womb,' to be preposterous" (172). On the other hand, Pérez-Firmat doesn't necessarily claim that poetics are not engendered. Rather, he tries to show that Guillén was echoing Petrarch and that he was playing with the "dolce stil nuovo."

12. LeoGrande provides information about the change in Cuba's foreign policy and its military aid to Angola and Ethiopia, which constituted the first large-scale commitments of regular Cuban combat troops abroad. Moore critically analyzes the impact of Cuban foreign policies in Africa on domestic racial policies (*Castro* 299–321).

13. Morejón states: "Cuando en nuestros días se analizan estas cuestiones, también hallamos, unido al prejuicio racial, un indiscutible e insoslayable prejuicio en el orden del sexo" (*Fundación* 26) [When we analyze these issues today, we also discover, alongside the racial prejudice, an indisputable and unavoidable gender bias (tr. Linda Howe).]

14. Morejón links themes of racial and gender prejudice in Villaverde's novel with social issues of contemporary Cuba. She states that "La óptica de Cirilo Villaverde, nuestro más brillante novelista del siglo XIX, nos obliga, sin duda, a reflexionar y volver sobre muchos temas que todavía hoy lastran nuestra vida cotidiana. Y, más allá de cualquier miopía temporal, sus objetivos—parcialmente logrados—nos alertan" (*Fundación* 27) [The perspective of Cirilo Villaverde, our most brilliant nineteenth-century novelist, forces us to reflect on subjects that still weigh heavily on our life today. Whatever shortsightedness might have been imposed by his times in which he lived, Villaverde's objectives, which were partially achieved, alert us to these issues (tr.Linda Howe).]

15. I use the 1985 bilingual edition of Morejón's poetry for the Spanish version of the poem and an updated, unpublished English translation by Kathleen Weaver.

16. Lorna Williams also points out how the active verbs signify the Afro-Cuban woman's assertiveness (2).

17. Marietta Morrisey points out how gender inequality characterizes the female slave experience, since "gender stratification remained relevant, expressing another tragic irony of Caribbean slavery: that with women working as hard as men, in the same jobs and generally as competently, gender was an important basis of social hierarchy" (16). With more comprehensive studies, like that of Morrisey (also those of Bush and Martínez-Alier), the image of the female slave

has changed considerably. In the words of the historian Barbara Bush, the female slave "has begun to emerge from historical obscurity" (3).

18. I elaborate on Morejón's use of the womanist theory in "Nancy Morejón's Womanism."

Chapter 4. Miguel Barnet's Creative Oeuvres

1. Cuban argot that refers to contemporary hustlers and prostitutes. It is believed that the word is derived from *jinete* (horseman). When there was an influx of Russian motorcycles in Cuba, Cubans labeled "jineteras" the women who made friends with motorcycle owners in order to have transportation (transportation is a precious commodity in Cuba). The word also referred to people who waited outside hotels to contact foreigners and to exchange pesos for dollars (which was prohibited by law until the mid-1990s).

2. *The Holy Family* was a satirical pamphlet against Bruno Bauer and the Young Hegelians that Marx and Engels published in 1845.

3. In *Antes que anochezca,* Arenas's autobiography, he provides minute details of his misadventures with the Castro government. In 2000 Julian Schnabel directed the poetic film version of the text and titled it *Before Night Falls,* after the English translation of the text.

4. In *El socialismo y el hombre en Cuba* Che Guevara expounds on his concept of the "new man" which replaced the notion of material gain with utopian ideas of cooperation, voluntarism, and solidarity to generate human development.

5. Pérez Firmat reminds us that like the sonnet, "the madrigal circulated on the courtly setting of the Renaissance love poetry, and it entered Spanish poetry in the work of the Petrarchist poet Gutierre de Cetina" (92).

6. We are reminded of Nancy Morejón's objective description and caustic criticism of Havana's dreary urban landscape, full of decay and hopelessness in *Paisaje célebre.*

Bibliography

Abudu, Gabriel Asoaba. "Transcurso poético cubano de Nicolás Guillén a Nancy Morejón: Lo social y lo político." Ph.D. dissertation, Temple University, 1992.

Acosta, Leonardo. "La música afroamericana; síntesis y reinterpretación." *Revolución y Cultura* 49 (Sept. 1976): 11–20.

———. *Del tambor al sintetizador.* Havana: CNC, 1983.

Aguilar, Alejandro. *Figuras tendidas.* Las Tunas, Cuba: Editorial Sanlope, 2000.

Almendros, Néstor, dir. *Improper Conduct.* Cinevista, 1984.

Amaro, Nelson, and Carmelo Mesa-Lago. "Inequality and Classes." In *Revolutionary Change in Cuba,* edited by Mesa-Lago, 341–74.

Arandia, Gisela. Interview with Linda Howe, Havana, 5 August 1992.

Arenas, Reinaldo. *Antes que anochezca.* Barcelona: Tusquets, 1992.

———. *El mundo alucinante: Una novela de aventuras.* Barcelona: Tusquets, 1997.

Auden, W. H. *W. H. Auden: Collected Poems.* Edited by Edward Mendelson. New York: Vintage International, 1995.

Bachiller y Morales, Don Antonio. *Cuba primitiva: Origen, lenguas, tradiciones e historia de los Indios en las Antillas Mayores y las Lucayas.* Havana: Miguel de Villa, 1883.

Ballagas, Manolo. Interview with Linda Howe, Miami, 1996.

Baloyra, Enrique A., and James A. Morris, eds. *Conflict and Change in Cuba.* Albuquerque: University of New Mexico Press, 1993.

Balutansky, Kathleen M. "Naming Caribbean Women Writers: A Review Essay." *Callaloo* 13, no. 3 (1990): 539–50.

Barnet, Miguel. *Akeké y la jutía.* Havana: Editorial Gente Nueva, 1978.

———. *Apuntes para el folkore cubano.* Havana: Consejo Nacional de Cuba, 1966.

———. *Autógrafos cubanos.* Havana: UNEAC, 1990.

———. *Bocetas de Haiku.* Havana: UNEAC, 1991.

———. *Biografía de un cimarrón.* Madrid: Ediciones Alfaguara, 1966.

———. *La canción de Rachel.* Barcelona: Editorial Estela, 1970.

———. *Carta de noche.* Havana: UNEAC, 1982.

———. *Con pies de gato.* Havana: Ediciones Unión, 1993.

————. "The Documentary Novel." *Cuban Studies / Estudios cubanos* 2, no. 1 (1981): 19–32.

————. "Entrevistas." *Casa de las Américas* (22–23 Jan.–April 1964): 139–49.

————. *La fuente viva.* Havana: Editorial Letras Cubanas, 1983.

————. *Gallego.* Madrid: Alfaguara, 1986.

————. *Isla de güijes.* Havana: Ediciones El Puente, 1964.

————. *Mapa del tiempo.* Havana: Editorial Letras Cubanas, 1989.

————. "Miosvatis." *New Yorker* (26 Jan. 1998): 70–74.

————. "La novela testimonio: Socio-literatura." *Unión* 6, no. 4 (1969): 99–122.

————. *Oficio de ángel.* Madrid: Altea, Taurus, Alfaguara, S.A., 1989.

————. *Orikis y otros poemas.* Havana: Letras Cubanas, 1980.

————. *La piedra fina y el pavorreal.* Havana: Ediciones Unión, 1963.

————. "Poesía anónima africana." In *Literatura y arte nuevo en Cuba,* edited by Iguasi Piera, 277–87. Barcelona: Estela, 1971.

————. *La sagrada familia.* Havana: Casa de las Américas, 1967.

————. Interview with Linda Howe, Havana, 2 August 1992.

————. Interview with Linda Howe, Havana, 27 July 1994.

————. *Viendo mi vida pasar.* Havana: Letras Cubanas, 1987.

————. *When Night Is Darkest: Selected Poems.* Bilingual edition with translations by Charles Hatfield. Havana: Editorial José Martí, 2002.

Barnett, Clifford R., and Wyatt Macgaffrey. *Twentieth-Century Cuba: The Background of the Castro Revolution.* New York: Anchor Books, 1965.

Bejel, Emilio. *Escribir en Cuba: Entrevistas con escritores cubanos, 1979–1989.* Rio Piedras: Editorial de la Universidad de Puerto Rico, 1991.

————. "Strawberry and Chocolate: Coming Out of the Cuban Closet?" *South Atlantic Quarterly* 96, no. 1 (1997): 65–82.

Belkin, June S., and Carmelo Mesa-Lago. *Cuba in Africa.* Pittsburgh: University of Pittsburgh Press, 1982.

Belsey, Catherine. *Critical Practice.* New York: Methuen, 1980.

Benedetti, Mario. "Anatomía de la obra de Nancy Morejón." *Granma* 50 (15 Dec. 1991): 5.

————. *Los poetas comunicantes.* México: Marcha Editores, 1981.

————. "Present Status of Cuban Culture." In *Cuba in Revolution,* edited by Bonachea and Valdés, 500–526.

Benítez-Rojo, Antonio. *La isla que se repite: El Caribe y la perspectiva posmoderna.* Hanover, N.H.: Ediciones del Norte, 1989.

————. "Nicolás Guillén and Sugar." In *Nicolás Guillén: A Special Issue,* edited by Vera M. Kutzinski. *Callaloo* 10, no. 2 (1987): 329–51.

Berman, Russell A. *Modern Culture and Critical Theory: Art, Politics, and the Legacy of the Frankfurt School.* Madison: University of Wisconsin Press, 1989.

Bernard, Jorge L., and Juan A. Pola. *¿Quiénes escriben en Cuba?* Havana: Editorial Letras Cubanas, 1985.

Bernstein, Richard. "'Dirty Havana Trilogy': It's Hard Work Being a Hedonist in Cuba." *New York Times,* 5 February 2002.

Bethell, Leslie, ed. *Cuba: A Short History.* Cambridge: Cambridge University Press, 1993.

Bianchi Ross, Ciro. *Las palabras de otro.* Havana: Ediciones Unión, 1982.

————. "Nancy Morejón: Soy muchas poetas." *Cuba International* (April 1991): 30–34.

Blight, James G., and David A. Welch. *On the Brink: Americans and Soviets Reexamine the Cuban Missile Crisis.* New York: Hill and Wang, 1989.

Block, Holly, ed. *Art Cuba: The New Generation.* New York: Abrams, 2001.

Blocker, Jane. *Where Is Ana Mendieta? Identity, Performativity, and Exile.* Durham, N.C.: Duke University Press, 1999.

Bolívar Aróstegui, Natalia. *Los orishas en Cuba.* Havana: Ediciones Unión, 1990.

Bonachea, Rolando E., and Nelson P. Valdés, eds. *Cuba in Revolution.* New York: Doubleday, 1972.

Bonilla Chongo, Noel. "Marianela Boán: Encarnación de lo dramático." *Tablas* 2, no. 64 (April–June 2001): ii–iv.

Bourdieu, Pierre. *Distinction: A Social Critique of the Judgment of Taste.* Translated by Richard Nice. Cambridge, Mass.: Harvard University Press, 1984.

————. *The Field of Cultural Production: Essays on Art and Literature.* Edited by Randal Johnson. New York: Columbia University Press, 1993.

————. *Homo Academicus.* Cambridge: Polity Press, 1984.

Bourdieu, Pierre, and Loïc J. D. Wacquant. *An Invitation to Reflexive Sociology.* Chicago: University of Chicago Press, 1992.

————. *Language and Symbolic Power.* Translated by Gino Raymound and Matthew Adamson. Cambridge, Mass.: Harvard University Press, 1991.

Boyce Davies, Carole, and Elaine Savory Fido, eds. *Out of the Kumbla: Caribbean Women and Literature.* Trenton, N.J.: Africa World Press, 1990.

Brent, William Lee. *Long Time Gone.* New York: Time Books, 1996.

Bunck, Julie Marie. "The Cuban Revolution and Women's Rights." In *Cuban Communism,* compiled by Horowitz, 443–63.

Bush, Barbara. *Slave Women in Caribbean Society: 1650–1838.* Bloomington: Indiana University Press, 1990.

Butler-Evans, Elliot. *Race, Gender, and Desire: Narrative Strategies in the Fiction of Toni Cade Bambara, Toni Morrison, and Alice Walker.* Philadelphia: Temple University Press, 1989.

Cabrera, Lydia. *Anagó. Vocabulario Lucumí. El yoruba que se habla en Cuba.* Havana: Editorial C. R., 1957.

————. *Cuentos negros de Cuba.* Madrid: Imprime Ramos, 1972.

————. *El monte.* Miami: Ultra Graphics Corporation, 1983.

Cabrera Infante, Guillermo. "Delito por bailar el chachacha." *Mundo Nuevo* (July 1968): 59–71.

————. *Mea Cuba.* Barcelona: Plaza and Janes, 1993.

————. "Un poeta de vuelo popular." *Vuelta* 160 (1990): 45–47.

Captain-Hidalgo, Yvonne. "The Poetics of the Quotidian in the Works of Nancy Morejón." *Callaloo* 10, no. 4 (1987): 596–604.

Carbonell, Walterio. *Crítica, como surgió la cultura nacional.* Havana: Ediciones Yaka, 1961.

————. Interview with Linda Howe, Havana, 16 July 1992.

————. Interview with Linda Howe, Havana, 18 July 1994.

Carby, Hazel. *Reconstructing Womanhood: The Emergence of the Afro-American Woman Novelist.* New York: Oxford University Press, 1987.

Cardenal, Ernesto, ed. *Nueva poesía nicaragüense*. Managua: Ediciones Nueva Nicaragua, 1981.

Carpentier, Alejo. *Ecue-Yamba-O! Historia Afro-cubana*. Madrid: Ediciones España, 1933.

Carrió, Raquel. "Teatro y modernidad: Treinta años después." *Tablas* 70 (2002): 33–39.

Casal, Lourdes. *El caso Padilla: Literatura y revolución en Cuba (Documentos)*. Miami: Ediciones Universal, 1971.

———. "Literature and Society." In *Revolutionary Change in Cuba*, edited by Mesa-Lago 447–69.

———. *Revolution and Race: Blacks in Contemporary Cuba*. Washington, D.C.: Woodrow Wilson International Center for Scholars, 1979.

Casaus, Victor. "Inventario de cólera y amor." *Casa de las Américas* 8, no. 48 (May–June 1968): 143–44.

———. "La más joven poesía: Seis comentarios y un prólogo." *Unión* 3 (July–Sept. 1967): 5–14.

Castañeda, Jorge G. *Utopia Unarmed: The Latin American Left after the Cold War*. New York: Knopf, 1993.

Castellanos, Isabel. "Commentary: Notes on Afro-Cuban Religion and Cuban Linguistics." In *Cuban Studies since the Revolution*, edited by Fernández 222–31.

Castellanos, Jorge, and Isabel Castellanos. *Cultura Afrocubana*. 3 vols. Miami: Ediciones Universal, 1990–92.

Castro, Fidel. "Cuba es más que blanco, más que negro." *Hoy* (28 March 1959): 1–3.

———. *In Defense of Socialism: Four Speeches on the 30th Anniversary of the Cuban Revolution*. Edited by Mary-Alice Waters. New York: Pathfinder, 1989.

———. *Palabras a los intelectuales*. Montevideo: Comité de intelectuales y artistas de apoyo a la Revolución Cubana, 1961.

———. Speech. *Revolución*. Havana, Cuba, 26 March 1959: 4–5.

Cavafy, C. P. *Collected Poems*. Translated by Edmund Keely and Philip Sherrand. Princeton: Princeton University Press, 1992.

Chanan, Michael. "Otra mirada." *Cine cubano* 127 (1989): 27–35.

Chaviano, Daína. *El hombre, la hembra y el hambre*. Barcelona: Planeta, 1998.

Christian, Barbara. *Black Feminist Criticism: Perspectives on Black Women Writers*. New York: Pergamon Press, 1985.

Collins, Patricia Hill. *Black Feminist Thought: Knowledge, Consciousness, and the Politics of Empowerment*. Boston: Unwin Hyman, 1990.

Connor, Steven. *Theory and Cultural Practice*. Oxford: Blackwell, 1992.

Contrera, Félix. *Porque tienen filin*. Santiago de Cuba: Editorial Oriente, 1989.

Coulthard, G. R. *Race and Colour in Caribbean Literature*. London: Oxford University Press, 1962.

Crahan, Margaret E., and Franklin W. Knight. *Africa and the Caribbean: The Legacies of a Link*. Baltimore: Johns Hopkins University Press, 1979.

Crow, John A. *The Epic of Latin America*. Berkeley: University of California Press, 1992.

Davis-Lett, Stephanie. "The Image of the Black Woman as a Revolutionary Figure: Three Views." *Studies in Afro-Hispanic Literature* 2–3 (1978–79): 118–33.

DeCosta-Willis, Miriam, ed. *Blacks in Hispanic Literature*. Port Washington, N.Y.: Kennikat Press, 1977.

———. "The Caribbean as Idea and Image in the Poetry of Nancy Morejón." *Association of Caribbean Studies* 7, nos. 2–3 (1989–90): 233–43.

———. "Self and Society in the Afro-Cuban Slave Narrative." *LALR* 32 (1988): 6–15.

de la Fuente, Alejandro. *A Nation for All: Race, Inequality, and Politics in Twentieth-Century Cuba*. Chapel Hill: University of North Carolina Press, 2001.

Depestre, René. "Carta de Cuba sobre el imperialismo de mala fé." *Casa de las Américas* 34 (Jan.–Feb. 1966): 33–61.

DesChamps Chapeaux, Pedro. *El negro en la economía habanera del siglo XIX*. Havana: UNEAC, 1971.

de Vega, Lope. *Obras de Lope de Vega*. Madrid: Real Academia de España, 1916.

Díaz, Jesús. *Las palabras perdidas*. Barcelona: Destino, 1992.

———. "El último puente." *La Gaceta de Cuba* (Aug.–Sept. 1966): 4.

Díaz Martínez, Manuel. "Carta de noche." *La Nueva Gaceta* 3 (1983): 20.

———. "Poesía cubana de hoy." *Revista Canadiense de Estudios Hispánicos* 13, no. 1 (1988): 111–25.

Dolores Espino, María. "Tourism in Cuba: A Development Strategy for the 1990s?" *Cuban Studies* 23 (1993): 49–69.

Domínguez, Jorge I. *Cuba: Order and Revolution*. Cambridge, Mass.: Harvard University Press, 1978.

Dopico Black, Georgina. "The Limits of Expression: Intellectual Freedom in Postrevolutionary Cuba." *Cuban Studies* 19 (1989): 107–42.

Duharte Jiménez, Rafael. *Seis ensayos de interpretación histórica*. Santiago de Cuba: Editorial Oriente, 1983.

Eisler, Robert. "Luca Signorelli's School of Pan." *Gazette de Beaux-Arts* 33 (1948): 77–87.

Escardó, Rolando. *Libro de Rolando*. Havana: Ediciones R[evolución], 1961.

Estévez, Abilio. "El enano de la botella." Unpublished monologue, 1994.

———. *Tuyo es el reino*. Barcelona: Tusquets, 1999.

Estorino, Abelardo. *Vagos rumores y otras obras*. Havana: Editorial Letras Cubanas, 1997.

Evenson, Debra. "Cuban Culture Goes to Market." *Cuba Update* 1–2 (1994): 21.

Fagen, Richard. *The Political Transformation of Political Culture in Cuba*. Stanford: Stanford University Press, 1969.

Fernández, Damián J., ed. *Cuban Studies since the Revolution*. Gainesville: University Press of Florida, 1992.

Fernández Guerra, Ángel Luis. "Edipo y Cayo (Para leer a Miguel Barnet)." *Casa de las Américas* 30, no. 180 (1990): 45–53.

Fernández Retamar, Roberto. *Calibán*. Minneapolis: University of Minnesota Press, 1992.

———. *Para una teoría de la literatura hispanoamericana*. Havana: Editorial Pueblo y Educación: 1984.

———. *La poesía contemporanea en Cuba, 1927–1953*. Havana: Orígenes, 1954.

Fernández Retamar, Roberto, ed. *José Martí: Páginas escogidas*. Vols. 1–2. Havana: Editora Universitaria, 1965.

Fernández Robaina, Tomás. "The Struggle against Racial Discrimination and Prejudice in Cuba, 1959–1991." Unpublished manuscript translated by Laurence Glasco.

———. *El negro en Cuba, 1902–1958*. Havana: Editorial de Ciencias Sociales, 1990.

———. Interview with Linda Howe, Havana, 16 July 1994.

———. Interview with Linda Howe, Havana, 12 July 1996.

Ferrer, Jorge. *Minimal Bildung*. Miami: Ediciones Catalejo, Inc., 2001.

Forgues, Roland. "El Camino de Damasco: Entrevista a Miguel Barnet." *Socialismo y Participación* 45 (March 1989): 55–70.

Foster, David William. *Gay and Lesbian Themes in Latin American Writing*. Austin: University of Texas Press, 1991.

Foster, David William, and Cynthia Margarita Tompkins, eds. *Notable Twentieth-Century Latin American Women: A Biographical Dictionary*. Westport, Conn.: Greenwood Press, 2001.

Foucault, Michel. *Power/Knowledge: Selected Interviews and Other Writings, 1972–1977*. Edited by Colin Gordon. New York: Pantheon, 1980.

Fowler Calzada, Victor. *La maldición: Una historia del placer como conquista*. Havana: Letras Cubanas, 2000.

———. "La tercera orilla." *Unión* 7, no. 18 (Jan.–March 1995): 68–73.

———. Interview with Linda Howe, Havana, August 1996.

Franquí, Carlos. *Vidas, aventuras y desastres de un hombre llamado Castro*. Barcelona: Planeta, 1988.

Fuentes, Norbeto. *Dulces Guerreros cubanos*. Barcelona: Editorial Seix Barral, 1999.

Fulleda León, Gerardo. Interview with Linda Howe, Havana, 20 July 1994.

———. Interview with Linda Howe, Havana, 28 July 1992.

García, Cristina. *The Agüero Sisters*. New York: Ballantine, 1997.

García-Lorca, Federico. *Romancero Gitano*. Edited by Derek Harris. Valencia: Gráficas Soler, S.A., 1991.

García-Pinto, Magdalena. "Entrevista con Pedro Pérez Sarduy en Columbia, Missouri en marzo de 1993." *Afro-Hispanic Review* 13, no. 1 (spring 1994): 23–33.

Geisdorfer Feal, Rosemary. "Bordering Feminisms in Afro-Hispanic Studies: Crossroads in the Field." *LALR* 20 (July–Dec. 1992): 40–45.

Gilard, Jacques. "La obra poética de Nancy Morejón: Un despertar de la negritud." *Hora de poesía* 16–17 (July–Oct 1978): 321–35.

Ginsberg, Allen. *Allen Ginsberg: Gay Sunshine. Interview with Allen Young*. Berkeley: Gray Fox Press, 1973.

Glanville Taylor, John. "The United States and Cuba." In Pérez Jr., *Slaves, Sugar and Colonial Society*, 114–16.

Gómez, Sara, dir. *De cierta manera*. ICAIC, 1974–78.

Gómez de Avellaneda, Gertrudis. *Sab*. Edited by Mary Cruz. Havana: Instituto Cubano del Libro, 1973.

González, Mike, and David Treece. *The Gathering of Voices*. New York: Verso, 1992.

González, Reynaldo. *Contradanzas y latigazos*. Havana: Letras Cubanas, 1983.

———. "Meditation for a Debate, or Cuban Culture with the Taste for Strawberry and Chocolate." Translated by William Rose. *Cuba Update* 15, no. 2 (May 1994): 14–19.

González, Tomás. Interview with Linda Howe, Canary Islands, Spain, 16 May 1996.

González Echevarría, Roberto. "An Outcast of the Island." *New York Times Book Review* (24 October 1993): 1–33.

———. "'Biografía de un cimarrón' and the Novel of the Cuban Revolution." *Novel* 13, no. 3 (1980): 249–63.

———. *Myth and Archive: A Theory of Latin American Literature.* Cambridge: Cambridge University Press, 1990.

———. "The Humanities and Cuban Studies, 1959–1989." In *Cuban Studies since the Revolution,* edited by Fernández, 199–215.

———. *The Voice of the Masters: Writing and Authority in Modern Latin American Literature.* Austin: University of Texas Press, 1985.

González-Wippler, Migene. *Santería: African Magic in Latin America.* New York: Doubleday, 1975.

Gosse, Van. *Where the Boys Are: Cuba, Cold War America and the Making of the New Left.* New York: Verso, 1993.

Graham, Richard., ed. *The Idea of Race in Latin America, 1870–1940.* Austin: University of Texas Press, 1990.

Granados, Manuel. Interview with Linda Howe, Paris, 9 June 1996.

Guerra, Ramiro. *Teatralización del folklore y otros ensayos.* Havana: Editorial Letras Cubanas, 1989.

Guevara, Ernesto Che. *Obra revolucionaria.* México: Era, 1971.

———. *Obra.* Havana: UNEAC, 1979.

———. *El socialismo y el hombre en Cuba.* Havana: Eds. R, 1965.

Guillén, Nicolás. *Antología poética.* Edited by Oscar Hermes Villordo. Buenos Aires: Editorial Abril, S. A., 1987.

———. *Motivos de Son.* Havana: Imp. Rambla, Bouza, 1930.

———. *Sóngoro Cosongo. Poemas mulatos.* Havana: Úcar García, 1933.

———. *West Indies Ltd. Poemas.* Havana: Úcar García, 1934.

Guirao, Ramón, ed. *Órbita de la poesía afrocubana, 1928–37 (Antología).* Havana: Ucar, García y Cía, 1938.

Gutiérrez, Carlos María. "Carmichael: Poder negro + Tercer Mundo." *Marcha* 29 (11 Aug. 1967): 16–18.

Gutiérrez, Juan Pedro. *Dirty Havana Trilogy.* Translated by Natasha Wimmer. New York: Farrar, Straus and Giroux, 1998.

Gutiérrez Alea, Tomás, Juan Carlos Tabio, Robert Redford, et al. *Fresa y chocolate* (Strawberry and Chocolate). Film. Burbank, Calif.: Instituto Cubano de Arte e Industria and Miramax Films, 1995.

Helg, Aline. *Our Rightful Share: The Afro-Cuban Struggle for Equality, 1886–1912.* Chapel Hill: University of North Carolina Press, 1995.

———. "Race in Argentina and Cuba, 1880–1930: Theory, Policies, and Popular Reaction." In *The Idea of Race in Latin America,* edited by Graham, 37–69.

Hernández Espinosa, Eugenio. *Teatro.* Havana: Editorial Letras Cubanas, 1989.

———. Interview with Linda Howe, Havana, 20 July 1994.

Hoetkin, Harry. "The Cultural Links." In *Africa and the Caribbean,* edited by Crahan and Knight, 20–40.

hooks, bell. *Yearning: Race, Gender, and Cultural Politics.* Boston: South End Press, 1990.

Horowitz, Irving Louis, comp. *Cuban Communism.* New Brunswick: Transaction, 1991.

Howe, Linda. "Afro-Cuban Intellectuals: Revolutionary Politics and Cultural Production." *Revista de estudios Hispánicos* 33, no. 3 (Oct. 1999): 407–39.

———. "The Fluid Iconography of the Cuban Spirit in Nancy Morejón's Poetry." *Afro-Hispanic Review* 15 (spring 1996): 29–34.

———. "Haydee Santamaría." In *Notable Twentieth-Century Latin American Women,* edited by Foster and Tompkins, 258–63.

———. "Nancy Morejón's 'Negrismo' in the Revolutionary Era: The Question of Gender and Race in Cuba." *Explicación de textos literarios* 24 (1995–96): 91–111.

———. "Nancy Morejón's Womanism." In *Singular Like a Bird: The Art of Nancy Morejón,* edited by Miriam DeCosta-Willis, 153–68. Washington, D.C.: Howard University Press, 1999.

Jackson, Richard. *The Black Image in Latin American Literature.* Albuquerque: University of New Mexico, 1976.

Johnson, Peter T. "Nuanced Lives of the Intelligentsia." In *Conflict and Change in Cuba,* edited by Baloyra and Morris, 137–63.

Klein, Herbert S. *African Slavery in Latin America and the Caribbean.* Oxford: Oxford University Press, 1986.

———. *Slavery in the Américas: A Comparative Study of Virginia and Cuba.* Chicago: Ivan R. Dee, 1967.

Knight, Franklin W., and Margaret E. Crahan. "The African Migration and the Origins of an Afro-American Society and Culture." In *Africa and the Caribbean,* edited by Crahan and Knight, 1–19.

———. *Slave Society in Cuba during the Nineteenth Century.* Madison: University of Wisconsin Press, 1970.

Kolakowski, Leszek. *Main Currents of Marxism.* Vol. 3. Oxford: Oxford University Press, 1981.

Kupchik, Christian. "Miguel Barnet: La realidad de las cosas." *Brecha* 149 (23 Sept. 1988): 22–23.

Kutzinski, Vera M. *Sugar's Secrets: Race and the Erotics of Cuban Nationalism.* Charlottesville: University Press of Virginia, 1993.

Lamming, George. *The Pleasures of Exile.* London: Michael Joseph, 1960.

LeoGrande, William M. "Cuban-Soviet Relations and Cuban Policy in Africa." In *Cuba in Africa,* edited by Mesa-Lago, 14–49.

Le Riverend, Ada Rosa. *Diccionario de literatura cubana.* Vols. 1–2. Havana: Editorial Letras Cubanas, 1984.

Lezama Lima, José. *Paradiso.* Madrid: Ediciones Cátedra, 1980.

Lima, Chely. *Triángulos mágicos.* México: Grupo Editorial Planeta, 1994.

Liss, Sheldon B. *Fidel! Castro's Political and Social Thought.* Latin American Perspectives Series, no. 13. Boulder: Westview Press, 1994.

Luis, William. "Cinema and Culture in Cuba: An Interview with Néstor Almendros." *Review* 37 (1987): 14–21.

———. *Literary Bondage: Slavery in Cuban Narrative.* Austin: University of Texas Press, 1990.

———. "The Politics of Memory and Miguel Barnet's *The Autobiography of a Runaway Slave.*" *MLN* (Hispanic Issue) 104 (1989): 475–91.

———. "Race, Poetry, and Revolution in the Works of Nancy Morejón." *Hispanic Journal* 14, no. 2 (fall 1993): 83–103.

Luis, William, ed. *Voices from Under: Black Narrative in Latin America and the Caribbean.* Westport, Conn.: Greenwood Press, 1984.

Lumsden, C. Ian. "The Ideology of the Revolution." In *Cuba in Revolution*, edited by Bonachea and Valdés, 529–44.

Macgaffey, Wyatt, and Clifford R. Barnet. *Twentieth-Century Cuba: The Background of the Cuban Revolution.* New York: Doubleday, 1965.

Machado, Eloy. Interview with Linda Howe, Havana, 25 July 1994.

———. Interview with Linda Howe, Havana, 15 June 1996.

Marie Bunck, Julie. *Fidel Castro and the Quest for a Revolutionary Culture in Cuba.* University Park: Pennsylvania State University Press, 1994.

Marinello, Juan. "Sobre nuestra crítica literaria." *Vida universitaria* 21, no. 219 (May–June 1970): 43–48.

Mario, José. "Allen Ginsberg en La Habana." *Mundo Nuevo* 34 (April 1969): 48–54.

———. "Novísima poesía cubana." *Mundo Nuevo* 38 (Aug. 1969): 63–69.

Mario, José, ed. *Novísima poesía cubana.* Havana: Ediciones El Puente, 1964.

Marrero, Levi. *Cuba: Economía y sociedad.* Vol. 9. *Azúcar, ilustración y conciencia (1763–1868).* Madrid: Editorial Playor, 1983.

Martí, José. *Our America.* New York: Monthly Review Press, 1977.

Martiatu Terry, Inés María. "María Antonía: Wa-ni-ile-re." *Tablas* 31 (1984): 35–44.

———. "Mayoría étnica y minoría cultural." *XI Congreso de ASSITEJ.* Havana, 25 February 1993.

———. Interview with Linda Howe, Havana, 23 July 1994.

———. Interview with Linda Howe, Havana, 15 August 1996.

———. "Prologue." *Eugenio Hernández: Teatro.* Havana: Letras Cubanas, 1989.

Martín, Raúl. *Nuestra mirada a los siervos.* Teatro de la Luna-La Prensa. Havana, Cuba, September 14, 1999.

Martínez-Alier, Verena. *Marriage, Class, and Colour in Nineteenth-Century Cuba.* Ann Arbor: University of Michigan Press, 1989.

Martínez Furé, Rogelio. *Conjunto folklórico Nacional [Ensayos].* Havana: Consejo Nacional de Cultura, 1963.

———. *Diálogos imaginarios.* Havana: Editorial Arte y Literatura, 1979.

———. Interview with Linda Howe, Havana, 2 August 1997.

———. Interview with Linda Howe, Havana, 10 March 1998.

Martínez Tabares, Vivian. "Marianela Boán: Mover la palabra, ritualizar el gesto." *Revolucion y cultura* 1 (Jan.–Feb. 2001): 45–48.

Matas, Julio. "Theater and Cinematography." In *Revolutionary Change in Cuba*, edited by Mesa-Lago, 427–43.

Matibag, Eugenio. *Afro-Cuban Religious Experience: Cultural Reflections in Narrative.* Gainesville: University Press of Florida, 1996.

Menton, Seymour. *Prose Fiction of the Cuban Revolution*. Austin: University of Texas Press, 1975.

Merino, Antonio. *Nueva poesía cubana (Antología 1966–1986)*. Madrid: Orígenes, 1987.

Mesa-Lago, Carmelo, ed. *Revolutionary Change in Cuba*. Pittsburgh: University of Pittsburgh Press, 1971.

Mesa-Lago, Carmelo, and June S. Belkin, eds. *Cuba in Africa*. Pittsburgh: Center for Latin American Studies, 1982.

Moore, Carlos. *Castro, the Blacks, and Africa*. Los Angeles: Center for Afro-American Studies, University of California Press, 1988.

———. "Le peuple noir a-t-il sa place dans la Révolution cubaine?" *Présence Africaine* 56 (1964): 15–68.

Morejón, Nancy. *Amor, ciudad atribuida*. Havana: El Puente, 1964.

———. *Baladas para un sueño*. Havana: Unión, Coleccion Ciclos, 1991.

———. *Botella al mar*. Zaragoza, Spain: Olifante, 1996.

———. *Le Chaînon-Poetique*. Translated by Sandra Monet-Descombey. Paris: Mediatheque Chanpigny-sur-Marne, 1994.

———. *Cuaderno de Granada*. Havana: Casa de las Américas, 1984.

———. *Elogio de la danza (poemas)*. México: Universidad Nacional Autónoma de México, 1982.

———. *Elogio y paisaje*. Havana: Union, Coleccion de la Rueda Dentada, 1997.

———. *Fundación de la imagen*. Havana: Editorial Letras Cubanas, 1988.

———. *Grenada Notebook*. Translated by Lisa Davis. New York: Círculo de Cultura Cubana, 1984.

———. *Mutismos*. Havana: El Puente, 1962.

———. *Nación y mestizaje en Nicolás Guillén*. Havana: Unión de Escritores y Artistas de Cuba, 1982.

———. *Octubre imprescindible*. Havana: Union, Contemporáneos, 1982.

———. *Ours the Earth (Anthology)*. Selected and translated by J. R. Pereira. Kingston, Jamaica: Institute of Caribbean Studies, University of West Indies, 1990.

———. *Paisaje célebre*. Carácas, Venezuela: Colección la Diosa, 1993.

———. *Parajes de una época*. Havana: Letras Cubanas, 1979.

———. *Piedra pulida*. Havana: Editorial Letras Cubanas, 1986.

———. *Poemas (Anthology)*. Selection and preface by Efraín Huerta. Mexico City: Universidad Nacional Autónoma de México, 1980.

———. *Poemas de amor y muerte*. Toulouse: Revista Caravelle, 1993.

———. *La quinta de los molinos*. Havana: Letras Cubanas, Coleccion Cemi, 2000.

———. *Richard trajo su flauta y otros argumentos*. Havana: Instituto del Libro, 1967.

———. *El río de Martín Pérez y otros poemas*. With illustrations by Rolando Estevez. Matanzas, Cuba: Vigía, 1996.

———. Interview with Linda Howe, Havana, 5–6 August 1992.

———. Interview with Linda Howe, Havana, 16 July 1994.

———. *Where the Island Sleeps Like a Wing*. Translated by Kathleen Weaver. San Francisco: Black Scholar Press, 1985.

Morejón, Nancy, ed. *Recopilación de textos sobre Nicolás Guillén*. Havana: Casa de las Américas, 1974.

Morejón, Nancy, and Carmen Gonce. *Lengua de pájaro*. Havana: Instituto Cubano del Libro, 1971.

Moreno Fraginals, Manuel. *The Sugarmill: The Socioeconomic Complex of Sugar in Cuba, 1760–1860*. Translated by Cedric Belfrage. New York: Monthly Review Press, 1976.

Morrisey, Marietta. *Slave Women in the New World: Gender Stratification in the Caribbean*. Lawrence: University Press of Kansas, 1989.

Mosquera, Gerardo. "Africa in the Art of Latin America." *Art Journal* 51, no. 4 (winter 1992): 30–38.

———. "El síndrome de Marco Polo. Algunos problemas alrededor de arte y eurocentrismo." *Casa de las Américas* 188 (July–Sept. 1992): 64–70.

———. "Introduction to New Cuban Art." In *Contemporary Art from Cuba / Arte Contemporáneo de Cuba*, edited by Marilyn A. Zeitlin, 23–29. New York: Delano Greenidge Editions, 1999.

Mosquera, Gerardo, ed. *Beyond the Fantastic: Contemporary Art Criticism from Latin America*. Cambridge, Mass: MIT Press, 1996.

Moure, Goria. *Ana Mendieta*. Barcelona: Ediciones Polígrafa, S. A., 1996.

Oppenheimer, Andres. *Castro's Final Hour: The Secret Story behind the Coming Downfall of Communist Cuba*. New York: Simon and Schuster, 1992.

Orovio, Helio. *Diccionario de la música cubana*. Havana: Letras Cubanas, 1992.

Ortiz, Fernando. *La africanía de la música foklórica de Cuba*. Havana: Ediciones Cardenas y Cía, 1950.

———. *Contrapunteo cubano del tabaco y el azúcar*. Caracas: Biblioteca Ayacucho, 1987.

———. *Los bailes y el teatro de los negros en el folklore de Cuba*. Havana: Letras Cubanas, 1951.

———. *Fernando Ortiz*. Edited by Julio Le Riverend. Havana: UNEAC, 1973.

Otero, Lisandro. "Notas sobre la funcionalidad de la cultura." *Casa de las Américas* 12, no. 68 (Sept.–Oct. 1971): 94–107.

Pacheco, José Emiliano, et al. "Declaration by the Contributing Editors, Casa de las Américas Magazine." *El Corno emplumado* (23 July 1967): 133–37.

Padilla, Heberto. *La mala memoria*. Barcelona: Plaza and Janes, S. A., 1989.

Padula, Alfred. "Cuban Socialism: Thirty Years of Controversy." In *Conflict and Change in Cuba*, edited by Baloyra and Morris, 15–37.

Padura Fuentes, Leonardo. *Máscaras*. Barcelona: Tusquets, 1997.

———. *Paisaje de otoño*. Barcelona: Tusquets, 1998.

———. *Pasado perfecto*. Barcelona: Tusquets, 2000.

———. *Vientos de cuaresma*. Barcelona: Tusquets, 2001.

Paquette, Robert L. *Sugar Is Made with Blood: The Conspiracy of La Escalera and the Conflict between Empires over Slavery in Cuba*. Middletown, Conn.: Wesleyan University Press, 1988.

Patterson, Enrique. "Cuba: Discusiones sobre la identidad." Instituto de estudios Cubanos. *Encuentro* 2 (1997): 49–67.

Patterson, Thomas G. *Contesting Castro: The United States and the Triumph of the Cuban Revolution*. New York: Oxford University Press, 1994.

Paz, Senel. *El lobo, el bosque y el hombre nuevo*. México: Ediciones Era, 1991.

Pedro, Alberto. "El Tercer Mundo exige una dramática decisión de los intelectuales." *Revolución y Cultura* 9 (30 April 1968): 33–46.

———. "Poder negro." *Casa de las Américas* 9, no. 51 (Nov.–Dec. 1968): 134–44.

Pereda Valdés, Ildefonso, ed. *Lo negro y lo mulato en la poesía cubana.* Montevideo: Ediciones Ciudadela, 1970.

Pérez, Louis A., Jr. *The War of 1898: The United Sates and Cuba in History and Historiography.* Chapel Hill: University of North Carolina Press, 1998.

Pérez, Louis A., Jr., ed. *Slaves, Sugar and Colonial Society: Travel Accounts of Cuba, 1801–1899.* Wilmington, Del.: Scholarly Resources Inc., 1992.

Pérez Firmat, Gustavo. *The Cuban Condition: Translation and Identity in Modern Cuban Literature.* Cambridge: Cambridge University Press, 1989.

Pérez-Stable, Marifeli. *The Cuban Revolution: Origins, Course, and Legacy.* New York: Oxford University Press, 1993.

Pick, Zuzana M. *The New Latin American Cinema: A Continental Project.* Austin: University of Texas Press, 1993.

Piedra, José. "Literary Whiteness and the Afro-Hispanic Difference." *NLH* 18 (1987): 303–32.

Piñera, Virgilio. *Obras completas.* Havana: Ediciones Cubana, 1961.

———. "Introduction." In *Libro de Rolando,* by Escardó, 9–27.

———. "Los Siervos." *Ciclón* (1955): 9–29.

Pipes, Richard. *Russia under the Bolshevik Regime.* New York: Knopf, 1993.

Pisani, Francis. "Cuba negra." *Nexos* 171 (March 1992): 8–13.

Ponte, Antonio José. *Contrabando y sombras.* Barcelona: Mandadori, 2002.

———. *In the Cold of the Malecón.* Translated by Cola Franzen and Dick Cluster. San Francisco: City Lights Books, 2000.

———. *Tales from the Cuban Empire.* Translated by Cola Franzen. San Francisco: City Lights Books, 2002.

Portela, Ena Lucía. *El pájaro: Pincel y tinta china.* Barcelona: Editorial Casiopea, S. L., 1998.

———. *La sombra del caminante.* Bogotá: Quebecor World, 2001.

Portuondo, José Antonio. "Sobre la crítica y el acercamiento recíproco de los artistas y el pueblo." Report to the First National Congress of Writers and Artists, Havana. In *Estética y revolución,* edited by Lourdes Casal, 70–81.

Portuondo Linares, Serafín. *El partido independiente de color.* Havana: Dirección de Cultura, 1950.

Prats Sariol, José. "Donde se habla de la poesía de Miguel Barnet a propósito de 'Carta de noche.'" *Unión* 4 (1983): 158–62.

Price, Richard. *Maroon Societies.* Baltimore: Johns Hopkins University Press, 1979.

Prieto, José Manuel. *Livadia.* Barcelona: Literatura Mondadori, 1999.

Quejereta, Alejandro. "Un mapa de medio siglo." *Ahora* (17 Feb. 1990).

Quiñones,Tato, dir. *Nganga Kiyangala.* Televisión Latina, 1991.

———. Interview with Linda Howe, Havana, 25 June 1992.

Quirk, Robert E. *Fidel Castro.* New York: W. W. Norton, 1993.

Reed, Roger. *The Evolution of Cultural Policy in Cuba: From the Fall of Batista to the Padilla Case.* Doctoral thesis, no. 456, University of Geneva (Switzerland), 1989.

Ripoll, Carlos. "Writers and Artists in Today's Cuba." In *Cuban Communism*, compiled by Horowitz, 499–513.

Rodríguez, Rafael. "Nancy Morejón en su Habana (Entrevista)." *Arieto* 32.8 (1983): 23–25.

Rodríguez-Núñez, Victor. "Hacia una nueva poesía cubana." *Plural* 12.3, no. 135 (Dec. 1982): 21–30.

Rosegreen-Williams, C. "Rewriting the History of the Afro-Cuban Woman: Nancy Morejón's 'Mujer negra.'" *Afro-Hispanic Review* 8, no. 3 (Sept. 1989): 7–13.

Santos Moray, Mercedes. "El teatro como reflexión: Diálogo con Gerardo Fulleda León." *Granma* (5 Sept. 1994): 5.

Saslow, James M. *Ganymede in the Renaissance: Homosexuality in Art and Society.* New Haven: Yale University Press, 1986.

Savory Fido, Elaine. "A Womanist Vision of the Caribbean: An Interview." In *Out of the Kumbla*, edited by Boyce Davies and Savory Fido, 265–69.

Schnabel, Julian, dir. *Before Night Falls.* New Line Studios, 2001.

Schulman, Ivan. "Social Exorcisms: Cuba's (Post)Colonial (Counter) Discourses." *Hispania* 75, no. 4 (Oct. 1992): 941–49.

Schumacher, Michael. *Dharma Lion: A Critical Biography of Allen Ginsberg.* New York: St. Martin's Press, 1992.

Scott, Rebecca J. *Slave Emancipation in Cuba: The Transition to Free Labor, 1860–1899.* Princeton: Princeton University Press, 1985.

Serviat, Pedro. *El problema negro en Cuba y su solución definitiva.* Havana: Editora Política, 1986.

Simo, Ana María. "Respuesta a Jesús Díaz." *La Gaceta de Cuba* (June–July 1966): 4–5.

Sklodowska, Elzbieta. "Miguel Barnet." *DLB* (1994): 1–15.

Smith, Barbara. "Toward a Black Feminist Criticism." In *The New Feminist Criticism: Essays on Women, Literature, and Theory*, edited by Elaine Showalter, 168–85. New York: Pantheon, 1985.

Smith, Lois M., and Alfred Padula. "Twenty Questions on Sex and Gender in Revolutionary Cuba." *Cuban Studies* 18 (1988): 149–58.

Smith, Verity. "Recent Trends in Cuban Criticism and Literature." *Cuban Studies* 19 (1989): 81–99.

Stubbs, Jean. "Cuba: The Sexual Revolution." In *Latin American Women*, edited by Olivia Harris, 18–19. London: Minority Rights Group, Ltd., 1983.

Stubbs, Jean, and Pedro Pérez-Sarduy. *Afro Cuba: An Anthology of Cuban Writing on Race, Politics, and Culture.* Melbourne: Ocean Press, 1993.

———. *Afro-Cuban Voices: On Race and Identity in Contemporary Cuba.* Gainesville: University of Florida Press, 2000.

Szulc, Tad. *Fidel: A Critical Portrait.* London: Hutchinson Ltd., 1986.

Taylor, Frank F. "Revolution, Race, and Some Aspects of Foreign Relations in Cuba since 1959." *Cuban Studies* 18 (1988): 19–41.

Taylor, Patrick. *The Narrative of Liberation: Perspectives on Afro Caribbean Literature, Popular Culture, and Politics.* Ithaca, N.Y.: Cornell University Press, 1989.

Thomas, Hugh. *Cuba or the Pursuit of Freedom.* London: Eyre and Spottiswoode, 1971.

———. *The Cuban Revolution.* New York: Harper, 1977.

Timerman, Jacobo. *Cuba: A Journey.* Translated by Toby Talbot. New York: Vintage, 1992.

Torrents, Nissa. "Images of Women in Cuba's Post-Revolutionary Narrative." In *Knives and Angels: Women Writers in Latin America,* edited by Susan Bassnett, 110–14. New Jersey: Zed Books Ltd., 1990.

Tucker, Robert C. *The Revolution from Above, 1928–1941.* New York: W. W. Norton, 1990.

Unruh, Vicky. *Latin American Vanguards: The Art of Contentious Encounters.* Berkeley: University of California Press, 1994.

Valdés, Nelson P., and Nan Elsasser. "Cachita y el Che: Patron Saints of Revolutionary Cuba." *Encounters* (winter 1989): 28–32.

Valdés, Zoé. *La nada cotidiana.* Buenos Aires: Emecé Editores, 1996.

Valdés Figueroa, Eugenio. "Trajectories of a Rumor." In *Art Cuba: The New Generation,* edited by Holly Block, 17–23. New York: Abrams, 2001.

Valle Omir, Amir. *Brevísimas demencias.* Havana: Ediciones Extramuros, 2000.

Vázquez Montalbán, Manuel. *Y Dios entró en La Habana.* Madrid: Aguilar, 1998.

Vega, Jesús. "El necesario oficio de Barnet." *El Caimán Barbudo* (Sept. 1988): 30.

Villaverde, Cirilo. *Cecilia Valdés.* Edited by Raimundo Lazo. Mexico City: Editorial Porrúa, 1972.

Vitier, Cintio, ed. *Las mejores poesias cubanas.* Havana: Primer Festival de Libro Cubano, 1959.

Wacquant, Loïc J. D., and Pierre Bourdieu. *An Invitation to Reflexive Sociology.* Chicago: University of Chicago Press, 1992.

Walker, Alice. *In Search of Our Mothers' Gardens.* San Diego: Harcourt, 1983.

Wallerstein, Immanuel, and Etienne Balibar. *Race, Nation, Class: Ambiguous Identities.* New York: Verso, 1991.

White, Steven F. *Culture and Politics in Nicaragua: Testimonies of Poets and Writers.* New York: Lumen, 1986.

———. *Modern Nicaraguan Poetry: Dialogues with France and the United States.* Lewisburg, Penn.: Bucknell University Press, 1993.

Williams, Lorna. "The Revolutionary Feminism of Nancy Morejón." Unpublished paper, 1993.

Williams, Sherley Anne. "Some Implications of Womanist Theory." *Callaloo* 9, no. 2 (1986): 303–8.

Williams, William Carlos. *Pictures from Brueghel and Other Poems: Collected Poems 1950–1962.* New York: New Directions, 1962.

Wynter, Sylvia. "Afterword: Beyond Miranda's Meanings: Un/silencing the 'Demonic Ground' of Caliban's 'Woman.'" In *Out of the Kumbla,* edited by Boyce Davies and Savory Fido, 355–70.

Yáñez, Mirta. "Miguel Barnet, el poeta." *Revolución y Cultura* (5 May 1985): 13–16.

Ziegler, Jean. *Les Rebelles.* Paris: Seuil, 1983.

Index